Cut the Connection

Cut the Connection

Disestablishment
and the Church of England

Colin Buchanan

DARTON·LONGMAN+TODD

First published in 1994 by
Darton, Longman and Todd Ltd
1 Spencer Court
140–142 Wandsworth High Street
London SW18 4JJ

ISBN 0–232–52059–3

A Catalogue record for this book is available from the British Library

Phototypeset in 10/12pt Century Roman by Intype, London
Printed and bound in Great Britain by Page Bros, Norwich

'Give to Caesar what is Caesar's and to God what is God's.' (Jesus Christ, in Mark 12:17)

Sciatis nos ... concessisse Deo et hac praesenti carta nostra confirmasse ... quod Anglicana ecclesia libera sit ... (*Magna Carta*, 1215)

Can anything be more demoralizing ... anything more destructive of the Church's religious influence than the mode of appointment adopted in the case of bishops? The *congé d'élire*, the Royal Letter, the assured obedience of the dean and chapter, enforced if necessary by the penalty of *praemunire*, associated as it is with solemn prayer for Divine direction – Sir, it is playing with sacred things, for political and secular ends which is perfectly shocking, and which goes far to paralyze the spiritual authority and influence of the Church. (Edward Miall in a speech in the Commons on 9 May 1871, quoted by David Nicholls in *Church and State in Britain since 1820* (Routledge and Kegan Paul, London, 1967), p. 91)

If the Church is to have new life ... it must have liberty. Those who are promoting this Movement are convinced that we must win for the Church full power to control its own life, even at the cost, if necessary, of disestablishment ... (Temple and others in the first public utterance of the Life and Liberty Movement – a letter published in *The Times* on 20 June 1917, reprinted in F. A. Iremonger, *William Temple: Archbishop of Canterbury* (Oxford 1948), p. 227)

I see there is to be another Church and State Commission. I cannot imagine anyone clever enough to be invited onto it being stupid enough to accept. (Alec Vidler in a letter to *The Times* prior to the appointment of the Chadwick Commission, quoted from memory)

There is another [radical and disestablishing] tradition in our Church's history. All Church and State Commissions, including this one, pay uneasy respect to the consciences of those who argue for the absolute claim of Christ to the allegiance of his Church. All Church and State Commissions including this one, return gladly to the claims of history. So it is the case that the more radical of our traditions has never been stated in an official report except by people who are rejecting it. (Valerie Pitt in 'Memorandum of Dissent' in *Church and State 1970*, pp. 68–9)

One thing is certain: if Church and State were starting their lives *de novo* in the twentieth century, no one would dream of suggesting any relationship between the two even remotely resembling that which currently exists, and even if he did no one would dream of taking him seriously. (Trevor Beeson, *The Church of England in Crisis* (Davis-Poynter 1973), p. 93)

Any Christian Church which still needs official state privilege for support in 1989 has chosen to manacle itself to a spiritual corpse. In their heart everybody knows it, but no one will admit it. (Clifford Longley in *The Times*, 2 December 1989)

... The most dangerous fact about Bishop Bell, however, was ... that he was loathed by Mr Churchill, and as the Labour Government tottered in slow motion towards defeat, it became increasingly obvious that Mr Churchill would again become Prime Minister.
    'Think of your future, Aysgarth!' implored my father. 'It's death to get on the wrong side of these politicians!'
    'Then I must die!' said Aysgarth cheerfully. 'I refuse to be an ecclesiastical poodle.'
    'But if you want to be a bishop or a dean – '
    'All I want is to serve God. Nothing else matters.'
(Susan Howatch, *Scandalous Risks* (1991), p. 24)

It is time for the Church and State to consider an amicable parting after four centuries of wedlock. (*The Times*, Leading article, 28 January 1993)

Contents

Introduction

This book is not a definitive study; it is a call for change. It is not detached; it is impassioned. It is not an ecclesiology; it is ecclesiastical politics. It is written by a journalist rather than a scholar. Its vested interests and its desired outcome stalk every page. From its title onwards there should be no mistake about that.

However, it is not the work of a passing whim. It is the fruit of at least seventeen years of reflection on the issue, of personal engagement in Synod, around the country, and in the media, on the need for disestablishment and the agenda of it if it is to come. In the process, I have encountered every kind of pro-establishment view, and had my own position not just tested but adjusted, reinforced and refined. And the Church of England being what it is, I have become used to reactions like:

'You are simply spelling the end of the Church of England'
'You can't be serious'

sometimes, 'You must be out of your mind' and, 'You are simply spelling the end of your own credibility'.

Sometimes I have wondered if I have been thought to be denying the resurrection . . .

So, although there are many other gospel issues facing the Church of England, and although there are many other issues on my own agenda leaving me little margin of time to pursue this particular venture, in the absence of anyone else having a go, I have put my hand to it.

Because the book is angled for a contemporary and practical purpose, it cannot and does not provide even a full outline of history. I have had to omit all reference to Constantine, Justinian, and upwards of a thousand years of 'Christendom'. Because the book is specifically for and about the Church of England, I have taken Henry VIII as the *starting point*, and have provided simply a minimum of history to disclose the determining causes of why the Church–State relationship today is what it is. And I need to start with a definition.

Definition

The word 'disestablishment' does not mean the same thing to all who use it. That is because there is unclarity about the meaning of 'establishment', a difficulty which has haunted almost all writings on the subject. The latest Church and State report, i.e. the report of the Chadwick Commission, *Church and State 1970*, carefully excluded visibly unhelpful uses of 'establishment'. These included 'those in authority' and 'the existing system' (uses which in a church context could well imply a *'Church* establishment' without any Church-and-State reference) – and by implication cut out 'those subtly entrenched in authority by reason of birth or privilege'. Clearly, the varying colloquial uses will snarl up communication, unless they are determinedly put aside. We need a clear and consistent meaning, even if it is at a tangent with some popular usage. When we have 'establishment' right, we can address 'disestablishment'.

The Chadwick Commission reached a result as follows:

> For us 'establishment' means the laws which apply to the Church of England and not to the other Churches.[1]

Such a stated intention as to how the word should be used is in principle a great help. Curiously the actual definition at first sight looks a little simplistic, though it does give a usage quite close to the regular ecclesiastical use of the word to mean 'something to do with State ownership of, or at least selective involvement with, one Christian Church – in England's case the Church of England'. At any rate I work from the Chadwick definition, honing it slightly with two provisos:

1. The Chadwick definition does not seem to allow of *degrees* of establishment – it suggests that if there are unique laws for the Church of England, few or many, then we are 'established', and if not, not. (Yet other Churches sometimes have unique laws – such as the Methodist Church Act 1929, the Act which secured Methodist union: but that unique law did not 'establish' Methodism.)
2. Until seventy years ago the Church of Scotland was always viewed as 'by law established', and had 'laws which apply to the Church of Scotland and not to other Churches', until 1921. It was then freed of State control *by State action*, so that the Church of Scotland Act 1921 is a law which

applies to the Church of Scotland alone, but is *not* evidence that the Church is 'established'. We may compare it – and this is a comparison to which I return – to that distinct Act of the Westminster Parliament which sets free a colony (or group of colonies). A famous instance was the British North America Act 1867, which created the Dominion of Canada, and ensured it was free of British control. A century later, in the great period of decolonization of British colonies, there were literally dozens of such Acts. But these Acts, whilst belonging to the named territories alone, did not colonize but rather decolonized.

In other words, I believe the most helpful use of the word 'establishment' is in relation to those laws (and sometimes conventions) which bring from the State upon the Church actual *control* in a way that it is not brought upon other Churches. This the Church of Scotland Act 1921 did not do – for, quite the reverse, like the decolonization process, it *lifted* State control. Thus I believe it is quite unhelpful to call the Church of Scotland 'established' – rather, it is 'by law disestablished'. And, in Anglican terms, that is the position of the Church of Wales also. This principle, that it is restrictive or controlling laws which characterize 'establishment', provides the basic verbal usage which undergirds this book. Thus a law such as the Church of England (Worship and Doctrine) Measure 1974, which devolves large powers over liturgy from Parliament to General Synod, is in principle a 'disestablishing' move – albeit one taken by law.

What the Church of Scotland does usually claim is that it is the 'national Church' of the land of Scotland. This is a different kind of statement and one which admits of less precise definition. Indeed it is a notably obfuscating term. Its currency may even derive from its imprecision – those using it are making strong positive claims (claims which nearly make other Christian bodies 'sects'), but, when the use of the term is rigorously inspected, people may be driven from one meaning and yet find another in which they can take refuge without having to renounce the claim to be 'the national Church'. For a Church making the claim is covertly stating that it is one or more (but not necessarily all) of the following:

1. the Church which is 'by law established';

2. the Church which stands closest to the government of the land;

3. the Church which can point to an unbroken historic continuity with the origins of Christianity in a particular nation;

4. the Church which has the largest proportion of the nation currently in membership;

5. the Church which has a territorial spread such as in some way to offer ministrations to all the inhabitants;

6. the Church which believes itself alone to be orthodox, such that all Christians in that land ought to belong to it;

7. the Church which has reason to think that the unchurched of the land look most towards it for ministrations to the fringe;

8. the Church which stands closest to the folk-culture of the land.

There may be other offers. But this range immediately demonstrates the difficulty of either making or allowing the claim, and particularly so if in any nation more than one Church makes it. The claim may perhaps be hesitatingly granted where only one Church makes it (especially if the other Churches there will allow it), but even then it must be recalled that there is a 'weasel' element to the term, and it may be received by the hearer as meaning something different from that intended by the user. On the whole it is clearer to use 'established', 'historic', 'majority' or other adjectives to identify which of the several possible meanings is intended. I have tried to use 'national' only sparingly and transparently.

Establishment in four Reports

The issue, through the sheer complex history of the establishment and of the gradual loosening of it in recent history, has been the subject of four major 'Church and State' Reports this century. These are:

1. The 'Selborne' Report (1916). This did the groundwork for the 'Enabling Act'.

2. The 'Cecil' Report (1935). This followed the 'Prayer Book Crisis' of 1927–8.

3. The 'Moberley' Report (1952). This asked for 'changes desirable in the present relationship'.

4. The 'Chadwick' Report (1970). This specifically handled authority in respect of forms of worship and procedures for the appointment of bishops.

There have also been reports on single issues (e.g. Canon Law, the Appointment of Bishops, etc.), but these four alone have been comprehensive. There are some general points to be made about them.

Firstly, the Commissions were limited in their terms of reference or their membership or both. They make unsupported statements like, 'We do not think the English people at this point in history look for or expect the disestablishment of the Church of England, but that does not, of course, mean that every detail of the present relationship is immune from criticism' or, 'The Church of England is generally satisfied and glad to be the Church by law established, and we would not dream of challenging that conviction'. This kind of basis for proceeding is the most soft-core defence of the establishment conceivable – for, whilst it may be marginally reinforced by citation of actual benefits, it is of itself without content, and might of itself be simply reproducing a widely held superstition as much as a Christian conviction. There is always need of toughened ideology in defence of establishment and the reports are short of it.

The second point runs on from the first. Until 1970 there was virtually no dissent. The Cecil Commission, for instance, did not include Hensley Henson, the then Bishop of Durham, who would not have been content with 'soft-core' arguments in any field. There was a tremendous weight of convinced establishmentarians on each Commission and they cautiously asked themselves whether the Church could properly move another inch towards independence, and then tended to settle for a millimetre. As a matter of inspection, the 1916 Report is bolder than either of the next two. In 1970 alone was there dissent – and the courageous writing of Valerie Pitt, Denis Coe, and Peter Cornwell actually reads like hard-core advocacy: here were people with their feet on a rock of principle attempting to build something of lasting substance, but to do so in minority opposition to smooth 'mainstream' hedging and fudging. The mainstream members of that Commission and their arguments look together like a prospectus for a Friday afternoon car which is permanently stuck in second gear, with a handbrake which will not release, whilst the legend reads 'Will take you anywhere with speed and freedom'.

However, there is a third general point to make about these Commissions. It is this: they have followed each other since the turn of the century at regular intervals – sixteen years, nineteen years, seventeen years, and eighteen years – but they have stopped dead since 1970. So, as I write, it is twenty-four years on since the last such Report was published, and, even if a motion in General Synod this July led to the setting up of a new Commission, it is doubtful whether it would convene, consult, report and be published much before 1998, and it would more probably be 2000. That is to identify a serious standstill in what ought to have been a progress; and it might yet be slower still. So I write with a sense of frustrated urgency.

Limitations

Not only is my history not exhaustive; nor is my range of current Church–State issues. I have endeavoured to treat of the most prominent rocks and shoals, and to clear a passage through a blocked channel. But I acknowledge that I have not dredged up every possible hazard, and, no doubt, those who do not wish to make the passage will fasten upon what I have not done. I gladly list a few of which I am aware: I have not discussed Ecclesiastical Courts, Oaths of Allegiance, State Chaplaincies, status of Royal Peculiars, the appointment of Deans, or Canon Professorships. Nor, if it comes to that, have I mentioned the protection of Sundays, Church Schools, or saying grace at Lord Mayor's Dinners – topics which, whilst varying in their Christian importance, are not necessarily 'Church of England' matters at all – for other Christian denominations have the same or parallel interests in them.

I acknowledge these and a range of other omissions. My only claim is that, in tackling head-on the most obstinate and obnoxious features of the present establishment of the Church of England, I have shown how a determination to achieve the end-result can in principle also lead to other obstacles being cleared away.

Reasons for urgency

It does strike me as odd that, despite the secularizing march
of time in this country and some provocations from the State,
yet there appears to be less overt unrest about the establishment than in the days of Temple's Life and Liberty Movement
over three-quarters of a century ago . But perhaps the needed
reforms have been slow because there has not been in recent
years any pressure group or disestablishing 'movement' and
this lack has left the State control of the Church in place as
long as it has. This is in total contrast to the period from
around 1850 to 1920, when outside pressures were strong, and
internal ones associated with Temple began.[2]

In any case, should not the lead come 'from the top'? There
have been hints in recent years that one in every two Archbishops of Canterbury would himself give a lead. However,
Temple (1942–4) was less persuaded than he had been a quarter of a century earlier; Ramsey (1961–74) dropped big hints in
his enthronement sermon, but perhaps was never sufficiently
interested in structures to pursue the matter; and Runcie
(1980–91), who had given more than hints when he was Bishop
of St Albans,* obviously found the change of perspective as
Archbishop affected his view, though he still came across
as only a reluctant defender of the present system. Whether
or not previous views bear upon the present stance of an
archbishop or not, it is obvious that the position he holds
almost entraps him. He is not only the spiritual leader of the
Church of England, he is also the first citizen of the nation
after the monarch, he is also by definition close to the Royal
Family, a spokesman for the Church in the House of Lords,
and the guardian of a very conservative, very slow-moving,
institution. Wherever else he may be prophetic, on this issue
an Archbishop needs to detect a strong ground-swell within
the life of the Church of England before it is appropriate to
stick his neck out. And the problem is not only that the Arch-

---

*I hope that St Albans Diocese will be part of a disestablished Church . . .
Those who support the Establishment claim that it does express still the
latent religious sentiments of the English people . . . We are frequently
told that nobody can do a Royal Wedding or a Churchill funeral like the
good old C. of E.; but honestly I do not think that such arguments can
sustain the case for the Establishment.' (Robert Runcie (ed.), *Cathedral
and City* (Martyn Associates 1977), p. 129.)

bishop's own position turns all but the doughtiest into establishment men; it is not only that the Archbishops who
alternated with the ones mentioned above i.e. Fisher (1945–61)
and Coggan (1974–80) were deeply committed establishmentarians; it is also that the last three Archbishops of York –
Donald Coggan (1961–74), Stuart Blanche (1975–83), and John
Habgood (1983 to the present day) – have also been strongly
in favour of the establishment. It would be a foolhardy Archbishop of Canterbury who gave a strong lead which he knew
his colleague at York would oppose; and it is likely that to no
Archbishop of Canterbury, whatever his personal views, has
the issue appeared to deserve a high priority or any determined advocacy. After all, most of the time things can proceed
quite peacefully without our having to worry about this fine
point of principle; so why rock the boat? Thus it is probable
that the matter will only be moved along by either a Church–
State crisis which drives an Archbishop into such taking sides,
or by a rising tide of nationwide alarm at the present colonized
state of the Church. It is, I suppose, possible that the major
Commission on the Church of England's organization, to be
chaired by Bishop Michael Turnbull, the appointment of which
has been announced as I write, will find itself up against
establishment issues, and may have to address them. But
equally it is to identify, harness, resource and swell a rising
popular tide that this book is written.

A personal note

Changing events have changed my own mind in forty years of
adult faith and sense of vocation. My conviction that I look on
a different landscape has no doubt an element of the subjective
about it; but the changes in the position of the Church of
England in society are hardly shaped by my particular
spectacles; no, they are objective and discernible to all the
world. It is my strong conviction that, in the course of those
changes, even a weakening establishment has crossed a watershed from the conceivably defensible to the self-evidently
harmful.

As it is known that in my own life I have personally suffered
through the directly intervening control of the State upon the
Church of England, it is a proper question as to whether I
write simply out of personal pique. It would be hard to refute

such a suggestion were it not that I have an open record of seeking disestablishment going back at least to 1977.* Certainly at times the points of principle I want to raise here are sharpened by particular contemporary events; and, equally certainly, I have myself been at the storm-centre of some such events (though at a great distance from others). Nevertheless, it *is* issues of principle which concern me here, and, if ever in the future I do write an autobiography, it will be clearly different from this.

I inevitably name many contemporary English Christians, some of them good friends, and most of them at least honoured opponents. I hope I have neither hurt nor misrepresented any. I have tried to rely upon direct and typical quotations to give expression to other people's views. If I confront differing views, and occasionally criticize them robustly, then I have sought to keep the process within the limits of 'speaking the truth in love'. No personal *animus* is intended, and my hope is to help the Church of God build itself up in love.

I am also at times asked: 'How can you live in the Church of England if you are opposed to the establishment?' To this I can only reply that I *can* live with our chains, that I cannot ever visualize going into dissent over what must count in gospel terms as a secondary point, but I cannot by any stretch of the imagination lie down and enjoy the captivity. Were I to fall for *that* form of making a virtue out of a grave defect, then I would be a captive indeed. I take seriously the utterances I quote elsewhere in this book that the Church must not connive by its silence at its humiliation. But the Church is in pilgrimage, and I can live with the establishment so long as I can protest and work for as swift a change as possible. This is precisely how proponents of the ordination of women as pres-

---

*'. . . the Church of England still presents a field of desperate inaction at many points where action is needed for a fair ecumenical encounter. We do too little too late to separate from the State's control; we leave the 1662 BCP in the hands of Parliament; we move only an inch a year over the State appointment of bishops; we still have our privileged position in the House of Lords; and the story could be prolonged.' (COB, 'The Unity of the Church' in Ian Cundy (ed.) *Obeying Christ in a Changing World: 2 The People of God* (Collins 1977), p. 123.) My record in General Synod in the years 1980–5 will support this, and motions I moved in Southwell Diocesan Synod in 1985 and Birmingham Diocesan Synod in 1987 should reinforce it.

byters have had to conduct themselves for the last two decades
– they did not secede, but hung in, and their deliverance has
come. I take courage before God from that.

I confess too that I owe much to State-appointed bishops,
including that wonderfully over-the-top Erastian, Gerald Elli-
son, who ordained me deacon and presbyter, and that mild
Erastian, Hugh Montefiore, who nominated me as his suffragan bishop. I have entertained great admiration for monarchs,
statesmen and prelates who have lived under the inherited
system and done much good in it. I can even thank God for
Henry VIII, let alone for Thomas Cranmer, Queen Elizabeth
and Richard Hooker. But my admiration of some and my gratitude for others do not compel imitation, when the context of
operation has so greatly changed. So I have attempted to write
in 1994 for the Church of 1994.

1. Phases of the Establishment: From the Reformation to the Enabling Act

No contemporary institution can be understood apart from its own history. The only credible explanation of the current link between the Church of England and the State is one that explains within an historical process its genesis, its growth, its distortion, and its passage into incredibility. But all history is told selectively and for a purpose and this is clearly no exception. All that the selective historian can do is to declare his hand – I marshal historical evidence and tell a particular story, because I believe it leads to a shrieking practical conclusion. Let there be no doubt, no suggestion of deceit, about the cause to which this book is directed. But, I should add, I do not believe I have so much written history to favour a cause, as I believe that reading history has driven me to that cause. It is the inescapable main features of Church of England history since the reign of Henry VIII which, intermingled with some theological reflection and a touch of political awareness, have driven me to espouse disestablishment as the overriding policy the Church of England ought to pursue in relation to the State today.

I approach the history through five demarcated separate eras, three of them in this Chapter, two in the next. I trust that the paragraph above and the constraints of space will suffice as an apologia for the broad brush-strokes I employ.

1. From Henry VIII's break with the Pope to the Glorious Revolution (1534–1689) – the nationalized monopoly

For more than twenty years after he inherited the throne, Henry VIII was, to all appearances, a loyal monarch of the papal order. Theologically, he was conservative, opposed to the continental Reformation, and rewarded with the award

from the Pope of the title *Fidei Defensor* for his book against
Luther, *De Septem Sacramentis* (1521). During the 1520s there
were groups at the Universities and elsewhere studying Eras-
mus' text of the Greek New Testament; there were English-
language New Testaments being sent into England by Tyndale
from Antwerp; and there were inevitably English people with
live contacts with both Lutheran and Reformed Protestant
circles on the continent. But on the surface all remained unre-
formed and safely papalist.

The troubles began with Henry's desire to marry Anne
Boleyn. He appealed to the Pope in 1527 for a decree of nullity
in respect of his union with Katharine of Aragon, on the ground
that she had been his deceased brother's wife before he married her and the papal dispensation obtained at the time was
a theological impossibility – if a union was null (and therefore
in this case incestuous), then no Pope could overrule the law
of God. We do not have to speculate on how far Henry had a
genuine conscience (shaping itself through a conviction that
he had no living male heir because God was judging him for
his sin), and how far he was driven by passion for Anne to
engage in a wholly cynical procedure. The simple fact that
emerged was that, however much another Pope in another era
could have helped a King of England in such a predicament,
in 1527 Pope Clement VII could not help at all – he was the
virtual prisoner of Charles V of Spain, Katharine's nephew,
who (perhaps with equal cynicism) would not allow the Holy
Father to rule against Katharine's interests.

It was at this point that Henry encountered a Cambridge
don called Thomas Cranmer, who made in his hearing the
famous suggestion that, instead of consulting the Pope further,
Henry should sound out learned opinion throughout the universities of Europe. This was, in principle, a proposal to make
a unilateral declaration of independence. It did not, of course,
emerge as such at the time, though the direction being set
must have been clear to those who implemented the plan. And
when Cranmer himself had fulfilled the itinerant brief, and
had returned with a majority opinion in Henry's favour (and
with a Lutheran wife), action on the basis of the opinion was
carefully organized to meet Henry's own timetable. Archbishop
Warham died, and Henry not only contrived that Cranmer
should succeed him, but also held off the UDI until Cranmer

was not only consecrated, but had also been to Rome and had received the metropolitical pallium from the Pope (and sworn allegiance to him) in April 1533. However, events were rolling fast, and by March that year Anne Boleyn was known to be pregnant, and official proclamation was made that Henry, having never been married to Katharine, had taken Anne as his queen. The process of casting off the Pope was furthered by the Act in Restraint of Appeals in 1533, the Ecclesiastical Appointments Act of 1534, and finally the Act of Supremacy of 1534. By the end of 1534 the UDI process was complete – the clergy owed their livings, their income and their freedom to Henry's person, and they had forsworn all fealty to the Pope. Their bishops were nominated solely by Henry himself, and he could act as abitrarily as he pleased. The Divine Right of Kings sanctioned his every whim – the temporal subjection of the clergy implemented it. The Church of England within two short years passed from being an England-located branch of a great trans-national company with headquarters in Rome to being a department of state whereby the monarch in Parliament catered for the religious welfare of his subjects. The monarch might be munificent or niggardly, benevolent or tyrannical – but before God and his subjects he was there to be 'head' of the Church of England. There was spasmodic reference to the Convocations of the Clergy, but for most purposes the Church was governed by the monarch in Parliament in exactly the way that taxes were levied, laws changed, or wars waged. Whilst the king might not normally take on ministerial roles or sacramental ministry, yet he *was* able, so the theoreticians had it, to recreate a line of bishops by his own say-so if the existing line ever expired without successors appointed!*
And this religious settlement was more or less monolithic – over the twelve years of Henry's monarchical supremacy (i.e.

---

*[Question] 14. Whether it be forfended by God's law, that (if it so fortuned that all the bishops and priests of a region were dead, and that the word of God should remain there unpreached, the sacrament of baptism and others unministered) that the king of that region should make bishops and priests to supply the same, or no?
[Answer] It is not forbidden by God's law.' (Cranmer 'Questions and Answers concerning the Sacraments and the Appointments and Power of Bishops and Priests', dated from Autumn 1540, reprinted in Thomas Cranmer, *Works: II Miscellaneous Writings and Letters* (Parker Society, Cambridge, 1846) p. 117.)

from the end of 1534 to the beginning of 1547) a Bible-loving Protestant might well die for his heresy, whilst a Papalist might die alongside him for his treason.

For our purposes it is sufficient to note that Henry VIII viewed the whole country as an organic unity, a many-membered body, which, by allegiance to its own laws, found itself bound to follow Henry whithersoever he might take them. When Henry issued decrees and his Parliament issued laws to which he gave the Royal Assent, then a Christian nation was regulating its own life in a way comparable to the governing of the land of Judah which had been practised in the days of the Davidic kings.

At this point we start to encounter a technical word, 'Erastian'. The term, however applicable it might have been in the first fifteen centuries of the Church, derives from Thomas Erastus, a Swiss theologian and physician (1524–83) who worked at Heidelberg, and, largely because of local controversies, wrote a thesis that ascribed to the State the right to exercise excommunication and ecclesiastical discipline, even to the point of overriding the leadership of the churchly community and its decision-taking bodies. However, we must not misread this; it seems fairly clear that in the sixteenth and seventeenth centuries there was an assumption that the civic rulers, even if not theologically learned and whilst certainly lay, would nevertheless be Christian. They would thus be broadly competent to exercise that control. However, by the eighteenth century there was no such automatic assumption about the beliefs of rulers, and the term slid over to indicate direct civil (and secular or irreligious) control of the Church of Christ. Indeed its use since then has assumed that the rulers were *not* Christian, and for this reason it has generally been reckoned to be a heresy, and can always safely be used as a 'boo' word, however morally neutral its origins.

But even in sixteenth-century terms, it is doubtful whether the term would stick on Henry VIII. The Crown in Parliament was not simply a civil power asserting authority over the people of God from outside. Rather the Church of England was governing itself corporately *from the inside* through the only organs of government then known or practised. So, whilst it might have been Erastianism in its original sixteenth-century sense, even then it was not that the organs of State were controlling a different body, the Church; for the State and the Church were one and same people, under one and the same legislature, a legislature with a God-given charter to control and direct the whole way of life of all the subjects of the king, whether fiscal, or moral, or religious. Nor was it entirely lay, for the bishops, as Lords Spiritual, took their place in the legislature. Thus the Church of England, through its Head and its organs of self-government, had both rid itself of any external claims to dominion over it from abroad, and had consolidated its own unity, as its very existence was merged into the common citizenship of the land. The whole Church of England was now sustained through the normal administrative power of the State organs of government over any department of State. But no feature of that arrangement could, in modern terms, be dubbed 'secular'. The Church of England was a department of State indeed, but an all-embracing department penetrating the life of every citizen, and not simply a seat of sectional interests.

It will be obvious that the 'nationalization' process in 1532–4 had very little overt doctrinal content. Apart from the inevitable denunciations of the Pope, and the exaltation of the religious office of the Crown, Henrician catholicism – e.g. in relation to the 'sacrament of the altar' or any other feature of its worship – was little changed in the years after the break from Rome from what it had been before. But a new *locus* of doctrinal authority had replaced the Pope, and it was now sheer coincidence, compounded by governmental caution or mere royal whim, which conformed the outward face of the Church to Roman Catholicism. There was no authority from Rome, none anyway which had any currency in England, which was requiring the Church of England to be thus. Accordingly, if the outward face of the Church of England remained relatively unchanged and comparable to Rome in Henry's day, that was no guarantee that it would do so in the reign of his son, Edward.

As the king aged, so the forces gathered. But the die was cast when the Prince's uncle, Edward Seymour, the Duke of Somerset, was named as Lord Protector during Edward's minority. And that cast die was itself imperilled when at the same time Henry named Princess Mary, his daughter by Katharine of Aragon, a Roman Catholic, as next in line to the throne if

Edward should die without issue.* This meant that the Council which ruled from January 1547, in the name of the ten-year-old King Edward VI, knew it stood but one heart-beat away from a Roman Catholic monarch. Clearly it would be years before the young king could beget a line of succession by physical descent from his own loins, and thus the Council went to work with extreme nervous energy to entrench a 'top down' Reformation as deeply as possible in as short a time as possible. The relocation of authority for belief in Henry's reign had laid eggs which hatched and came home to roost in Edward's. If ever a country was caught in *cuius regio, eius religio* ('he who holds the throne decides the religion'), that country was England. In England it meant not so much that a king was likely through *force majeure* to get his own way, as that the king's way was, by definition and as a doctrinal norm, God's way and beyond question. This view admittedly created occasional problems for royal advisers and counsellors when monarchs pressed their divine right beyond the limit, or when the people questioned that which was beyond question.

Through successive reigns for 155 years the vision of a country and Church which were co-terminous hung before the eyes of monarchs, bishops and legislators. It was wonderfully if horrifically put by Edwin Sandys, Bishop of London, in 1575, when charging five Dutch Anabaptists with heresy: as reported by Anabaptist sympathizers, he threatened to 'expel them from his church'; a prisoner asked 'How can you expel us ... when we have never yet been one with you?' – and to this Sandys replied that 'this was all the same ... [for] in England there was no one that was not a member of God's church.' So he condemned them to death, a fate two of them duly suffered.[1]

Even the Civil War of the 1640s did not destroy this ideal – for, though it divided the nation bitterly in half, each half had an ideal of a 'Church of the nation' which victory would bring

---

*Mary, of course, had been illegitimized by the nullifying of Henry's marriage to her mother, and therefore had no dynastic claim to the throne whatsoever. But Henry swept aside all such considerations and, with Parliament's support, settled the succession in his will. In the preamble he stated that he had full power of nominating the order of succession in himself, and then in the heart of the Act he did so nominate – simply stating that Edward, Mary and Elizabeth in that order would follow him, without any mention of *why* each took his or her place.

in. The Commonwealth period (1649–60, following the execution of Charles I) was in theory a time when an alternative understanding of a national Church flourished. The point is simply that a programme for a national Church (albeit a non-episcopal and largely aliturgical Church) was in the forefront of the Puritan programme. The regime may have made its own ideals hard to realize, but the ideals were certainly there. And the Restoration of the monarchy in 1660 saw not only a restoration of the episcopal, liturgical and monarchical Church of England, but also a theoretical monopoly of church life vested within it. Non-conformity of course existed, and it was immensely strengthened by the swingeing character of the 1662 Act of Uniformity. But the Act was looking for a genuine 'uniformity' of religious belief and practice for all the citizenry, a church which embraced them all alike, even if by coercion, and a unity of Church and State which were coextensive in their membership and subject to the same monarchical and parliamentary rule.

Whilst this concept of a Christian nation under a 'godly prince' was common to most leaders of this whole period, it was given its most forceful exposition by Richard Hooker. His *Laws of Ecclesiastical Polity*, first published in 1597, set out an ideal of a unitary Christian nation, in which the monarchy and other organs of government protected and upheld both a theological concept of the State and the actual corporate worship and faith *of the same people*, but now in their churchly role. As with Henry VIII, the issue was *not* by any stretch of imagination whether or how an alien State machinery should govern the company of believers – from the outside, so to speak – but rather how, in a Christianity-believing State, the members could govern themselves, from the inside.

The points at which the system broke down most obviously were when the lawful heir to the throne was a Roman Catholic, and therefore incapable (so it would seem) of both acting as supreme head on earth or governor of the Church of England, and of receiving the allegiance of others in that capacity. This extraordinary freak of succession happened twice – once in the person of Mary (1553–8), and once in the person of James II (1685–9). Mary came sufficiently early in the period to try to put the whole system into reverse, and monarch in Parliament surrendered the autonomy Henry VIII had seized, bowed the

knee to the Pope, and turned the Church of England back into
Provinces of the Roman Catholic jurisdiction. It is pointless to
speculate on what the effect of a long reign would have been;
as it was, she died after five years, and the nation, led by the
young Queen Elizabeth, went back to its reformed ways and
in particular restored the legislation of Henry VIII which separated England from the papacy. Elizabeth differed from Henry
largely in taking the title 'Supreme Governor' (rather than
'Head'), and in adopting Cranmer's second Edwardine Prayer
Book. In due course the Pope responded with an excommunication, and even a decree that whoever put Elizabeth to death
would do God service (in the bull *Regnans in Excelsis* 1570).
From then on the independence of the Church of England in
relation to the papacy was assured – Roman Catholicism was
driven underground, and papists were automatically set in
opposition to the Queen and her Church. The unitary theory
returned.

James II, the second Roman Catholic monarch, inherited a
far more entrenched Church of England, a far more suspicious
Parliament, and the worst of all possible international contexts
for promoting Roman Catholicism in England – for in France
1685 was the year of the revocation by Louis XIV of the Edict of
Nantes. This was the Edict issued in 1598 whereby Protestant
Huguenots were granted freedom to practise their religion.
When the Edict was revoked there was a massacre and a flight
to England of the Huguenots. This in turn raised great alarms
about what a Roman Catholic monarch might initiate in
England. James had to find a sensitive way – any way at all
– to fulfil his incompatible double role – as Supreme Governor
of the Protestant Church of England and as a loyal member of
the Church of Rome with its inbuilt exclusive claims and its
consequent hostility to the Church of England. James was not
sensitive, nor even wanting to be. But the double role was
impossible anyway, and had he not provoked his people so
obviously and so soon, he would probably still have done so less
obviously and slightly later. He brought about his own downfall
with his promulgation in 1688 of the Declaration of Indulgence,
a proclamation intended to relieve non-Anglicans (and therefore Roman Catholics) of the penalties previously imposed for
not conforming to the national Church. The story of the refusal

of seven bishops to handle it, of their trial for treason, and of their triumphant acquittal, is well known. A secret invitation went to William of Orange and he landed in Devon on 5 November 1688, the time came for James to flee, the throne was declared vacant by Parliamentary vote, men abandoned their oaths of allegiance to James, and invited William of Orange and his wife Mary, James' daughter but a Protestant, jointly to occupy the throne.* The Divine Right of Kings perished in the process. The sacredness of oaths took a battering, and a new day dawned for non-conformists. 1689 was the end of an era – and the beginning of the end of the establishment of the Church of England.

2. From the Glorious Revolution to the Reform Parliament (1689–1830) – the era of privilege

Once William and Mary were on the throne, Roman Catholicism in England and Wales became again a semi-underground movement, tainted with the likelihood that its adherents were secret or even open 'Jacobites', that is, people owing allegiance to James and his heirs. The Coronation Oath was altered and laws of succession enacted (notably in the Declaration of Rights (1689), and the Act of Settlement (1701)) to ensure there should never again be a papist monarch, and the stance on that front became very clear. However the leaders of Church and nation were faced in 1689 with two options in relation to non-conformity. They undoubtedly owed a debt to men and women whom only a few years before they had harried with legal discrimination and harsh penalties. These same people had stood with them in resisting James, and had even shared in opposing the Declaration of Indulgence – the terms of which had been designed to benefit non-conformists as a covert means of promoting Roman Catholicism! So how was the debt to be repaid? Clearly there could never be a return to the penal laws.

The obvious answer lay to hand in a policy of comprehension. In effect this was what the Puritans had sought in 1662, when the Restoration juggernaut had crushed them. The policy had

---

*The majority in the House of Lords for declaring the throne vacant was merely three – and the bishops who had not abandoned their oaths to James were absent, or they might have swung the day. Anything might have happened then.

much to commend it, and would in theory have resulted in a
single, somewhat diverse, Church of England. A conference
produced a draft 'Liturgy of Comprehension'; laws to enable
non-conformists to find their way back into a broad national
ecclesiastical fold were drafted; encouraging noises were made.
But it all came to nothing.

It looks as though the church leaders did not want to broaden
their base. They were sensitive lest the claims to be the 'true'
Church of England pass to the non-jurors. These – the non-
swearers – were led by the nine bishops and 400 presbyters
who, from a sense of conscience about the sanctity of oaths,
had declined to nullify their oaths of allegiance to James by
making new oaths to William and Mary, and were thus depart-
ing from the dioceses and parishes. They included Sancroft,
the Archbishop of Canterbury, and four others of the seven
bishops who had in 1688 come as heroes through the treason
trial. On the whole – as their scruple of conscience shows –
they were strict churchmen, who were not themselves going
to soften one jot or tittle of what being a churchman meant,
and were going to claim both the moral and the ecclesiastical
high ground. It became a time when the established Church
could give little away towards comprehension, and the project
failed.

An alternative programme was therefore followed. Non-conformists were offered a new concept, toleration. They were
going to be allowed to be themselves, though at a certain cost
in civil disadvantages. They could not go to the Universities,
sit in Parliament, or hold public office. But they *could* have
licensed places of worship, and they *could* assemble, meet and
worship in them. They could be free from the fear of arrest for
ridiculous offences. They took their chance.

The era was inevitably launched by heavy Parliamentary
action. In particular this fell upon the Church of England in
a clumsy and wounding way – for Parliament had to decree
that dioceses led by bishops who had not altered their oaths
of allegiance were now vacant, and had to take legislative steps
to deprive the occupants of those sees. With the Archbishop
of Canterbury himself proving one of the most obstinate of
opponents – simply on the issue of the sacredness of oaths
of allegiance – there was no possibility of a 'Church' process
that could have sorted out the troubles.

The fifty years from the Glorious Revolution to the beginnings of the evangelical revival (John and Charles Wesley had their hearts 'strangely warmed' in 1737) are mostly notable to ecclesiastical historians for the collapse of religious seriousness in the land. The collapse encompassed the non-conformist denominations as well as the established Church. It may well have been occasioned by the loss in 1689 of a sense of being embattled on God's behalf in a conflict which at root was his conflict, a confidence enjoyed by both sides when in conflict with each other as in Charles II's reign, and experienced no less strongly when churchman and non-conformist were embattled together against the king in James II's time. Perhaps the end of the Divine Rights of Kings was significant also. Religious passion died away in a generation, and apathy set in.

There was in that period another constitutional point which has been of importance to the Church of England in the almost three centuries which have elapsed since. In 1707 the Parliaments of Scotland and England were united. However, for obvious reasons the Churches of the two countries were not simultaneously united by that very move – the national Church of Scotland by law established was Presbyterian, whilst the Episcopal Church of Scotland was Jacobite, semi-underground, and certainly not by law established. Neither could be fused by law with the Church of England, and the possibility was never seriously considered. So separate Churches continued in the two nations. Thus in turn, for the first time, the Parliament which ruled the Church of England was not co-extensive in its constituency and membership with the geographical borders of England and Wales. The principle of unrepresentative persons taking counsel for the good (or at least the life) of the Church of England may have passed somewhat unremarked at the time, and in the history books – but it was the thin end of a very curious wedge, of which the thick end has latterly become visible. From 1689 onwards the Church of England is less numerically than all the people of England and Wales: from 1707 onwards it is also ruled by a body which in part comes from beyond the elected representatives of the people of England and Wales.

This paradoxical outcome was not repeated when the Irish

Parliament united with the Westminster Parliament in 1800.*
Instead the Church of Ireland did become united with the
Church of England by the very Parliamentary process, and
remained for seventy years 'The United Church of England
and Ireland', governed by the one Parliament of the 'United
Kingdom'. This was, of course, to have great significance when
that Parliament took unilateral action in respect of the Irish
part in 1833, and by that action triggered Keble's Assize
Sermon, and thus the Tractarian movement.

In theory the Church of England still had its own organs of
clerical self-government – the Convocations. These bodies had
shown some vigour in Stuart times, but in 1717 when they
opposed the Latitudinarian (i.e. 'Liberal') Bishop Hoadly they
were prorogued – a polite term for a permanent closure. They
maintained a shadowy existence, and in theory were convened
every time a new session of Parliament was inaugurated. But
they were only able to respond to Letters of Business issued
by the monarch, and no such Letters were issued from 1717
onwards. Business for the Convocations was not restored until
well into the next time phase. Indeed the actual changes in the
law affecting the Church of England which were implemented
during this period arose through straight initiatives in Parliament. Instances were:

(a) Banns of Marriage (regarding the place in the service
for calling them), 1753;

(b) banning of Clergy from membership of Parliament,
1801;

(c) building of 'Waterloo' Churches by Parliamentary allocation of £1 million in 1818, and £800,000 in 1824.

It was in this period that the shift in meaning of the word
'Erastian' occurred. Whether or not its sixteenth-century usage
could be properly applied to Hooker and the Tudor and Stuart
eras, the shift in meaning in the eighteenth century certainly
marched *pari passu* with a shift in the realities of Church and
State in England – and thus provides us with a word which

---

*It is irrelevant to this consideration that the Irish Parliament was both
before and after the union of 1800 highly unrepresentative of the Irish
people, in that no Roman Catholic could sit for any constituency. The
English contituencies in those days had their strong share also of rotten
boroughs, vote-rigging, and (of course) highly selective and privileged
franchise.

can be used with intense accuracy about the twentieth century establishment in England. Since the eighteenth century it has meant the constitutional rule by a secular State over a Christian Church. The very existence of the word, and the sheer applicability of it to our establishment, are the good weapons that come to hand at the outset of any confrontation with the establishment of the Church of England – for all agree at the outset that Erastianism is a heresy.

The writing was on the wall long before the end of this phase. We have seen how the Church of England lost its practical hold on the affections and religious loyalty of the land in the first half of the period. In neither depth of devotion nor breadth of numbers was this ever regained. And, as the impact of nonconformity rose through the Methodist Revival, and the Methodist and other 'Revivalist' evangelical groupings went into separation, and as the need for the emancipation of Roman Catholics surfaced through the political union with Ireland, so the Church of England was *de facto* losing not only numbers but also the high ground of originally defensible privilege from which it had begun. The end of that era was in sight.

3. From the Reform Parliament to the coming into force of the Enabling Act (1830–1920) – the era of Church self-discovery

The Reform Parliament came in 1830. It had itself a reformed composition in that Roman Catholics could now take their place in the Commons, in the same way that they were taking a proper place in society. (Free Churchmen also were now given permanent rights, though in practice they had been allowed by annual dispensations for the previous hundred years.) Ideas for church reform marched alongside this, and in 1833 Thomas Arnold, the Headmaster of Rugby from 1828 to 1842, produced his *Principles of Church Reform*. Whilst no one could ever have devised a scheme for an established Church broad enough to comprehend Roman Catholics, in other respects Arnold matched the broadening political scene with a scheme (not unlike what might have been attempted in 1689) for a comprehensive Church. Thus the Church of England could expand (papists apart) to meet the sociological and ecclesiastical realities, and the unity of Church and State could be not just minimally sustained, but actually substantially recovered.

The Reform Parliament quickly set about a programme of political reformation. Early in the programme was the enforced union of Southern Irish bishoprics and the resultant redistribution of income to more needy parts. The purpose was wholly beneficent – and the process, though it was entirely Parliamentary, was (it might be argued) much needed. But it was a step taken entirely on the political presuppositions which had run on from the previous century – that Parliament took counsel and took action for the good of the English Church, and now, since 1800, the Irish Church was under the same authority. When the High Churchman, John Keble, came to prepare his Assize Sermon, to be delivered in St Mary the Virgin, Oxford, on 14 July 1833, he had plenty of Parliamentary initiative against which to direct his artillery.

Keble's starting points are the direct opposite of Arnold's. The Church of England is the historic Church of the nation. The nation is now religiously pluriform, and Parliament sadly reflects that. In such a situation, Parliament is not only useless as the guardian of the Church, but actually misleads those who think the Church's credentials rest on its legal parliamentary support. Such is not the case, and the Church must be ready for parliamentary support to be withdrawn or to wither – in which case the true foundations of the Church in its apostolic succession will emerge clearly for all to see. The implication is that it does not matter terribly whether three-quarters of the nation or less than 1 per cent adhere to the Church of England, what the Church cannot do is compromise its apostolic inheritance and become comprehensive simply for the sake of numbers.

It cannot be said that the Tractarian Movement, or the anglo-catholic party as it became, ever stood consistently by this defiance of the state machinery as the chief legislative authority in the Church. Even the Assize Sermon reads as though Parliamentary authority *has been acceptable* until 1830; and it would be of some academic interest to know what Keble's reaction would have been if it had been the pre-1830 Parliament which had decided to unite Irish bishoprics. It is of course obvious that, in general terms, the high and sharp-edged profile which the Tractarians wished to give the Church of England would not sit well with a broad and inclusive national membership, and something would have to give. It is also obvious that the ever higher doctrine of the 'threefold' orders of ministry – i.e. bishop, priest (or presbyter) and deacon – which the same people were preaching would not sit well with mere Parliamentary (i.e. 'lay') authority. The Tractarians were further provoked to oppose secular rule over the Church, in that, when issues concerning their teaching and practice arose, recourse to the courts led straight on to appeal to the Judicial Committee of the Privy Council. The Judicial Committee was inevitably labelled 'secular' and denounced as being without theological justification or moral authority, and, as its findings proved time and again to be contrary to the 'catholic' innovations, it became policy not to recognize its jurisdiction in ecclesiastical cases and not to be bound by its findings. No matter that the two Archbishops themselves might be members of the Judicial Committee – it was a state-constituted court, and it had no authority. On the other hand, it would be difficult to find instances where the right of the monarch to nominate diocesan bishops was queried.

There is, however, a delightful and trenchant exception in Tract No. 59, 'Church and State' by Hurrell Froude, in which Froude lists the Prime Ministerial nomination of bishops as a sub-item under 'State interference'. What *was* occasionally asserted in relation to the appointment of bishops was that deans and chapters should be ready to defy the royal nomination and reject the actual nominee; and the opposition to Hampden becoming Bishop of Hereford in 1847, including a minority vote against him at the election by the dean and chapter, witnesses to this. It appears that the Crown was viewed as certainly having the right to name a name; but this right was not unbounded but was limited both by a sense of Christian responsibility towards God on the part of the monarch and – if this was insufficient – a fall-back ecclesiastical protection whereby either the dean and chapter could decline to elect or the Archbishop of the Province could decline to consecrate. This was realistic in the sense that it dealt with powers and procedures as they actually existed, and it could just be squared with their ecclesiology – but it still lacked something in sheer realism as to whether anyone would or could ever invoke such sanctions successfully, or at all. Realism

was not the usual currency of anglo-catholic discourse and
they generally preferred a bold and even visionary polarizing
as between God's Church and a pluralist or secular State.
Indeed it was this fairly determined unrealism in their polarizing, in relation to Parliament and to secular courts, which was
always part of their romantic and colourful attractiveness.
Perhaps their very romanticism bred a fraction too much sentiment in favour of the throne, and that gave limits to their
revolt. At the turn of the nineteenth and twentieth centuries
we can sense the relief with which Davidson, Archbishop of
Canterbury from 1903 to 1928, secured a *Royal* Commission
on Ecclesiastical Discipline, when for some years Parliamentarians had been calling for a Parliamentary one. Davidson
knew that a Parliamentary Commission would be anathema-
tized before it was even formed, but had hopes (perhaps partly
realized in the event) that a Royal Commission would hold
some vestige of moral authority in a generally lawless Church.

Statistics of affiliation and attendance

This period was also notable for the first accumulation of
reliable figures for church attendance. The findings of the
Census of Religious Worship of 1851 fell like a hammer-blow
upon the Church of England. The population of England and
Wales was around 17 million people, and these proved to be
divided for church-going purposes into three almost equal
groups: one third were worshipping on the day of the Census
in the Church of England, one third worshipped in other
Churches (90 per cent of them being Non-conformist and 10
per cent Roman Catholic), and one third were not in worship
at all.

It is no part of the present task to reflect on what this finding
meant for the missionary impetus of the Church of England
(as a matter of fact, the general nineteenth-century approach
was to treat non-worshippers as somehow lapsed and about to
return – so the vital response was to work for there to be
enough seats to seat them if they did return). But this grass-
roots finding was also stray evidence that the Church of
England was having an ever-growing problem in claiming to
be the Church of the people; and in many areas it was outnumbered by the other Churches, and the proportions of the apparently unchurched were becoming horrifying.

Church organs of self-government

As the conviction grew among churchmen that Church and State were not co-extensive and were not properly amenable to a single parliamentary form of government, so the calls went up for the restoration of the Convocations. These organs depended upon the royal writ for their convening, and upon Royal Letters of Business for their agenda; but they did have the form of 'sacred synods', they were by definition clerical, and were therefore clearly confessional in their composition and theological in their deliberations. There was precedent (as, e.g. in 1661 in the revision of the Book of Common Prayer) for the Convocations being the originators of legislation which was then rubber-stamped for the legal proprieties by Parliament, and it was precedent which the Victorian churchmen were keen to invoke for the restoration of real life in the Convocations. In the event Canterbury Convocation began deliberations in 1852 and York in 1861. One of the first fruits of this process was the Clerical Subscription Act of 1865, originated in Convocation, and terminating in not only an Act of Parliament, but also in the more strictly ecclesiastical outcome – amendments to Canon Law which altered the existing Canons 36, 37, 38 and 40 in conformity with the Act of Parliament, but were themselves 'enacted' solely on the authority of the Convocations with Her Majesty's licence. The Church of England once again had legislative bodies which, even if they were subject to the monarch, and in certain respects subservient to Parliament, nevertheless helped define the Church as a 'spiritual body' over and against the State.

It was unfortunate, to say the least, that almost immediately after the revival of the Convocations Parliament passed the 1874 Public Worship Regulation Act without recourse to the Convocations, and against the judgement of most church leaders; but this simply demonstrated that where powers exist, they are always liable to be used – and also that such a method of imposing laws on the Church of England lacked consent from those on whom they were imposed, and was therefore not only without moral authority but also unworkable in practice. If Parliament was meant to be the lay voice of the Church of England, then it was now not only actually unrepresentative of the Church in the Members' own plurality of beliefs, but was also ready arbitrarily to legislate without consulting the clerical Convocations.

In 1887 there came the first representative lay assembly from the Province of Canterbury; and the first signs of a fully representative 'church' organ – at least for deliberation – came when existing provincial lay bodies met with the Convocations in 1903, and took the title of the Representative Church Council. It was a further indication that the Church of England was identifying itself as a Church with its own internal organization, as over the State which, as an obvious corollary, was *not* to be viewed as the Church, nor was Parliament 'representative' of it. It was this Council which in 1913 passed the following Resolution:

> That there is in principle no inconsistency between a national recognition of religion and the spiritual independence of the Church, and this Council requests the Archbishops of Canterbury and York to consider the advisability of appointing a Committee to enquire what changes are advisable in order to secure in the relations of Church and State a fuller expression of the spiritual independence of the Church as well as the national recognition of religion.

There are some wonderful touches of unreality in this resolution: is not 'recognition' really 'ownership'? And is not 'religion' really 'The Church of England'? And is there really 'no inconsistency'? But, leaving debating points aside, we record that the 'Selborne' Committee was set up on the basis of this request, and it in turn ushered in the end of the era.

Disestablishment in Ireland and Wales

During this period there were two notable exercises in disestablishment. The Church of Ireland was disestablished in 1871, and the dioceses of the Canterbury Province which were located in Wales were disestablished and re-formed as a separate Province of the Anglican Communion, the Church in Wales, in 1920. It is no part of this book to explore these two steps in detail, but the actual processes of disestablishment which were used do bear upon contemporary questions. The two separate processes of disestablishment were in fact, despite many close parallels, in great contrast with each other. Thus, for instance, the disestablishment in Ireland was the upshot of an almost single-issue electoral victory by the Liberals in 1868, whereas Welsh disestablishment had difficulty sustaining Parliamentary attention, being originally charted before the First World War, being held in suspension during the War, and only focused for action after the Armistice.

In both cases the following conditions obtained:

(i) The desire for disestablishment arose from outside the Church concerned, and was generally resisted by the Church. There seems to be almost a principle of history that church leaders in established Churches have great difficulty in thinking positively about disestablishment.

(ii) Nevertheless, it is worth noting that very few points of principle were raised in defence of the two establishments, but the main fears aroused were: (a) that seemingly unjust disendowment would be bound in with it; and (b) that there would be a loss of some more intangible 'spiritual' advantage which the respective Churches held whilst established but would forfeit on disestablishment.

(iii) No one seems to have raised as a problem that Churches thus liberated would have to choose their own bishops and other leaders, and would have to form some pattern of synodical government to run their corporate lives.

(iv) Despite occasional grumblings, both Churches seem to have taken to disestablishment like ducks to water, and the publicity and debate surrounding the actual events seem to have raised their profiles and advertised their purposeful voluntary life very well. They also coped with a financial division of assets without shrinking.

(v) Each time the question was asked 'If disestablishment is good for the Irish (Welsh), why it is not opportune for the English?' The answer given to everyone's satisfaction was 'In England the majority of the inhabitants profess to be "C of E", and the establishment properly reflects and protects that situation.'

> 'We English,' said *The Times*, 'rest our Church on its popular basis – that is, on the basis of numbers.'[2]

> 'Can any one suppose that if the members of the present Church of England dwindled down to a twelfth of the population, the people would for one moment consent to

that Church remaining the Established Church of the
country?"³ (F. F. Trench (Rector of Newton, Co. Meath)

Rather amusingly, the Conservative opponents of Irish
disestablishment saw the appeal to numbers as politically
dangerous, and threw their weight against it for that reason.
How was it that it could be *politically* dangerous? Why,
because it would lead logically to universal suffrage . . .!
Once again, opponents have had to shift their ground in the
light of later history.

It is no part of this book to follow at any length later church
history in these two countries, in respect of their two disestablished Churches. No case for or against disestablishment of
the Church of England is going to be based on the experience
of these two Churches. The limitations of any parallels are
gladly acknowledged. Nevertheless the following markers need
to be put down:

(i) Both Churches, not only immediately after disestablishment but consistently since, have shown themselves at least
comfortable and at most excitedly enthusiastic about their
new status as 'free'.*

(ii) Neither Church saw itself, or allowed others to describe
it, as a 'sect'. Indeed both have been firmly insistent on their
standing as part of 'one holy catholic and apostolic Church',
Certainly all other Churches – Anglican or otherwise – have
continued to regard them exactly the same as before.

(iii) Neither Church suffered decline in numbers out of proportion to that suffered by other Churches in the same

---

*If we seek signs of retrospective grief among communities which had so
thoroughly opposed disestablishment in advance, then an isolated
example of a wonderfully pessimistic spirit is to be found in one of the
deservedly least known of Mrs Alexander's hymns, reported as sung in
Derry Cathedral on New Year's Day 1871:

Look down, Lord of heaven, on our desolation!
    Fallen, fallen, fallen is now our Country's crown.
Dimly dawns the New Year on a churchless nation,
    Ammon and Amalek tread our borders down.

The Bible itself gives a short book to Lamentations, but hope of a new
Jerusalem is a much weightier theme. One dares to hope that the disappointed Mrs Alexander got this out of her system once and for all, and
the very record that it was sung in that place on that day suggests
strongly that it was sung nowhere else and on no other date.

period, and, in the case of Wales, it is at least arguable
that the Church in Wales holds a relatively more prominent
position in the country compared with 'the chapels' than it
did seventy-five years ago.

(iv) Paradoxically the United Kingdom government found
itself with four territories to govern, one with an episcopal
established Church, one with a Presbyterian, and two with
no established Church at all. Whether this actually means
that the union Parliament is, as English apologists often
state, officially confessing Jesus Christ as Lord, appears
doubtful. It might be equally expounded as a Parliamentary
system which has a couple of established Churches, both
very different from each other, still attached to it by accident
of history, but which has no vested interest in that kind of
arrangement and which is institutionally indifferent on the
matter.

(v) Just as paradoxically, the Church of England is now
ultimately governed by that same Parliament, in which not
only do there sit for English constituencies people of every
belief and none, but equally people of similar variety of
views from *right outside England* are constituted by the
establishment as guardians and governors of the Church of
England. Furthermore, at intervals even a Prime Minister
comes from outside England – the most recent examples
being Alec Douglas-Home (1963–4) and Jim Callaghan
(1976–9). There have also been many instances right up to
the present day of other political parties having leaders from
outside England aspiring to inhabit 10 Downing Street –
and the names of David Steel, Neil Kinnock, and John Smith
come immediately to mind. In terms of legislation, there can
be little that is odder than the sight of Ian Paisley, the
Democratic Unionist MP for North Antrim and minister of
the Free Presbyterian Church of Ireland, laying down the
law for the Church of England, a Church with which he had
neither geographical nor ecclesiastical affinities and very
few visible sympathies.

The end of the era

Before the First World War it was not only 'ecclesiastical discipline' and Welsh disestablishment which were occupying the
Church of England. The difficulty in getting church legislation

through Parliament and other frustrations within the life of
the Church itself led to the 'Selborne' Committee, mentioned
above. The Committee's report in 1916 proposed a considerable
devolution of powers from Parliament to the Representative
Church Council, and its recommendations became the subject
of the advocacy of an unofficial pressure group, the Life and
Liberty Movement, in 1917. The First World War was itself
altering the face of the Church of England, and chaplains
returned from the War with new ideals. Alongside the Church
of England, the established Church of Scotland was negotiat-
ing with the United Free Church of Scotland to find a pattern
of united church life in which the national establishment would
remain, but total freedom from State control would be assured
– and this reached consummation with the Church of Scotland
Act 1921.* So minds in England could not help but move in
step with that. In the event the 'Selborne' Report and the Life
and Liberty Movement led to a quicker result than could ever
have been visualized: a precipitating factor here was undoubtedly the impatience of Parliament with having to handle
detailed church legislation. The Church of England might not
be governing itself fully – but it was at least now able to
identify itself as a distinct and even spiritual entity.

---

*The preamble to this read:

This Church, as part of the Universal Church wherein the Lord Jesus
Christ has appointed a government in the hands of Church office-
bearers, receives from Him, its Divine King and head, and from Him
alone, the right and power subject to no civil authority to legislate, and
to adjudicate finally, in all matters of doctrine, worship, government
and discipline in the Church. (11 & 12 George 5, cap. 29 (Church of
Scotland Act 1921))

If a preamble to a Parliamentary Act actually expresses Parliament's
ideology (and it certainly reads like a universal principle), then all the
groundwork for the freedom from State control of the Church of England
was laid over seventy years ago.

2. Phases of the Establishment: From the Enabling Act to the Present Day

The year 1920 is a hinge point in Church–State relationships in England. The separation and disestablishment of the Welsh dioceses was peripheral to this, for the main change was the creation of an official – and Parliamentarily sanctioned – identification of a Church of England which was now formally and visibly less than the whole nation of England. From 1920 onwards there exists an ecclesiastical entity carrying the name 'Church of England' which from parish to nation exists within the civic society, but is by no stretch of imagination co-extensive with it. Indeed the Church of England numbers only a fraction of the count of the civic community. The quest for an ecclesial and synodical, as distinct from a nationalistic or atmospheric, identity was in large measure fulfilled in 1920. Certainly a trend was set which has a virtually inevitable end. And the period since 1920 itself divides naturally into two parts, thus completing the five phases of the establishment which my section-headings advertise.

4. From the Enabling Act to synodical government (1920–70) – the era of growing incredibility

The technical title of the Act of Parliament which devolved powers to the Church was the Church of England Assembly (Powers) Act 1919, but it is always known as the Enabling Act. The Act followed closely the recommendations of the 'Selborne' Commission and the goals of the Life and Liberty Movement, and came to pass after the War with astonishing speed. The Church of England now had, in its National Assembly and its relation to Parliament, a wholly new pattern of self-government. It is worth noting the structure of this new edifice.

We begin with the parishes. In them there had to be not only Parochial Church Councils but also – and necessarily –

an electoral base from which the laity to represent the parish
on the PCC, on the Ruri-decanal Conference, and the Diocesan
Conference, were to be elected. There existed, of course, the
ancient 'vestry' meeting which, jointly with the incumbent,
chose the churchwardens and received reports on certain charities.* At an early stage in the creation of the Enabling Act it
was determined that each parish would have its own electoral
roll, and that people would have individually to apply for membership of their respective parish rolls. The roll in each parish
would then provide a defined base of 'members', from whom
and by whom the requisite elections could be made. The issue
was then one of the qualifications for inclusion on the electoral
roll.

Here we may illustrate the options available by setting out
two polarized opinions. At the one end was Hensley Henson,
Bishop of Hereford from 1917 to 1920, and of Durham from
1920 to 1939. In 1919 he was totally opposed to any moves
towards distancing the Church of England from the State, and
he viewed the whole creation of electoral rolls with distrust.
His own image of the whole land, the whole population
(*exceptis excipiendis*), of England as being by definition the
Church of England was threatened by the creation of the electoral rolls. Those who enrolled would, from his standpoint,
form an ecclesiola within the ecclesia and thus erect a two-tier
pattern of church membership. In the two tiers the voluntarily
enrolled would always have pretensions to *be* the Church, and
would thus inexorably 'unchurch' the merely passive parishioners. This view was overridden (it would have been fatal
to the whole 'enabling' concept), but it helped create the cli-
mate in which only minimal qualifications were to be required
for enrolment. Thus a parishioner had merely to be baptized
and state that he or she was a 'member of the Church of
England' and that would suffice. Neither confirmation nor any
attendance at worship was required. Those from outside the
parish could qualify by six months regular worship in the
parish. The application to be included on a roll and the stating
therein by the applicant 'I am a member of the Church of
England' did not *make* the applicant a 'member' – the statement simply set out in writing that which was deemed to be

---

*See the fuller discussion in Chapter 8 below.

already the case. It was thus possible, though perhaps with some discomfort, to hold to the Hensley Henson view that somewhere around thirty million adults should be viewed as 'members of the Church of England', even whilst bringing into force the electoral rolls. Candidates for the PCC and higher bodies had to be not only on the electoral roll but also confirmed, and the House of Laity of the National Assembly was then elected indirectly by the lay members of the Diocesan Conferences.

Hensley Henson also gave warning that the provision of the rolls would not only create a two-tier pattern of church membership, but would also reveal how very few in number were prepared to apply for enrolment. This indeed proved to be the case.

The opposite view was put forward by Charles Gore, Bishop of Oxford. He, from his anglo-catholic background, viewed with alarm the creation of a roll with such a minimal requirement for inclusion. His own understanding of initiation meant to him that confirmation had to be added to water-baptism for admission to adult membership.* He wished the rolls to include only communicants, which again pointed to confirmation as their basis. His thesis, if it had been adopted, would have provided a smaller figure still than was actually registered when the rolls were begun, but would have perhaps given a more realistic picture of actively participating 'members'. It would have created a 'membership' figure for the Church of England which would have indicated negatively that 75 or 80 per cent of the random thirty million baptized were *not* to be reckoned as members, and positively that the Church of England consists of the true worshippers, with much less fuzziness at the edges. Gore failed in his advocacy – and resigned his see (not wholly because of this, but not without reference to it).

Thus there came into statutory prominence in 1920 the National Assembly of the Church of England (usually called by its popular title 'Church Assembly' hereafter). It was not of course invented in 1920, nor was it created by the Act of Parliament. The title of the Act almost makes this explicit –

---

*Gore believed in the 'two-stage' anglo-catholic theory of sacramental initiation, i.e. that confirmation is a second half and a 'completion' of water-baptism.

the Church of England Assembly (Powers) Act. It was the conferring by Parliament upon an already existing Assembly (i.e. the Representative Church Council) of legislative powers that was deemed to be occurring. The leaders of the Church of England, whilst wholly bound into the State machinery and the State connection, still baulked at a move so nakedly Erastian as the State *creating* church governmental bodies. Thus the very point of origin of our fourth period witnessed in its inception to a nervousness amongst the bishops about Parliament's exercising powers over the Church of England – and also witnessed thereby to their own semi-subconscious convictions: (a) that Church and State were two separate institutions; (b) that the Church must not too obviously be subservient to the State; and yet (c) that the Church could only get peaceably the powers it desired if those powers were devolved by lawful process from Parliament; and it could only get the increased freedom it desired if it were prepared to be content with a lengthening rather than the elimination of the leash on which it was held. Compromise was required in both drafting and conscience.

The upshot was the joining of the two Houses of both Northern and Southern Convocations with the House of Laity to form a single, but complex, National Assembly of the Church of England. The Assembly received from Parliament powers to draft legislation, insofar as the Church of England was governed by statute. The powers included total freedom to revise and amend such drafts in ways which replaced all Parliamentary procedures, saving only the equivalent of the third reading in each House of Parliament. At this final reading no amendments were to be moved, and the powers of each House of Parliament were limited to saying 'yea' or 'nay'. Such legislation, whether in draft or after enactment, was to be known as a Measure, and the procedure is still in operation down to the present day. A Measure is fully part of Statute Law, and often amends existing Acts (as was inevitable from the start, as all previous Church legislation took the form of 'Acts' – as, e.g. the very Act of Uniformity 1662). The only sifting by Parliament of Measures sent to it from the Assembly has been that, under the Enabling Act, Parliament has an 'Ecclesiastical Committee' which receives a Measure from the Assembly and adjudicates as to whether it is or is not 'expedient' for the

Measure concerned to be laid before the Lords and Commons. If the Committee deems it 'not expedient' (perhaps as inconsistent with itself or in opposition to existing statute law and the rights of citizens) then it has to send the draft Measure back to the Assembly (or nowadays the Synod). Otherwise the Committee takes responsibility for introducing the Measure into Parliament, though, obviously, within the Lords it would usually be a bishop who moves it.

It is a matter of history that the system very nearly defeated itself at an early stage of its implementation. In 1920, at the very point when the Enabling Act came into force, the Convocations had recently replied to the Royal Letters of Business issued in response to the Report of the 1904–6 Royal Commission on Ecclesiastical Discipline. But the Home Secretary who received their reply indicated that he thought that, now the new machinery for church government was in place, the proposals for liturgical revision in the reply should be placed before the newly empowered National Assembly, to be authorized by the new procedures, i.e. by 'Measure'. This course was followed; the Assembly considered proposals from 1920 till 1925; the House of Bishops took over and re-wrote the proposals almost from scratch; and they brought the new proposed Prayer Book to the Assembly in 1927. It was accepted there, and duly went (as a schedule attached to a Measure) to the Lords and Commons. The Lords passed it, but the Commons defeated it on 15 December 1927 by 238 votes to 205. There was dismay and an outcry that somehow the Commons could not have understood what they were being asked to do. It was their *duty* to approve what the Church Assembly resolved. It has to be said that the Commons acknowledged no such duty – they only observed that they had a discretion they could exercise and should do so responsibly. The bishops, convinced that the Commons had acted on a kind of random midwinter madness, re-touched the Book minimally, took it through the Assembly again (though with a greatly reduced majority), and then lost it in the Commons for a second time, with less *brouhaha* but an increased margin of defeat – 266 to 220. The new deal of the Enabling Act was being tested, and the Commons, unable to respond to Measures save by 'yes' or 'no', had duly said 'no' – twice.

A 'Church and State' crisis broke out, to understand which

we need a fuller view of the issues raised by the 1927–8 Prayer
Book. The broadest possible view would be that the Church of
England was endeavouring to come to terms with the existence
within its ranks of a large and increasingly strident anglo-
catholic party. This party, within the period of just under a
century since it had started, had departed from the original
charter which gave it birth – a strict, even wooden, reading of
the text and rubrics of the Book of Common Prayer – and was
imitating Roman ritual in dozens of ways. Hence had sprung
the Royal Commission on Ecclesiastical Discipline, and from
its findings in turn had sprung first a variant on the 'Orna-
ments Rubric' and then, almost by mistake, the key features
of a new eucharistic rite, and, finally, a complete alternative
Prayer Book. The overall effect was to broaden the liturgical
base of the Church of England so as to comprehend the existent
anglo-catholicism. However, the matter had arisen not from
an anglo-catholic liturgical initiative, but from quite the
reverse – strong Protestant complaints about liturgical
illegalities, and a consequent quest for 'Ecclesiastical discipline'. The only way, therefore, that there could be any broadening of the liturgical base (such as, for instance, to allow some
restricted use of permanent reservation of the sacramental
elements of communion) was by setting very firm limits to the
new broadening. So the broadening was to please the anglo-
catholics, the limits to it to pacify the evangelicals. It had
exactly the opposite effect – the evangelicals objected to the
broadening, the anglo-catholics to the limits.

The bishops were landed with the problem of the double
defeat by the Commons. They had gone to Parliament, under
the deal worked out only eight years before by the Enabling
Act, saying: 'You have the final powers, and we now need *your*
authorization of this Prayer Book.' The Commons said 'no' in
December 1927, apparently on the grounds that the Book
sailed too close to popery. The bishops then, in effect said: 'You
do have the final powers, and we *do* respect your right to say
"no", and you have done that, and we would not dream of
moving in liturgical revision until we have your "yes"; so now
we have tightened the rubrics slightly so as to draw in those
limits a little in accordance with the Protestant tone of your
debate; therefore *please* now give us by a "yes" the Book we
want and need.' And again the Commons said 'no'. So what

were the bishops to do? Could they, for instance, just pull in their horns and say '1662 alone is legal, and its rubrics and text bind us all absolutely, so everyone must dutifully come into line'? They couldn't reasonably take this position, not only because there was no way the anglo-catholic movement would go back securely behind 1662 walls, not only because for upwards of twelve months they had been explaining in public and to all comers how desperately the new Book was needed, but also because voices were rising on all sides to bid them not to surrender to the butchery of an ungodly, prejudiced, and theologically incompetent House of Commons.

In the event they cooked up a notion that the bishop of each diocese is, in his own diocese, the 'lawful authority' to which the Declaration of Assent then referred.* They made a public statement that 'in the present emergency and until further order be taken' they would not view the use of services within the 1928 'Deposited Book' as inconsistent with loyalty to the Church of England. The 'emergency' was one they proposed to solve not by further liturgical drafting, and the trying of further texts on Parliament – no, the intention was to find ways of circumventing Parliament so that liturgical texts should never again be the subject-matter of Parliamentary debate and decision. So the question was how to get powers devolved from Parliament to a more obviously 'Church' legislative body. The Cecil Church and State Commission which was set up in the wake of the debacle reported in 1935 and recommended that such powers should be devolved in and through a revision of Canon Law. This latter process was then set in hand by the appointment of a Canon Law Commission in 1939. This Commission could not meet, because of the War, until 1943, and did not report until 1947.

The sense of shock, pleasant or unpleasant, created by the unexpected Parliamentary vetoes in 1927 and 1928, was profound. One of those most wedded to the establishment,

---

*The Declaration of Assent until 31 August 1975 ran:

I assent to the Thirty-Nine Articles, and to the Book of Common Prayer, and of the Ordering of Bishops, Priests, and Deacons. I believe the doctrine of the Church of England as therein set forth, to be agreeable to the Word of God; and in public prayer and administration of the sacraments I will use the form in the said book prescribed and none other, *except so far as shall be ordered by lawful authority*. (Italics mine.)

Hensley Henson, did a complete U-turn and, with his aphorism 'end it or mend it', joined the opponents. Anglo-catholics who, for over eighty years, had been denouncing State authority over the Church of England as wicked, welcomed the results even if not the means; while evangelicals, whose whole stance had been '1662 alone', welcomed not only the result but also the means, and were thereafter subtly entrapped into an over-ready identification of Parliament with God's just ways of governing his Church – in contrast to the bishops and the Church Assembly whom the evangelicals regularly viewed as either spineless or conniving in the face of anglo-catholic aggression.[1]

This notable victory by Parliament against the wickedness of church leaders helped to entrench deep in evangelical minds the absolute – even the doctrinal – necessity of the State link to keep the otherwise wayward Church orthodox. This view of evangelicals was certainly still around in the 1960s, though it has been subject to slow death (in the face of State and ecclesiastical realities) since.* In the upshot, people saw a distinct line between Church and State much more clearly than had previously emerged. The famous statement by the House of Bishops, delivered to the Church Assembly on 9 July 1928 by Archbishop Davidson, witnessed to this:

> It is a fundamental principle that the Church – that is, the Bishops together with the Clergy and the Laity – must in the last resort, when its mind has been fully ascertained, retain its inalienable right, in loyalty to our Lord Jesus

---

*An amazing event in October 1993 demonstrated how some evangelicals at least can live in a world of constitutional unrealities – the Church Society, a somewhat coelacanthine institution quite improperly described in *The Church of England Year Book* as 'The senior evangelical society of the Church of England', went to the High Court to get an injunction declaring that the Commons would be acting *ultra vires* if they debated the Ordination of Women Measure, as this would touch the fundamental doctrinal character of the Church of England – a power not devolved by Parliament in the original Enabling Act. This was sheer madness, and it is a relief that the application failed. Had it succeeded, it would have invited Parliament to return to the days of the Public Worship Regulation Act 1874, and simply impose constitutional and doctrinal changes upon the Church of England unbid. What a make-believe world in which to protect the truth of God.

Christ, to formulate its Faith in Him and to arrange the expression of that Holy Faith in its forms of worship.

The presuppositions of this statement reveal clearly that we are at an advanced stage of separation of Church and State. The Church is defined almost explicitly as those who, in the Assembly and through Diocesan Conferences, had actually asked for the Book and had endorsed the expression of the faith in it. Equally, and again almost explicitly, no space is given in this statement for any theory that the electors of England are the true Church of England people, that they are properly and best represented in Parliament, and that therefore a Parliamentary decision *is* a, slightly concealed, *Church* decision. No, on this occasion at least, all pretence was swept away – there were two distinct and even opposed forces at work: namely, the Church and its organs of decision-making, and the State and *its* legislative body. The only pretence was that the Church was in the last analysis free.

One of the major effects of 'the Prayer Book Crisis' was to focus issues of Church–State relationships particularly upon the question of authority over forms of worship. This was where the battle had been fought; and this was where the need of change was great, but the means for change were closed to the bishops. In that *impasse* there was desperate need of, not so much new texts but new procedures. The bishops were entirely clear they would not send liturgy back to Parliament, for it to fall into such disrespect in the Commons when away from their own control. So instead the policy adopted was:

(i) to publish the 1928 Book as a kind of private publication, with a note stating that its publication did not of itself imply that it was authorized for use in worship;

(ii) to allow its use through the notion that bishops were for these purposes 'lawful authority';*

(iii) to press on with seeking new procedures for authorization of liturgy, procedures, that is, that would bypass Parliament.

Part (i) of the policy occurred later that same year, and the 'Deposited Book' has since been readily available in print, has been known as 'The Prayer Book as Proposed in 1928', and has had its own extended span of life in Series 1 Alternative

---

*See the Declaration of Assent then in use, in fn. on p. 39 above.

Services, with its last footprints in Rite B communion in the ASB.

Part (ii) of the policy found its anti-Erastian outworking in the resolution of July 1929 in the Upper House of Canterbury Convocation which said that the bishops would have regard to

> ... the following principles:
> (1) That during the present emergency and until further order be taken the Bishops, having in view [the whole sequence of events leading to the defeat in the Commons of the 1928 Book], cannot regard as inconsistent with loyalty to the principles of the Church of England the use of such additions or deviations as fall within the limit of these proposals ... [2]

It has to be confessed that this was the bishops defying Parliament and calling acceptable what Parliament had rejected.

Part (iii) of the policy led to the setting up in 1930 of the Cecil Commission on Church and State.

Because the issue of control of forms of worship had been *the* great issue which had filled the headlines in 1927–8, it was a solution to that issue which was sought. It bulked large in the 1935 Report of the Cecil Commission and from there found its way into the 1947 Report of the Canon Law Commission. At each point, the steady intention was to find the 'new procedures' by retaining the Declaration of Assent from the 1865 Clerical Subscription Act, and within it redefining 'lawful authority'. In the 1947 Report there was a long memorandum appended on the subject by Mr Justice Vaisey, which referred back to the Cecil Commission.[3] And Draft Canon XIII within the 1947 proposed code, over and above Royal Warrant and Parliamentary legislation, in effect would have newly conferred 'lawful authority' on any forms simply passed by the Convocations of either Canterbury or York, to be used within their respective Provinces. This would have allowed new forms to be devised without being submitted to Parliament – exactly the desired end.

To complete this story, it is worth noting that the proposed Canon took another nineteen years to come into force. It was debated and amended in the Convocations and House of Laity and the recommendations of the Moberley Commission on Church and State in 1952 had to be taken into account in order to give the House of Laity a say in authorizing what were now 'alternative services'. The Prayer Book (Alternative and Other Services) Measure 1965 went through the Church Assembly in July 1964, and the Commons in March 1965, and came into force on 1 May 1966. It became one of the first points in the constitution, subsequent to the original all-embracing 'Enabling Act', in which Parliamentary powers were devolved upon the Church Assembly.

However, it has to be said, in the light of history, that the haunting fascination exercised by the ghost of 1928 over-concentrated minds on powers in respect of liturgy. This had the effect of delaying unnecessarily a proper weighing of other powers that remained with Parliament. And even the Chadwick Commission which reported in 1970 gave all too much weight in its evaluating of Parliamentary powers over the Church of England to this same issue of liturgy. The 1965 Measure had built in, among its many other safeguards, a top limit of fourteen years currency for any one category of service (as, e.g. Holy Communion). Its whole validity was therefore due to perish in or around 1980, and a further treatment was vital. The chapter in the Chadwick report on 'The relation with Parliament' simply ignores all powers other than those connected with liturgy and doctrine; and its major thrust concerns whether all powers over worship should be devolved, or whether some residual powers should remain with Parliament.[4] One looks in vain for a discussion, let alone recommendations, on the general point of principle as to whether Parliament ought to have any powers over Church legislation. The Commission found it abhorrent that Parliament should have a veto over any proposed official forms of worship, but said nothing that would have borne upon whether or not Parliament ought to be able, for instance, to veto provision for women to be ordained as presbyters.

A fair view of our fifty years reveals on the official liturgy front one 'Prayer Book crisis', nearly forty years of 'the present emergency', three Church and State Commissions, one Canon Law Commission, eighteen years bringing a new Canon into force, the beginning of the Liturgical Commission (1955), and the authorizing of the first 'alternative services'. Liturgy is certainly a major feature of the public life of the Church of England in the period, and it is marked not only by the shape

and priorities of the report of the Chadwick Commission, but
also and inevitably by a constant stream of books, debates,
journalism and conflicts about liturgy. Yet there were other
issues to tackle through the central organs of the Church of
England in the period, and the Chadwick Commission did not
help; it had two categories of legislative issues, and it
addressed them as firstly 'The relation to Parliament' (Chapter
2, which is all about and only about liturgy) and secondly as
'Organization and property' (Chapter 5, which inevitably
raises in passing at every point of detail the relationship with
Parliament). The upshot was that, except in the dissenting
notes, the general principle of Parliamentary control was not
addressed in itself, and the very shape of the report subtly
contributed to an over-cautious handling of core principles in
the Church and State relationship.

The post-War years saw considerable official change. Canon
Law revision was the major preoccupation of the Fisher years
(1945–61); but in the 1960s not only did the new code of Canon
Law come into force, but elections to the Convocations were
detached from Parliamentary elections, a great cluster of
powers were devolved from Parliament to the Church authorities in the Pastoral Measure 1968, there was a beginning of
consultations in vacant dioceses prior to the nomination of a
new bishop (following the Howick Report of 1964), and finally
The Synodical Government Measure No. 1 1969 brought the
new era into being. Internally the Church of England was
also concerned with the Paul Report on *The Payment and
Deployment of the Clergy* (1964), with the Anglican–Methodist
Conversations, with the reform of patronage, with John Robin-
son, with falling numbers of ordinands, with opening shots
over open communion and even the ordination of women, with
new possibilities of relating to a post-Vatican II Church of
Rome, and with the (often stormy) story of the authorization
for actual use of services brought forward under the Alternative Services Measure. There was much business to be done.

The story of these fifty years as I have told it largely concerns
constitutional issues, with 1927–8 as a centre-piece. However,
it had to be added that through the period, and especially after
the Second World War, the Church of England was visibly
losing its distinctive position in the land. It is likely that
the War itself hastened the overall trend towards practical

atheism, despite many individual lives which would witness to the contrary. Infant baptism and other occasional offices still ran strong after the war – infant baptism being given in the Church of England to 67 per cent of live births in England in 1950. But the trend in all the statistics was downwards as the second half of the century progressed, and by 1970, our last watershed, a very different picture was emerging.

5. From 1970 to the present day – the end of pretence

The year 1970 was a watershed in many respects. In constitutional terms it saw the Church of England beginning on synodical government. Whilst General Synod only continues the powers of the Assembly in relation to the State, its coming has given a new sense of a coherent single central organ of government to the Church of England. It has brought Bishops, Clergy and Laity into closer and more integrated relationships with each other, and has stepped up the proportion of elected members within the House of Clergy. It is clear now that, whatever defects await correction in the structures of synodical government, the General Synod is, as a body, fully competent to attain the formal autonomy which a break with Parliament would entail. Its existence is taken for granted in the rest of this book, and a fuller defence of it is deployed in Chapter 6.

It was also in 1970 that there was published the latest Church and State report, *Church and State 1970*, the fruit of the Chadwick Commission. From that report have come two major results. The first is the Church of England (Worship and Doctrine) Measure 1974, which devolved most powers over liturgy to the General Synod, whilst still leaving the 1662 Book of Common Prayer parliamentarily entrenched. That process went through fairly cleanly (with some mutterings from the Lords and Commons which led to a reaction in the early 1980s). It represented the penultimate stage of getting 1927–8 out of the Church of England's system; and, as has been shown above, because it was the matter which had engrossed the interest of most Church and State interactions since 1920, the coming of a solution has correspondingly little place in the chapters which follow.

However, the other major outcome of the Chadwick Commission's report was a new convention for the consultation process which precedes the appointment of bishops. The political leaders retained strong powers for the Prime Minister of the day, and, although the Crown Appointments Commission method of the Church providing a short-listing procedure was adopted, this is clearly far from a truly churchly method of appointing bishops, and comes in for considerable critical analysis below. The actual operation of the convention, in which Prime Ministers have utilized the powers of discretion given them by it, has also served to demonstrate that the Church of England is still held on a Parliamentary leash, and diocesan bishops are still the appointees of the State.

The period has also seen the Commons twice defeat Church Measures, thus rubbing in the direct control of the Church of England, a power still held in Parliament. The Church for its part has been quite undefiant of this flexing of Parliamentary muscle, and has not only had to assimilate these bruisings, but most recently of all has had to wait for a year before the ordination of women as presbyters could be put through Parliament, in the course of which various leading members of General Synod and its Standing Committee have been subjected to somewhat humiliating cross-examination by the Ecclesiastical Committee of Parliament.

These national constitutional issues occupy four more chapters below. However, it may well be that a more significant change was what was happening in the country at street level. Here I can only give an impressionistic view, and it is, of course, open to other interpretation.

Perhaps the best way to illustrate this is to contrast the 1990s with the 1950s (well within living memory to large numbers of Anglicans, and to most Church leaders). If in the process the 1950s appear as though the establishment was then in good repair and even fairly credible, then readers would do well to remember that this a purely relative finding. The country is so far gone from Christianity, and so near the end of inherited Christianity as folk religion, that the 1950s appear as a period of Church strength in contrast to the present. But it *is* a relative phenomenon.

The Church of England today retains much of the trappings of a once great national Church, and apparently still lays claim to this inheritance, namely that it is the soul and conscience of a Christian nation, the source of spiritual care for all the citizens, there in a personal way beside all who are dying or distressed. This involves claims of overweening unreality. But I think that in my own schooldays, forty to fifty years ago in suburbia, the claim had still some semblance of credibility. I was not an Anglican myself – and for the larger part of my teens not a Christian believer – but distinct impressions of the establishment were sharply etched in my mind. Thus the parish church was in a special way the church of the parishioners. They knew it was there; they knew that it was in that parish that they lived; they were vaguely conscious that perhaps they ought to be attending there; they took their infants there for baptism (at 4 p.m. on a Sunday afternoon); they might very well have tried out the Sunday school for their children; quite a few had their children confirmed there (my choice of words is deliberate); most expected their daughters to get married there; and equally that the vicar would officiate at their funerals (and funerals very regularly did involve a service in church). At Christmas and at Easter numbers in church leapt up. The Christian faith was part of the atmosphere of that kind of suburbia, as was evidenced by school worship assemblies. To be English was to be, at least vaguely, Christian; and, although zealots might actually 'opt in' to some other Christian 'voluntarist' denomination (and thereby 'opt out' of the Church of England), it was generally reckoned that all those who had not thus opted out were perfectly good, if rather passive, Anglicans.

The same pattern was more or less true of the countryside, and a very high proportion of the parishes and the clergy of the Church of England were in the countryside. It was less true of the 'working-class' areas of towns, where the 'atmospheric' participation in Christianity was lower, the distancing of the people from the Church more obvious, and the active attendance at worship very poor indeed.

However, those days have ceased, and it is little good sighing for them. I believe the following factors distance the 1990s from the 1950s:

1. The vague atmosphere of the citizens' national Christianity of my youth may have tinged people's thinking, but gave them little grasp of God and his truth. In most parishes attendance at church did not of itself imply much about commitment. It is at least arguable that it was Billy Graham in his Harringay Campaign in 1954 who first made

'conversion' a term which ran beyond evangelicals and had general application to the Church.*

2. In the 1940s and 1950s the Church of England was enormously clericalist. The background was an inheritance of hundreds of years of the clergyman *being* the Church for most purposes. This inheritance was rooted in the rural society of pre-Industrial Revolution England; and in such a society the clergyman knew all the parishioners over many years, related intimately to their lives, and had scope to minister to them personally in their particular needs. For the last two hundred years this concept has been transferred to the urban scene, where most English people now live. It has been broadly incredible and unworkable, but it has hung on.

It was actually dependent upon a pastoral strategy which was linked to a sociological theory, which has itself now expired. The theory was this: that people lived in nuclear families; that fathers went out to work and earned a salary; that mothers, with or without children, were at home during the day and could be visited; that having the children in Sunday school was the foundation for first of all their own confirmation (at age ten to thirteen) and thereafter their own churchgoing lives. Thus the clergy energies went into three main channels: firstly, running Sunday services and Sunday schools; secondly, visiting homes during the day midweek (and particularly pressing there that children should attend Sunday school); and thirdly fulfilling the requirements of 'occasional offices' (funerals Mondays to Fridays, weddings on Saturdays, and baptisms on Sunday afternoons at around 4 p.m). If Sundays could be served by a good choir and good Sunday schools, and the visiting could be served by a vicar and two or more curates, then it was likely that the job could be done within the limits of its own vision, and the parish could well be 'successful'. Preaching need not be demanding (upon either preacher or hearers), youth clubs were a bonus, and schools could be invited on

---

*To be fair, there was an official precursor in the report *Towards the Conversion of England* (1945). But this report clearly used the word 'conversion' to shock, and was both well ahead of its times and predictably unsuccessful in getting the point across in the early years after its publication.

to church premises at intervals and thus be kept in touch with what 'church' was about. And the theory behind it all was that, in some sense, all the parishioners belonged, all were (at least subliminally) Christian, and the vicar, either directly or through his curates, was exercising a pastoral care over all.

3. Another feature of church life in the 1950s was that it was very cheap in financial terms. Incumbents lived on benefice income plus fees, plus (perhaps) an Easter offering. Curates were young, single, hard-worked, often living in digs, and surviving on very tiny incomes (which were usually paid by the parish). Giving might be needed to support the church fabric or to give the organ an overhaul or buy more choir robes, but it did not have to run far beyond that, and it could usually be sustained sufficiently on a penny or a sixpence in the plate, even from the relatively prosperous. In many places, dances or jumble sales or raffles would provide for special needs, or even, in the country, a special need, as with an organ repair, might well have been met by a wealthy squire or patron. The lack of call on lay giving all assisted the sense that the Church of England was simply 'there', resourced in ways inaccessible (and fairly uninteresting) to the average attender, but very secure. In broad terms, it was generally thought to be State-paid and State-supported – and rightly so.

4. Clearly such a Church had a very big 'fringe'. One measurable instance of this is the statistic that in 1950 67 per cent of live births in the country received baptism at Church of England fonts. That is a breathtakingly widespread folk religion at work. Furthermore, the Church of England went on measuring such baptized people as belonging to the Church of England thereafter. Indeed it was all too likely to be giving out the message that being baptized was *the* crucial point of being in touch with God and his Church, and everything else was rather secondary.

The same was true of confirmation. Genuinely adult confirmations were very rare before 1960, and the overwhelming proportion of candidates were ten to thirteen years of age. For large numbers it was their leaving certificate, and was known to be such. It was simply like getting a passport – useful to have if the need came up, and so worth having, but of no special need in the ordinary run of things. Confirmands too were counted, so that the Church of England somehow knew that in any one year it had, say, 23 million baptized members and 5 million confirmed ones.

Another way of measuring the fringe would have been to look at the 'midnight communions' on Christmas Eve. It is not only that these services tended to sprout two or three times as many communicants as a normal Sunday, but that they were also attended by large numbers of non-communicants who nevertheless had a yen to be there that night. Up to a point the same was true at Easter (which the Prayer Book declared to be the one time when parishioners *should* receive communion). Pentecost did not have the same appeal – not only because it never had 'folk' associations like mistletoe and Easter eggs,* but also because in the immediate post-War years it was the Spring Bank Holiday weekend, which moved with Pentecost, thereby depriving it of any religious significance to the fringe. (The classic third point in the folk observance of the Christian year was always harvest – not present in the Prayer Book, not over-magnified in the countryside (!), but a 'must' in suburbia ...)

It is fully arguable that, alongside this 'fringe' factor, the Church of England was far from welcoming to occasional churchgoers. Its regulars guarded their own seats; its robes and processions and ceremonial appeared highly esoteric; its Prayer Book was nearly impossible for the uninstructed to follow; its music was of a particular cultural genre; and its sidesmen were almost trained not to over-do the welcome or help people feel at home. However, when the occasionals came, they generally hoped to be anonymous and unseen, sitting well back so as to be able to follow others, holding a Prayer Book but not necessarily following anything in it. All this could be represented as a kindness to English reserve, to people who did not wish to be lionized or helped, but simply to be shown a seat and left to it!

In many congregations almost everybody was 'fringe'. It is not that the Church of England was catering for unbelievers – it is rather that the Church of England at large

---

*An exception to this came in the Manchester and South Lancashire areas, where 'Whit Walks' had a wide appeal, far beyond the ordinary churchgoers.

did not like to think the English included much in the way
of unbelievers, and it would certainly have been improper
to suggest it. Rather the level of church life was designed
(by accident of providence) to provide for the spiritual needs
of a vaguely believing nation at the intensity at which the
man in the street was thought to be ready for it.

5. The kind of Christianity such church life bred was personal, private and spiritually uncommunicative. Because
church life was 'going to church', and at church all was
formal and hierarchical, the vast proportion of worshippers
never ever found themselves testifying to their personal
faith in Christ, leading extemporary prayer, or even engag-
ing in group Bible study. Within the liturgy all sat in straight
rows and kept their head and eyes to the front, said nothing
of a personal sort to the people sitting near them, and simply
conformed to the parade-ground style of 'well-ordered'
worship. Thus in most parishes people's actual beliefs and
personal pilgrimages were treated as embarrassing: Christianity was for very private people, and it was profaning it
to make it the subject of informal conversation or mutual
sharing.

This kind of parish church life of the 1950s catered for a
lingering folk religion. It did keep doors open to all sorts and
conditions of people. It did reflect and even sustain a residual
national role for the Church of England. It did, in principle,
give the Church – and even the vicar – a known and honoured
place within the life of the nation, the community, or the
village.

But one has to say that the last days of such folk-lore and
folk-orientated religion *were* the last days. The Church of
England was already in the 1950s taking internal steps which
would in time move it on from this pattern. The Parish Communion, born on Tyneside in 1927, and boosted by Hebert and
Dix in the 1930s, returned after the war to spread almost
uncritically round the country. It had at its heart the Liturgical
Movement cry 'Let the Church be the Church'. Parish and
People, an organization specifically of the 1950s, promoted this
liturgical change. Holy Communion, which had been for the 8
a.m. zealots and golfers before the War, now became the main
service of Sunday mornings. It was backed by the slogan 'The
Lord's Service for the Lord's People on the Lord's Day'. It

nudged evening worshippers towards the morning. It gave audible hints of church being about togetherness. It divided between insiders who received, and outsiders who did not – and thus both gave a message of commitment on the one hand and of something lacking in non-communicants' lives on the other. It contained a whisker more of the rationale that the Church is to be found gathered *here* in worship, and correspondingly less of the notion that the whole country is subliminally Christian and C. of E. anyway.

Alongside this movement a quite different trend, quite unrelated to it, was also at work. This was the re-growth of evangelicalism. Evangelical Anglicans in the 1950s took new heart and numerical increase from three separate developments: the sustained work by the Inter-Varsity Fellowship to get evangelicalism above ground intellectually, and thus able to engage in scholarly combat with other schools of theological thought; the ever-growing impact of the Varsity and Public Schools camps (with their flow of converted teenagers into first National Service and then Oxford and Cambridge); and thirdly the bombshell of Billy Graham's first major campaigns in this country in 1954 and 1955 – some of the effects of which were that several thousand or tens of thousands of attenders, often people already churchgoing, professed instant conversion. Whilst evangelicals were usually as clericalist as any other part of the Church, they *were* sure that the nation at large was not born again, nor was the nation Christian simply because people had generally been baptized. On the other hand, they did tend to value the State connection more than it warranted, both because of the supposed opportunities it gave for ministering the gospel, and also because their own folk memory of the 1928 deliverance by Parliament from the wicked machinations of church leaders remained green. So their influence was uncommonly like that of the parish communion practitioners – they paid genuine outward loyalty to a parish system which their theological positions and parish policies were bound in time to undermine.

On the whole the 1950s were a decade of complacency for the Church of England. Little change was in the air; politically the country was Tory, and likely to stay that way; employment was high, and if internationally our imperial mantle had passed to the USA, yet the new Elizabethan era in Britain felt good. The Suez adventure (and subsequent fuel crisis) caused a temporary blip. But it was a time when the Church of England could not only believe itself to be unchanging, but could also believe itself to be set in a relatively unchanging society – and could believe the stability of each was good for the other. The flow of ordination candidates was at a post-War peak in the latter half of the 1950s, and the future looked secure.

If we now set today's Church of England against the description of the 1950s I have set out above, there is a vast swing to record:

1. The broad vagueness of Church of England belief has given way to strong supernaturalist conviction. The opening of a gulf between what the Church believes and what the 'world' does has sharpened the Church of England's own adherence to its faith.

2. Great effort is going into equipping and empowering the laity of the Church of England. This is not only in Synods, nor only in liturgy, but throughout every part of church life. There has been a realistic awakening to the fact that the ministers cannot and must not *be* the Church, but that the Church is an active *body*, with tasks or ministries for every member to fulfil. In the process, the concept that the minister was a kind of national spiritual health service officer with benefits to hand out to all who came has perished. The vicar who assumes the world will come to church if the choir is good, or will come to the vicarage if in trouble or need, has either gone from the scene, or needs to have gone. He or she is now more probably the leader and equipper of a loving company of the servants of Jesus Christ, and the distinction between the Church and the world has widened enormously.

3. Since 1970 the finances of the Church of England have undergone a revolution. In the 1990s the historic assets still pay for clergy pensions – and for working bishops. But the trend which has been running for many years (and is now exacerbated by the Church Commissioners' losses of £800 million capital in the late 1980s) is for the living Church to have to pay for all its working clergy and stipendiary lay workers, and to pay too for their vicarages, and for the cost of sustaining church buildings of every sort. Most such finances are handled by means of parish quotas through Diocesan Boards of Finance, but there are also items – such as the fees and support of ordinands and the sustaining of a central administration for the Church of England – which are handled by the Central Board of Finance, which draws upon Diocesan Boards for its income. At the same time, as compared with the 1950s, an equalization policy for clergy stipends has ironed out the wildest absurdities, and has brought the minimum (for assistant curates as well as incumbents) into the realm of the realistic.

The effect of these changes during the 1970s was that all round the country parish quotas were rising at twice the rate of inflation – and doing so when inflation itself was in some years near to 30 per cent. The Church of England groaned and complained and, although it was in slow numerical decline, sustained the increases. The Church which had never previously had to give money on any scale quickly learned to give. It may not yet give enough, and it is easy to point a finger – but against all the odds it did learn to give, and in the process changed its own view of itself. For councils which handle money exercise power, and councils which have power take themselves seriously as institutions. So there has been a growing church-consciousness in Parochial Church Councils and Diocesan Synods as finance has come to figure large on the agenda. As the burden of finance has been transferred from historic assets to the living Church, so the living Church has had to discover and identify itself. Councils which disburse money do so on behalf of Christians who have given it, and not only expect the clergy and other recipients of the money to be accountable, but also tend to identify the givers with the living Church. There is a very clear idea that the outsiders *are* outsiders; and in the process the Church of England at parish level has come to look and sound far more like a 'free' or voluntarist Church.

4. The 'fringe' factor has greatly changed in forty years. The general expectation of the 1950s, that those who do not attend church may yet think they belong to it in some way, and know what it is about, is clearly false in the 1990s, even in suburbia. It may still be just true in some rural communities. The Christian Churches are surrounded much

less today by a Christian penumbra and much more by
secular thinking which is without clues as to the Christian
faith, by superstitions (such as spiritualism, occultism and
astrology) which are actually hostile to the Christian faith,
and by other world religions which are uncomprehendingly
distanced from the Christian faith.* The upshot is seen in
broad terms in our schools. Secular teachers have declined
to lead acts of worship, or teach the Scriptures as though
they believed them; non-Christian superstitions have spread
through teenage dabbling; and the arrival of other religions
has confirmed the difficulty of giving Christianity a special
place in the school agenda – there were even stories in
December 1993 of the banning of Nativity plays! Of course
there are shining exceptions, sometimes State schools, sometimes Church schools, where an individual or group with
Christian convictions has kept a flame alive. But it is *not*
the story of the generality of our schools, and secondary
schools in particular have proved to be easily prised away
from the Christian faith.† It is an open question, and not
one I address here, as to whether the Christian faith can be
plausibly taught by unbelievers on the one hand, or can
be taught in a value-free way by believers on the other. It is
sufficient to note for our purposes that State Anglicanism
needs at least widespread folk Christianity in the community
to be viable; but conversely such folk Christianity, as and
when it does occur in particular schools or even districts,
does not entail or imply anything about the establishment
of the Church of England. Indeed, disestablishment would
not materially affect it.

What then of those 'occasional offices' which once brought

---

*One minor distressing feature of our being known as a 'Christian nation'
(a concept which is due to being 'Western' as much as to having an
established Christian Church) is that immigrants to this country who are
not Christian imagine that the *mores* of society stem from the Christian
faith, and immigrants who *are* Christian are desperately disappointed in
what they find.

†I do not here evaluate the provision in the 1988 Education Act for the
teaching of the Christian faith. The run-down of Christianity in schools
under the 1944 Act has been due to the erosion of Christian belief in the
teachers and the homes of England, not to defect in law – and it is
doubtful if the provisions of the 1988 Act can do more than buttress
conviction *where it can be found*. It will not do much to help it exist.

every Tom, Dick or Harry to church? The baptismal figures
shown a decline in infant baptisms of 1 per cent per annum
for forty years from 1950 to 1990 – that is from 67.5 per
cent of live births in the former year, to 27.5 per cent in the
latter.[5] Even in the mid-1980s, I knew a parish in inner
Birmingham (not especially Islamic or Sikh but genuinely
'mixed') where there was *no* enquiry or request from outside
the congregation in twelve months about infant baptism.
That is obviously exceptional, but it points to a complete
cessation of Christian folk religion, and my experience more
recently in the Medway suggests that Birmingham's present
is urban Kent's near future.

Marriages in church have held up, it seems, because the
Register Office alternative is so chill and perfunctory, and
not because of Christian conviction in young couples. The
vast majority of those who attend weddings of parishioners
who are not known as Christian seem to know no Christian
hymns, and certainly never to have sung in church before.
Parishioners still have legal right to be married in church;
the Church of England gains considerable fees from couples
(and pastorally takes advantage of applications by trying to
prepare people properly for marriage); but the sentiment
towards church weddings would appear to be more about
'what makes a good wedding' than anything to do with God.
It is folk culture rather than folk religion which is at the
root of it, and, in view of the widespread premarital and
extra-marital sexual experience of so many, it is doubtful
whether vows in the presence of God carry much weight.

Funerals are moving steadily away from the Church of
England. The clergy are quite probably unaware of the
slowly growing requests for wholly secular cremations and
burials (it is worth asking local undertakers – they know).
But the clergy know they are hired because the undertakers
offer to hire them, and the bereaved usually accept it as
(culturally?) appropriate. Very rarely in towns is there a
request for a service in church; very rarely is there a funeral
where the minister had actually met the deceased when
alive; and it is exceptional when Christian truth actually
enters people's lives through such services. The matter is
complicated by what are now very substantial fees, and the

clergy need to be earning those fees to keep the life of
the Church of England in being.*

The last relics of 'fringe' Christianity may well be found
in village churches (where a large proportion of the villagers
may consider they have a vested interest in the parish
church, whether they attend it or not, or support it finan-
cially or not). There also continue echoes amongst the over-
50s in suburbia (for they may have attended Sunday school,
or been choir boys), in the Public Schools (where teenage
confirmations remain vastly out of proportion to what occurs
in parishes), and in the millions who, we are told, faithfully
watch *Songs of Praise* on the TV on Sunday nights. Obviously the folk religion factor declines at different rates in
different places – and in different families – but the trend
is unmistakeable. The transition from Christendom to
pagandom, which began in 1689, may well not be totally
complete till the middle of the next century. But it is at its
eleventh hour.

5. The style of Church of England congregational life is now
far more networked, overtly believing, mutually supportive,
and concerned for the spiritual life than was the case forty
years ago. This too has raised the consciousness that the
worshippers *are* the Church, with the corollary that the
others are genuinely not.

The above are points of comparison and contrast with the
points about the life of the Church of England in the 1950s
which I raised earlier. But if comparisons with the past are
set aside, and a straight look is taken at the active life of the
Church of England of today, and at the residual Christianity
in the population today, then the story is different again. In

---

*There are of course all sorts of conversions and restorations which come
about through funerals, and the style of the minister and even the tone
of voice may be instrumental in bringing people to faith. The issue is not
whether such occasions are good opportunities, but whether the original
request for a Christian funeral has any detectable Christian faith behind
or within it – and time and again I am sceptical. But at intervals I find
myself with up to 40 per cent of adults who are being confirmed at one
time deriving their newfound faith from events and reflections following
the death of someone much beloved. I in no sense recommend that we
should cease to respond to requests for funerals, though the lack of
Christianity amongst mourners again affects not only hymn-singing but
the whole atmosphere and understanding of what is occurring.

1990 2.4 per cent of the population of England were adults who worshipped reasonably regularly with the Church of England; electoral rolls were slightly higher than attendance (1,396,000 as against 1,143,000); communicants were three-quarters of a million. And the 2.4 per cent were desperately unevenly distributed throughout the country and throughout the layers of society. It is certain that there was a great preponderance of women, and almost as certain that there was a serious weighting towards the middle-aged and elderly. It is likely that the 'working classes' were very poorly represented, and probable that the ethnic minorities also did badly. The implication is that to find as Christian worshippers in any congregation good numbers of young working-class men (let alone those from ethnic minority groups) is as likely as a snowstorm in July.

Nor, if our analysis is correct, are those outside only just outside – the truth is that they are very far distant indeed. Nothing in the *mores* of workplaces, or the atmosphere of popular music, or the lifestyle of young people, or the implicit message of the media, or even the basic values of politicians gives any hint that Jesus Christ was the incarnate Son of God, died for our sins, was raised from the dead on the third day, and lives today as King over the earth and Saviour of those who trust in him. The echoes of God have almost gone from the land, and it is difficult to uncover or demonstrate a widespread wistfulness or yearning to reinstate them. If individuals are being converted from this atmosphere – and they are – then those persons must rank as exceptional. There is no visible mainstream swing back to a search for God. It would be truer to assert a nearly universal spiritual anorexia, punctuated by occasional scattered persons with a spiritual hunger, a small proportion of whom find orthodox Christianity, whilst others find various superstitions, false sects, or other religions.

How stands the establishment of the Church of England in all this? It will suffice for the moment to point out how any defence of it has had to be highly volatile. There is no way that the rationales of Hooker and the Tudors can possibly justify the establishment today. Furthermore, there is hardly a stronger case for the simple assertion that the majority of the nation are 'C. of E.', as those fearful of disestablishment urged in the last century. If, for reasons which escape me, the structure of establishment is still required to stand, then as foundation after foundation for it crumbles, new foundations have first to be constructed and then to be awkwardly inserted under the tottering edifice.

So have we not indeed reached what I have titled this 'fifth phase' – that is, 'the end of pretence'? Conversely, does not the very establishment of the Church of England itself mean a shying away from reality? Indeed does it not reek of sustained pretence?

Pretence is a prevalent way of defending the establishment. There is pretence that we are in 'partnership' with the State, when we are in fact in captivity; there is pretence that, if in any one or two years we have not encountered that State control in its most virulent form, it has actually gone away; and there is the ostrich-like insistence that all reforms which have happened up until the present moment have been enlightened and welcome, but all proposed for the future are destructive of the fabric of the Church or of society or of both. Are we really arrived at the most enlightened form, the most delicate balance, of relationships between Church and State that all changes proposed for the future must be harmful? Or can we actually call an end to pretence and a dawning of reality?

If my analysis is accepted, then the establishment issue which is my theme can be addressed by our posing here three questions, and it may then be left for the later chapters to resolve.

1. Is there any plausible way in which the country can still be said to have a majority of Anglican Christians? It will be recalled that the assurance that the Church of England should not be disestablished in 1870 or 1920 sprang from the confident awareness that a majority of the population were truly C. of E.

2. If there is no plausible way of affirming that such a majority exists, can any case be made for the establishment of a *minority* Church?

3. If no case can be made in this way *for* the establishment, does it not follow that disestablishment is the only proper course?

I begin an attempt at these questions in the next chapter.

3. An Established Church in a Secular State

Biblical models for Church and State relationship

The Reformers, when justifying their unitary Church-State, naturally leaned to Old Testament models where, though kings and priests had different functions, there was a unitary politico-religious state. Such a model justified the independence of the State from the Pope, justified the doctrine of the Divine Right of Kings, justified making uniform State provision for religious exercises, and sustained a monolithic polity against threats of civil tensions or civil wars. It was necessarily imposed in a 'top down' way, and it was constantly under threat from private questioning of its truth, its validity, or the limits of its divine sanction. It was, of course, full of fatal cracks, as Cranmer found in Mary's reign when he wrestled in jail with how to give unquestioning obedience to the divinely appointed monarch, when it was clear to his biblically formed doctrinal conscience that she was unambiguously wrong. The theory finally collapsed when a monarch had to be run off his throne, when a nation was allowed by law to be non-conforming and at religious odds with itself, and when mere State-supported privilege ran on for the Church of England with neither Christian nor democratic rationale. It was a theory which had indeed been cogently expounded by the mighty Hooker:

> But Hooker was too late; already the foundation stone of his theory, although buttressed by force of law, was being eroded by the tides of religious diversity ... [1]

The question is: if that theory is inapplicable, what theory or model can replace it?

The obvious answer is a New Testament model. Here the Church is an international society, very specifically bonding together Jews and Greeks, Scythians and Barbarians. It sits within the Roman Empire, normally ready to obey its laws, pay its taxes, and honour its authority. But for the life of its own ecclesial society it makes its own choices, sends out its own missionaries, arranges its own priorities, makes its own appointments, takes charge of its own finances, and views itself accountable to God alone for its manner of life. It has a mission of good news to bring to those outside it, and by both faith and baptism it has a clear picture of who are its members and who are not. It believes it has the aid of the Holy Spirit, and in the last analysis it has to obey God rather than men. Its members reckon that they have a stewardship from God of their own lives and goods and of the good news, and that they must be ready to render account to God for the exercise of this trust.

Such a Church, though a 'people for God's own possession', can almost certainly operate within a modern State, albeit with some compromise if it has to come to terms with political or economic systems which it believes to be wrong. But our issue is not whether it can freely operate, but whether, far beyond that, the patterns of life of the Church should be *owned and directed* by a modern secular State? The obvious answer is: 'Theologically and morally they cannot be'. So how are we to square that kind of answer with the sheer hard fact that, theology and morality notwithstanding, the Church of England *is* owned and directed by a modern secular State? There are two possible answers – one occupies the high ground, breathing a somewhat rarefied atmosphere, and denies that England is secularized; the other occupies the low ground, where not a little fog or marsh-gas persists, so that it is simultaneously both accessible and yet also elusive. It is elusive in that it alternates its denials between saying that theology and morality do not preclude State control, and saying that it is not really State control at all anyway.

The high ground – still a Christian nation?
We begin with the hardy occupants of the high ground. The most committed exponent of all is Enoch Powell – he can climb Everest without oxygen, and thus does not notice that the rest of humanity is unable to go with him:

> The Church of England is that Church of which the Supreme Governor on earth is the Crown of England. This description applies to no other Church, or part of the Church, and

it applies to the Church of England irrespective of all other characteristics and of doctrine. Its essential nature is thus not doctrinal but political . . .

Not one of the other Churches in the Anglican Communion is governed by the supreme lay or secular authority in its own territory. They are self-governing or synodical Churches . . . The Archbishop and the General Synod of the Church of England are thus unique among the prelates and synods of the Anglican Communion, in that they are, by the essential nature of the Church of England, respectively appointed by the Crown and subordinate to the governorship of the Crown . . .

For the Church of England is territorial . . . It was over that Church in England that the Crown became Supreme Governor. Logically its governorship extended no farther than the outer limits of its territorial sovereignty. Equally logically it applied to everybody within that territory, whence, despite the rise and toleration of other churches and of irreligion, the Church of England is still the Church of every resident in every parish throughout England: he may not claim it, but if he does his claim is upheld by the law. It is the Church of all the English, of all in England, precisely because, and only because, the supreme authority in it is the supreme secular authority . . .

[The representation of the laity in synods is misconceived because] The most fundamental defect . . . lies in the nature of the underlying electorate itself . . . are those persons [i.e. those on the electoral roll], in the necessary sense, the people – the *laos* – of the Church of England? The contrary would follow automatically from my earlier proposition that the Church of England is the right and possession of all the people of England, both those who do and those who do not avail themselves of it, so that all the people of England are, as such, potentially members of the Church of England in a sense in which they can not be potentially members of the Roman or any other Church. But that is not what I am arguing here. I am making a more limited claim that those whose worship and attendance are occasional, who are not even annually communicant, but who look to the Church of England to hallow the great events of their lives, are also entitled to be regarded as its laity and to be included in

its representation. If so, the electorate which underlies the
indirect, pyramidal election of the House of Laity is too
narrow and partial to sustain a claim by that body to
represent the Church of England for the purpose of consent-
ing to changes in its law ...

[So we come back to Parliament] Let it first be reiterated
that Parliament legislated, and legislates still, for the
Church of England not as being representative of it but
because the Crown, the Church's Supreme Governor, makes
all law through Parliament and only through Parliament ...

There is thus nothing in the character or composition of
Parliament or the House of Commons which makes grotesque
in practice its constitutionally logical function as the
legislator for the Church.[2]

Who can relate to this? It is provocatively typical Powell (and
there is plenty more of it). Its only concession to ordinary ways
of thought in the Church of England is when he calls all the
English *potentially* members'. That does look like a hole in
the argument, for it raises the question, who then are *actually*
members? Is it 'those ... who look to the Church of England
to hallow the great events of their lives'? These are, he says,
'also entitled to be regarded as its laity and to be included in
its representation'. Or is it some more committed grouping?
The author who functions without added oxygen at this great
height coolly discusses membership (or a kindred concept)
without reference to baptism, adult profession of faith, or faith
of any sort; and he does so in relation to a group which on his
hypothesis are overtly non-communicant, and thus seemingly
self-excommunicate. And what are we to make of tens of millions '*potential* members'? Does that, if we accept it, make us 'A
Christian nation'?

What of those on the high ground who have taken extra
supplies of oxygen with them? Here I find Hugh Craig:

... the majority still call themselves 'C. of E.' ... They still
look to the Church for a lead that they nowadays rarely find.
They still hanker for a faith that they could see as relevant
to the life they have to live. They still argue ... on the
basis of the Christian ethic. And they still recognize as the
authentic Christian gospel the historic faith of the Church
of England, and wish they could hear it again from the

majority of our pulpits. They may still turn to the Church in times of real need ... If we ignore or exclude the 'fringe' members of our Church we will hasten the very end we wish to avoid.

To clothe these statements with some numbers, one can deduce from published statistics that while some 40,000 churchmen or so form the electorate of the House of Laity of the General Synod there were over 1,600,000 on Anglican church electoral rolls in 1989. Probably between four and five million attend Anglican Churches at least once a month and at the very least fifteen million regard themselves as 'C. of E.'. Add to these perhaps eight million who claim to be Roman Catholics, Free Churchmen, or who belong to other Christian Churches, and the claim that we are no longer a Christian nation looks at best a trifle premature.[3]

So here Hugh Craig virtually claims what Enoch Powell does not – Powell says that the English are *members* (or nearly); Craig says they are Christian *believers* (or nearly). In the process he has put so many hands in the scales that the number of believers has grown in a way comparable to the early chapters of the Acts of the Apostles. The fantastic feature is the assertion about 'four to five million' – as in 1991 the 'usual Sunday attendance' was 1,137,000 (including children), he would have to assert that *no one* came more than once a month if there were to be, as he asserts, 'between four and five million' *different people* there on a once a month basis. Add his 'at the very least fifteen million' vaguely 'C. of E.' and 'perhaps eight million' vaguely of other Christian denominations, and one can see that the most invigorating oxygen has carried him up to such high ground. Indeed he may have achieved the majority he needs for his thesis. But those of us down below him, looking at the realities at our level, and the realities in terms of church attendance, cannot believe he could live at that height without his artificial figures. The *whole* adult attendance at Christian worship in all congregations on 15 October 1989 is reckoned at 3,700,000 in the Church Census. These were close to one-third Anglican, one-third Roman Catholic, and one-third Free Church of various sorts.[4] How the latter two categories can be added together to 'perhaps eight million' defies belief. Nor can Hugh Craig really have any idea how many lapsed Roman Catholics or Free Church people there might be, who would count towards his statistic.

We are in fact past the point where it is polite or affirming to call other people 'Christian', and more and more the word objectively describes those who have an actual faith in Christ – and more and more those without such faith do not want to call themselves Christian. There is only one small benefit to the argument which the 'high ground' advocates can bestow on us; it is this: their heading for the high ground derives from their own underlying recognition that the low ground is no place for a self-respecting establishmentarian. They are witnesses that, if they cannot make the high ground, they will have to concede the case. They may be wholly unrealistic about their own chosen ground – but they thereby witness silently to the impossibility of the low ground.

The low ground – an established Church in a secular state

We thus come to the major issue of this chapter. If we cannot live on the high ground that says this is a 'Christian nation', can we find low ground which would sustain an established (and thus privileged and protected) Church in a secularized or religiously pluralist nation?

It is clear, of course, that no one could ever credibly propose the establishing *de novo* of a minority Church in a secularist State. The low ground can only plead that we have an inherited protected role in the nation, and it is desirable not to lose it. The pleading has in the background the possibility that an egalitarian approach by some government in the future may lead to disestablishment; and the defences are designed to persuade Church and State alike not to touch the delicacy of the present relationship between the two.

The most notable protectors of the present pattern of establishment are the Archbishop of York, John Habgood, and the Second Estates Commissioner, Michael Alison, who is, in effect, the leader of a loose group of Church of England supporters in the Commons, and is in his own person a convinced proponent of the present establishment. So we should look at the reasons advanced.

John Habgood, by the very title of his first book on the

subject, *Church and Nation in a Secular Age*, made it clear
that he was not pretending that we are a 'Christian nation' –
and he began the book 'The aim is ... to explore the role
of a national Church in a secular, pluralist society.'[5] There
is one chapter on establishment, and he does not so much pro-
pound a theory, as treat the existing pattern as in possession
and invite others to criticize it. He then picks up major criticisms levelled and heads them off harmlessly. In the throes
of this, he would seem to be concentrating on the following
apologias:

> To be conscious of belonging to a national Church is to be
> given a broad sense of responsibility for all and sundry.[6]

> There are nowadays very few restrictions on the freedom of
> the Church of England ... on the rare occasions when there
> are tensions between Church and Parliament, the key issue
> is always whether a relatively small elected body of church
> activists is competent to speak for the inarticulate religious
> life of the nation.[7]

Along with these he argues against disestablishmentarians
that privilege is over-stated (and its obverse is
responsibility), that really Prime Ministers are not able to
force the wrong people as bishops on the Church (and if they
tried then the Archbishop of the Province could decline to
consecrate), that ecumenism is not badly hindered by the
establishment, and that:

> One almost inevitable consequence of disestablishment
> would be the alienation of large numbers of people whose
> residual allegiance to the Church of England is bound up
> with the perception that in some obscure way it represents
> 'England'.[8]

What are we to say to these things – ten years on from when
he wrote them? Clearly, he is not handling the full weight of
the case against the establishment, but choosing only medium-
weight charges to resist. There is no treatment of whether a
Christian Church ought to be answerable for its spiritual life
and organization to a secular State, no discussion of what I
have called Old and New Testament models, no recognition of
the widespread collapse and end of even wispy Christian folk

religion. He is even prepared to see the Commons as the reposi-
tory, indeed the mouthpiece, of the 'inarticulate religious life'
of the nation, as over against 'a relatively small elected body of
church activists'. Now diocesan bishops and archbishops are
not *elected* members of General Synod, but they were surely
strongly in evidence voting *for* the Appointment of Bishops
Measure in 1983, and the Clergy (Ordination) Measure in
1989, the two notable examples of conflict in recent Synod–
Parliamentary relationships? John Habgood wrote this book
just before the first of these incidents, so was unaware of the
application of his principles – but would he really say that
the Synod votes were irresponsible and unrepresentative
forays by 'a relatively small elected body of church activists'
and that Parliament, led in one instance by Ian Paisley and
Enoch Powell, was speaking for the inarticulate religious life
of the nation? Or, if we go back to before he wrote the book,
when in 1981 *both* Houses of Parliament gave a first approval
to the 'Prayer Book Protection Bill', which was resisted by the
Bishops in the Lords, who were then the unrepresentative
activists and who the voice of the right-thinking inarticulate?

Is there anything in his first defence that belonging to a
national Church has given us a broad sense of responsibility
for all and sundry? The 'broad sense of responsibility' to which
he refers is self-evidently not held by every non-attender who
reckons in some way to 'belong' to the national Church – it is
the responsibility held by what I think he would call the 'activists' (from archbishops down to those who run soup-kitchens
or staff playgroups). The issue is whether such people, individually or together, would feel less responsibility if they were
disestablished. I strongly suggest not; for

(a) in his statement of principle, the concept of 'established'
has slipped over into being called 'national'. And 'national'
means, as far as I can tell, spread into all parts of the nation,
or found in all parts of the nation's life, or rooted in the
nation's past.*

These are *positional* (and perhaps *dispositional*) statements, not constitutional ones. They may arise from the
past establishment, but they are independent of the present

---

*For a fuller description of possible meanings of 'national', see the Intro-
duction on pp. 3–4 above.

Church–State relationship and would run on as they do now (well or badly) without it. I imagine that the Roman Catholic Church might view itself as the 'national' Church in Eire or France or Portugal – but its constitutional relationship to the State differs greatly between them. The claim to be the 'national' Church is exactly the claim the (arguably not really established) Church of Scotland makes in Scotland. But those statements, whilst certainly carrying 'responsibility', do not make the various Churches 'established'. 'National' is a very different thing from 'established', and the latter should not be tucked into the former like an armed soldier into a wooden horse.

(b) Is a 'broad sense of responsibility' the unique possession of the Church of England – one which disestablished Churches all over the earth's surface have either forfeited or never gained? The 'sense of responsibility' of the Christian Church comes not from its links with any State, nor even its own constitutional foundation documents: it comes from its faith in Jesus Christ, from submission to his mission, and from a lively internal debate about how an acknowledged responsibility can be faithfully carried out: it springs from such Scriptures as, 'I am debtor both to the Jews and to the Greeks', 'it is required that those who have been given a trust must prove faithful'. Clearly, if we want examples, the Church of the Province of Southern Africa has had a 'broad sense of responsibility for all and sundry'; so has the Church of the Province of Kenya; so in Amin's time as well as at present has the Church of Uganda. We would be fools to think we alone (by which, presumably, must be meant the Church leaders and the 'activists' alone) were fully responsible, and only so because we are by law established.

The second apologia deals with the Parliamentary issue which I have already examined in passing – who *are* the activists, pray, and who the inarticulate religious? But the issue is *not* whether Parliament rarely or ever restricts our freedom, or blocks our policies. It is whether the powers should reside there at all. Or let me put it this way: the issue is *not* whether we can get a Measure through Parliament without arousing opposition or causing fluttering in dovecots; it is simply whether Parliament is God's ordained instrument of ecclesiastical policy-making, to which, as a matter of *theology*, we *must* be subject, or whether it is a secular court inappropriately giving judgement in spiritual things. Parliament is considered in Chapter 6.

The last reason given by the Archbishop for not getting disestablished is that disestablishing the Church of England would, it is urged, give a message of our nationally repudiating Christianity. I believe this to be a wrong forecast, and I offer an alternative scenario. The outcome depends upon which of two routes to disestablishing is followed.

The first route is the stealthy, step-by-step, move. No one 'out there' noticed when the Worship and Doctrine Measure was approved. No one 'out there' noticed when Parliament gave away the right to divide dioceses. The world, the fringe, and the half-committed are not avidly reading *Hansard* and forming their own religious beliefs in reaction against the Church of England's distancing itself from Parliament. They simply do not know it is happening. And if such a process led to a last single weak strand of linkage being broken, again it would hit no headlines, and break no bruised reeds.

But there could be a second route. If the Church of England, either by its own action, or by being simply dropped by the State, found all its bonds severed in one great glorious action, then, it is true, the event might catch a few headlines between the scandals of the private lives of Parliamentarians and anger about unemployment. But those headlines would be the Church of England's opportunity – with imaginative press releases, TV documentaries, videos, and local evangelistic initiatives. It is true that we might appear as marginally disadvantaged in worldly terms – but that would be very good publicity. Only if we botched the whole business would we suffer disadvantage. And as to those people who think the 'C. of E.' 'represents "England" ', I can only think they are aristocrats or Rip Van Winkles – they do not inhabit the parishes I have known in inner Birmingham or now know in the Medway basin.

And, of course, the issue of 'repudiating Christianity' is a very different one. When British Telecom was privatized, and Mercury was allowed to compete with it, this was not viewed as *repudiating* telephones. It was simply putting two 'denominations' (one previously State-protected) newly on a legal par with each other. It is certainly easy to find elements in the present state of the law where (as in the Education Act) Christianity is overtly recognized and favoured (perhaps even unfairly so); but that kind of recognition is *not* part of the establishment of the Church of England, and a promoting of Christianity could proceed (as it does in Wales and Northern Ireland) even where no Church is 'established'. On this front, the Churches together would have to advertise what they offered to the nation, and the disestablishment would be well marked by good ecumenical progress – which indeed is one of the reasons it is needed.

John Habgood has written further on the issue since. In *The Confessions of a Conservative Liberal* he has provided a broadcast talk he gave during the 1984 miners' strike entitled 'Church and State'. However, despite the title, he there sidesteps the constitutional issues, and says that such discussions 'can easily be trivialized into squabbles about how Parliament treats the Church of England, or the precise method of appointing bishops, or the implications of Mr Enoch Powell's views on Henry VIII'.[9] His enthronement sermon on 'Public Faith' opens the book, but, although it sounded at the time as though it touched on our established role, it does not in print read quite like that. So that book skirts round the establishment issue.

In a more recent collection of addresses, *Making Sense*, he has another paper on 'Church and State', a relationship which, he says, must be approached 'to a large extent pragmatically'. He asserts the need in a nation for 'a common language of hope, aspiration and penitence' – and states that 'a formal public commitment to religious faith at least provides a basis on which cohesion can be built'.[10] We appear to be approaching a wholly pragmatic basis for establishment, an establishment in which the Church accepts State control *for the sake of the State*. Certainly he wants no theoretical ideal of Church and State; his offer is instead to note the establishment is there and then defend it with three 'considerations' about its value and significance. These prove to be:

1. An established Church is a permanent reminder of the religious basis of civil power. Disestablishment would therefore be 'repudiation' (as asserted in his earlier book).

2. The establishment is important to the Crown.

3. The establishment makes us – or perhaps should make us – 'an open Church with a large fringe membership'.

Of these, I would want to say that the first 'consideration', harmless though hardly applicable universally, is so set out that, once you have it, you can *never* change and be without the establishment. I neither believe that, nor think that change would be read as 'repudiation', nor even think it necessarily appalling if it were. For the State to make an honest disclaimer that it was no longer 'C. of E.' has integrity, and passes on to the citizenry *their* duty to discover their own stance. This 'consideration' also evades the question as to whether none of the changes made down to the present involved 'repudiation', and only those which could be proposed for the future would do so. Is it that the first 90 per cent or 95 per cent or 99 per cent of disestablishment moves are not repudiative, but the last tiny percentage is? If so, I am sure we could find some formula which took us to virtually total disestablishment in fact, but could be defended as leaving some tiny thread of establishment still in place. This consideration looks very like the argument examined earlier, that establishmentarians tend to argue that all changes effected in the past and right up to this present moment are right and good, whereas every change proposed for the future is menacing and doom-laden and must be resisted.

The second 'consideration' involves a logic which starts from a wanted end-result: the monarchy must be bolstered at all costs – the Church is the only or the best support the Crown can have – it is best if the Church is tucked into the State, as *this* is the way to salvage the Crown. I suspect events have outdated this one; and I devote Chapter 7 to the Crown.

The third consideration is that the relationship to the State ensures 'an open Church with a large fringe membership'. This seems to me to be highly questionable as a matter of experience, highly problematical as an aim in any case, and obtainable by means other than establishment if it is a worthwhile aim. Certainly, from the days when the nineteenth century anglo-catholic movement pressed the need to be in communion, and then invoked the confirmation rubric and so debarred all unconfirmed parishioners from communion, it has been difficult to demonstrate this 'open church' notion evenly across our parishes. The fringe attachment, I submit, depends upon historical factors more than current policy, and arises from psychology, emotional need and personal traditions rather than from law. Then, insofar as contemporary policy in a parish or diocese may tend towards either a more 'open' or else a concentrated 'purposeful' type of church life, which of those tendencies is followed in turn does not depend upon establishment. And this reply is clinched by the existence of 'open' church styles among Free Churches in England and Anglican Churches overseas.

John Habgood also set out four reasons for holding onto the establishment in his letter to *The Times* of 30 January 1993, in which he was answering a leading article four days earlier – entitled 'Break the chains':

> First, such a development would rightly be seen as signifying that the nation was formally repudiating the Christian heritage . . .
> Secondly, beyond the ranks of the regular week-by-week Anglican churchgoers, there are millions who instinctively regard the Church of England as 'our' Church, and who seek its ministry . . .
> Thirdly, for the most part members of other Christian Churches, and indeed of the other faiths now present in this country, are not in favour of disestablishment . . .
> Fourthly, it really will not do to cite the disestablishment of the Church in Wales as an example. Given the strength of Nonconformism in Wales, Anglicanism was never a carrier of national identity in the sense in which this has been true in England.
> [He added a fifth which responded to *The Times*' suggestion that he was influenced by current royal behaviour – and excluded such a question from consideration.]

Here we see the same themes recurring, and, where that is so, they do not need to be answered again. But there are two further make-weights: the other Churches do not necessarily want us to be disestablished, and the Church in Wales has no bearing on the English situation. To these we must reply that traditionally – yes, and today – there have been many Free Church people who have stood away from the Church of

England *solely* or mainly because it was established. The well-
known Methodist leader, Rupert Davies, is one of those.* And
even those who profess to be glad that we are established,
whilst they themselves belong to a Free Church, are saying
very little of any weight: I am, for instance, very pleased that
there are people who work night-shifts, or labour underground,
and if I am glad, it is because I get certain benefits. But I see
little to recommend in the jobs themselves, would hate to have
to do one, and have no right to urge the benefits which *I* get
upon any such workers who are unhappy with their lot. Nor
did I see much sign that the Free Churches were interested
in taking our establishment on board when reunion talks were
on. I revert to this in Chapter 9.

The Wales issue is relevant because John Habgood is saying
that a minority Church in Wales might just as well be disestablished, but the English dioceses are (I presume he means this)
'a carrier of national identity'. This assertion of a kind of
mascot-cum-coat-of-arms role for the Church of England might
even have some accuracy in it as a matter of observation. But
it has no warrant in the New Testament, appears to lose sight
of Jesus Christ himself, and in passing dispenses with any
argument from numbers – we can be but a tiny minority, it
seems to be saying, but if that tiny minority (perhaps, say, like
Yeomen of the Guard?) can encapsulate from history some role
of 'carrying national identity', then we have shrugged away
the numbers game too. Then there never ever could be a reason
to disestablish, and once again the argument is cut short as it
begins. And perhaps that is the difficulty John Habgood's writings raise: we are left in no doubt that the present establishment is a Good Thing; we are told that any arguments against
it are misconceived; a spectre is raised of the appalling
implications of its dissolution; and we are then gently – even
paternalistically – steered away from this distraction into the

---

*See, for instance, his references to problems which *hold denominations
apart*, especially those 'so far deemed intractable ... like the English-
Anglican insistence upon the appointment of bishops by the State' in
Keith Clements, Rupert Davies and David Thompson, *The Church in Perspective* (Epworth 1992). It is interesting that he experiences this as not
just having our bishops appointed by the State, but as insisting it must
be so! See also his *The Church of England Observed* (SCM 1984) *passim*.

real issues which right-minded people should address. You can almost feel his steering hand upon your shoulder.

So we come to the Parliamentarians, Michael Alison and Frank Field, one Tory and one Labour. Both are concerned primarily for the good of the nation. I use two sample quotations:

Michael Alison:

> The State in all Western societies now is becoming increasingly secularized, increasingly the victim of pressure groups of every sort from every side. I think that the State needs the support and interaction with the Church more than ever before in our history.[11]

Frank Field:

> [the establishment] ... *has* over the centuries kept that rumour, that mystery of God alive ... and then one has to ask about the contact that there has been in the ordinary rank and file Englishmen and women in this country. They may not turn up to church but, as we have heard this evening, do regard themselves as members of that Church.[12]

It appears from these statements (which I think are typical) that Michael Alison thinks that standards of morality will be preserved in society by the establishment, whilst Frank Field expects the rumour of the knowledge of God to be preserved that way. To this we have to press the point that, if the cost of the Church doing the State some good is that the State must own it, appoint its leaders, and sit in judgement over it, then the cost is too high. We are still on the low ground; it is acknowledged that it is a country still in unbelief within which the Church is to be established *for society's good*. The MPs are quite clear that there are two entities, State and Church. The effect of these approaches they advocate is to urge the Church graciously to be willing to remain established because of the different kinds of good it may do to society. That is all very well – but the twist in the tale is that the only way the State can visualize us having that role is *if we are captive to the State*. There is a kind of knee-jerk illogic by which, even as they say the State needs us, they are quietly insisting that the State must have us on terms which make us subservient.*

Is our strength, our ability to serve, locked into being established?

I fear that the establishment Parliamentarians (there are, according to a recent poll, more anti-establishment MPs than there are those in favour) are both over-wishful on the one hand, and severely paternalistic on the other. Very sure of their own Christian faith, which I applaud, they simply want to manage the place of the Church in society (by Parliamentary means when necessary) to give the best possible spiritual and social good to the communities of England. They thus expound their establishment theory to their own evident satisfaction.

The truth of the matter is that the Church of England has at least five great strengths in relation to English society which, although they may have arisen from establishment circumstances which cannot be defended as appropriate for today, shaped our life in the past in a way that can still be of

---

*This kind of reasoning does produce cloud-cuckoo-land ways of arguing. When the see of Canterbury was going to be vacant in 1990, I was asked to respond to a pre-recorded interview on video with Michael Alison to make up a programme that was to be broadcast on TVS. He did not put much emphasis on the Crown Appointments Commission, but instead went straight and without embarrassment to the role of the Prime Minister. He acknowledged that Mrs Thatcher would be making the determinative choice. He pointed out that, when Paul said 'The powers that be are ordained of God' (Romans 13:1), Nero was the Roman Emperor to whom Paul must have been referring. If then, he said, God worked through Nero, how much more through Mrs Thatcher? We should simply trust God that he was using her as an agent of his will. I was left to protest to the video-recording that Paul did *not* expect or allow that Nero could or should appoint apostles! Romans 13:1 cannot simply be a blank cheque for any old powers the State may wish to assume in relation to the Church of God, and anyone who thought through its implications for a Church in a totalitarian State would recognize it at sight. So much pro-establishment argument is suspended upon an unspoken premise that we British are different, we British know how to run a State Church in a fair and trustworthy way, and it is difficult to see why anyone should not trust, say, Mrs Thatcher. That is all right in a way, but it is not a universalizable argument, and it is jumping from one kind of argument to another to say aloud 'St Paul canonizes Nero's administration' and 'Whatever aliens may do, you can trust the British to do it properly and fairly'.

service to the gospel, yes, and to the nation in a disestablished Church as much as in an established one. The important point is that we should not identify these strengths with being established. So here goes on them.

1. It has a full nationwide organization. The ideology that 'everybody is in a parish which has a responsibility to all its parishioners' is perfectly sustainable (though a 'cure' of 9,500 'souls' does look a bit pretentious ...). It is not dependent upon being established.

2. It has bishops. The standing of, say, a bishop of Bradford in the city of Bradford, is *not* directly derivable from his being a bishop of the 'established Church'. No, it arises from his being a permanent and responsible church person, with a citywide purview, and an evident concern for the quality of life in the city. The regard (or disregard) in which he is held derives from a whole cluster of intangible factors. It may be helped or hindered by personal qualities. It would hardly in fact be altered by further moves towards disestablishment. But the distinguishing feature of the bishop is *not* that he belongs to a residually established Church; it is centrally that he is a *bishop*! The only comparable persons are Roman Catholic bishops, and they are much thinner on the ground and thus have much larger areas to oversee. They self-evidently are running a chaplaincy service to their own people, and, although they are nowadays much more widely respected than before Vatican II, they have a tradition of belonging to a highly separatist and exclusive (and not quite British!) Church. So they currently enjoy much less of easy public confidence and of lines of communication into society than do Anglican bishops. The Anglican bishop has a long start on his Roman Catholic counterpart. Furthermore, I write here about points of contact and impact in relation to secular society – but, of course, the heirs of John Keble will see in the episcopate not just an abiding profile and a firm public front, but also, through the episcopal succession, the guarantee of true catholicism; just as formidable a presence even if the State support were ever to be removed. By their presence the bishops reassure us even now, that we are not simply a State creation, but a historic part of the Church catholic.

3. The Church of England has far greater material resources than other denominations. Of course, these could be in part removed in a disestablishment package, and that would make a difference. It is worth noting what the inherited resources, along with present-day giving, actually bestow on us – and on the nation. The number of parishes – between one and two thousand – which have two or more ordained staff is prodigious. We also have a vast set of supra-parochial resources in diocesan staffs, cathedral staffs, diocesan officers, and administrative and secretarial back-up to all these. Furthermore there is a powerful central organization at Church House, again far outstripping anything any other Church can offer. These resources in principle not only make an enormous contribution to the health of parishes (not all parishes would agree!), but also give us a long start in terms of mission to the whole of society. In addition to these official resources, there are semi-official trusts such as the Church Urban Fund, and also vast numbers of independent ones in the 'societies': home and overseas missionary societies, religious orders, theological colleges, societies for renewal, trusts to provide for travel, for school fees, for hospital treatment, retreat houses, youth movements, a much ramified church press and publishing industry, and great stakes also in many inter-denominational societies, such as the Bible Society, Scripture Union, and a host of others.

4. We hold thousands of medieval buildings, which, whilst they are often a financial burden, and sometimes threaten to turn incumbents into curators, yet also keep the organization before people's eyes, so that, in many parts of the country, they do actually know where the church building is. The Church of England starts with a great local advantage, at least compared with other Christian Churches, simply through that fact. Our ancient cathedrals share in this 'accessibility' factor also, though they are always in danger of being submerged under hordes of tourists.

5. We inherit a concern for life in society. Sometimes it simply means that the vicarage gives sandwiches to gentlemen of the road; sometimes it means space is offered on the premises to counselling or advice centres, sometimes it produces activists who are picketing the local Borough Council on behalf of road safety, or bus fares for the elderly, or home-help provision for the shut-ins. Sometimes it is

tackling major national issues, such as war and peace, or
nuclear deterrents. Such work by the Church of England is
unspectacular, it is not different in principle from what the
Free Churches or Roman Catholic Church may offer, but it
is *there* and there in great strength, and it resources the
Church of England for a proper upfront role in mission to
the nation even when disestablished.

The presence of these resources, material, human, spiritual
and traditional, of itself means that the continuities would
hugely outstrip the discontinuities in the event of disestablishment. The *canard* that is sometimes raised, that apart from
the State we should become a 'sect', is palpably absurd, and
amounts to mischievous propaganda. The word 'sect' is a
classic 'boo' word – a put-down – in ecclesiastical language. In
this case it can only have survived through a combination of
wickedness and inertia! The wickedness is Goebbels' principle
that if you want a lie to be believed, you simply go on repeating
it; and the inertia lies in the fact that so many Anglicans have
not got round to confronting the problem of establishment that
they allow the lie to go unchallenged. No other Church in
England would allow that they are a sect because not established. No Anglican Church outside of England would allow
that they are a sect because not established. No learned works
on ecclesiology relate State control to the *esse* of being a
Church. Nothing of course in the New Testament could possibly warrant such a notion. On no definition whatsoever of
'sect' would a disestablished and thus free Church of England
be a sect; and the corollary of the assertion – that is, that it
is State undergirdings that currently make us a Church – is,
in logical terms, unthinkable, in theological terms unwarranted, and in moral terms actually abhorrent. The abusive
term 'sect' should be banished from the discussion.

A disestablished Church?
So what kind of relationship between a self-directing Church
and an honestly secular State is to be imagined? Adrian
Hastings, Roman Catholic Professor of Theology at Leeds,
writes:

In principle there are three alternative models. Religion can be wholly integrated with society in such a way that it might be said, for instance, in traditional Africa that to be a Kikuyu was itself a religion. The character of Christianity makes it almost impossible for this ever to be quite the case, unlike the character of Islam, but in practice medieval society, and, in theory, the doctrine of Justinian and Hooker went as far as could be in this direction. Religion may also be wholly differentiated from secular life in dualist terms. However, a fully sectarian programme of withdrawal from 'the world' can easily land one back pretty close to our first model. Life among the Closed Brethren or the Mormons or in a large contemplative monastery . . . becomes in practice rather like the life of a tribe . . . [13]

It may be simple, but surely the key to the answer is there in his second model 'wholly differentiated from secular life in dualist terms'? There are two autonomous societies, the State with apparent sovereignty over all institutions in its territory, and the Church, with its only obedience to Almighty God – even if at intervals that obedience may entail defiance of an autocratic or unjust State. That is the position of virtually all denominational bodies within Britain and Ireland, including the Church of Scotland, save only the Church of England.

Hastings' category of dualism indicates that we are not considering two institutions which have polarized from each other – the differentiation is of two institutions still closely juxtaposed, still keen to bring influence to bear on the other. Hastings' warning about the Closed Brethren flags up a warning – we are not talking, and cannot be talking, about a Church which flees from a public role, puts its head down, and lapses into a tight round of self-regarding pietistic exercises in total separation from the world. No, we are talking of a reinvigorated and in principle 'national' Church, which holds a missionary responsibility for the transformation of society in the name and into the likeness of Jesus Christ. This is a dualism in practice. And a disestablished Church, taking its own decisions, finding and appointing its own leaders, in critical intimacy with the organs of government and the State, but with its answerability for its life being to God alone – that Church of God begins to come above the horizon as a live possibility. It would be a Church with all the assets we have listed above, a Church with fairly clear boundaries, a visible community life of its own, a mission to the nation and great international links as well – and a freedom in the sight of God.

This is simply to work from the New Testament model, keeping our existing structures where we see fit, and reforming them where they do not serve. It is not actually enormously adventurous – virtually every other Church in the world has already done it or has the end-result without having had to do it. It is treating ourselves as no longer children, but grown up and needing independence from nurse – as no longer content to be a colony, but bound instead to call for de-colonization.

The chapters which follow address the bonds which have to be broken, and carefully suggest ways in which the Church could provide for itself once they had gone.

4. The Appointment of Diocesan Bishops: The State's System

We come now to the specific features of the present-day bonds which subject the Church of England to the State. The historical material in Chapters 1 and 2 is here taken for granted, though at intervals it has to be further expanded in relation to particular issues. We begin with the most obnoxious of all the links with the State – the appointment of our chief pastors.

The Henrician legislation

When Henry VIII removed the Church of England from papal control, he made sure that he would personally appoint the bishops from then on, and that no link of any sort with the papacy should remain. However he retained in other respects the pre-Reformation procedures (see Chapter 1, p.13). The legal system set in being by the Ecclesiastical Appointments Act 1534* has been scarcely modified until the present day, though it has been largely affected by a series of conventions. The major legal reform has been the abolition in the late 1960s of the penalties of *praemunire* (i.e. those for high treason) for cathedral chapters which defy the monarch's instruction.† And, whilst the anglo-catholics of the nineteenth century did object strenuously to the appointments of

---

*This is the main title of the Act, and the original sub-title is 'The Absolute Restraint of Annates, Election of Bishops, and Letters Missive Act'. The supposed 'short title' 'The Appointment of Bishops Act' nowhere appears in the original as far as I can tell. A large part of the text is reprinted as an Appendix to the Howick Report. The date is often put at 1533, but 1534 appears accurate.

†The penalties, even if they did not run to hanging drawing and quartering, certainly included imprisonment and sequestration of all goods. But no cathedral chapter ever qualified to see whether the full exactions would be made. It is wonderful to read in the Howick Report that a Church Assembly Measure in 1938 would have abolished *praemunire* then, but the Ecclesiastical Committee of Parliament deemed it 'not expedient' and the Assembly did not press the point. Did the Committee expect the Commons to want the penalties to stand and be employed?

Hampden to Hereford in 1847 and of Temple to Exeter in 1869,
and did in each case persuade a minority on the chapter to
vote against the monarch's nominee, it is not clear that they
objected in principle to the monarch having the choice, and it
does not figure strongly in their attacks on the Erastianism of
the Church of England. A wonderful exception, to which reference is made in Chapter 2, is Hurrell Froude in Tract 59:

> The appointment of all our Bishops . . . is vested in the hands
> of individuals irresponsible and unpledged to any opinion of
> conduct; laymen, good or bad, as it may happen, orthodox
> or heretic, faithful or infidel. The Bishops, every one of them,
> are appointed by the Prime Minister for the time being, who
> since the repeal of the Test Act, may be an avowed Socinian,
> or even Atheist . . . [an unflattering description follows of the
> ceremonies of election and confirmation and of consecration
> by the Archbishop] . . . Such is the legal urgency which has
> been substituted for the violence of former times: and thus,
> as the law exists, we have actually no check on the
> appointments of a Socinian (if it so happen) or Infidel Minis-
> ter, guided by the more violent influences of a legislative
> body, for which I feel too much respect as a political power,
> to express an opinion about certain persons of its members.[1]

The twentieth-century procedure

It is only in the twentieth century that the procedure has come
seriously into question in a sustained way. For this we need to
understand *in some detail* how bishops have been appointed.
This includes the provisions of the 1534 Act, but also embraces
processes with the sanction of conventions. In the years from
1900 to 1960, the procedure was as follows:

1. Death or resignation of existing diocesan:

2. Informal consultation between Prime Minister and Archbishop of Province of vacant see (save for a vacant archbishopric of Canterbury*) (convention):

---

*Whilst Archbishops of Canterbury may have been consulted about vac-
ancies at York, the reverse was not the case, and it is clear that Winston
Churchill simply used his own discretion in choosing Fisher and refusing
Bell in 1945. Furthermore the convention itself *could* through oversight,
or even deliberately, be ignored in the appointment of other bishops (see
Edward Carpenter, *Archbishop Fisher – His Life and Times* (Canterbury
Press, Norwich, 1991) pp. 217 and 219).

3. The Prime Minister (coached or assisted by his Appointments Secretary) determines on a name, and approaches him to see if he is willing (convention – this convention and the next developed with the office of Prime Minister during the reigns of the early Hanoverians, and from that political development there developed these conventions).

4. The Prime Minister forwards the name of the cleric who has accepted the nomination to the Palace, and there the name is published (convention).

5. The monarch sends a licence to the dean (or provost) of the cathedral of the vacant see to convene the greater chapter (i.e. including honorary canons) and then after prayer for the guidance of the Holy Spirit to elect a suitable new chief pastor (Henry VIII's Act). This licence is known as the *congé d'élire*.

6. The monarch by the same post sends 'letters missive' to tell the chapter whom to elect (Henry VIII's Act).

7. A ceremony of 'confirmation' is then held, whereby it is publicly certified that *this* cleric, publicly produced, is the man elected by the chapter as above (Henry VIII's Act). The man, even if not yet consecrated bishop, is then the legal diocesan bishop.*

8. If the man is not already a bishop, he is then consecrated, the chief consecrator being the Archbishop of the Province, or such other bishop as shall be instructed by Royal Mandate to officiate (Henry VIII's Act).

9. The new bishop then pays homage to the monarch (Henry VIII's Act), kissing hands and swearing allegiance as follows:

> I. . . .
> lately. . . .
> having been elected, confirmed and consecrated Bishop of. . . .
> do hereby declare
> that your Majesty is the only Supreme Governor of this your realm

---

*Because this involves a kind of ecclesiastical anomaly, the confirmation ceremony, for those not already consecrated as bishops, is usually held in the afternoon prior to the consecration day. It is, of course, whilst technically public, a somewhat hidden and arcane ceremony, but, yes, it *does* make him, there and then, the diocesan bishop!

in spiritual and ecclesiastical things
as well as in temporal
and that no foreign prelate or potentate
has any jurisdiction within this realm
and I acknowledge that I hold the said bishopric
as well the spiritualities as the temporalities thereof
only of your Majesty
and for the same temporalities I do my homage presently
   to your Majesty
so help me God
God save Queen Elizabeth*

It is from the paying homage that the new bishop receives his 'temporalities' ('all the possessions and profits spiritual and temporal' – Act, clause 5) under the Act, and that includes his parish patronage, which until that point remains with the Crown which holds the patronage during vacancies. I have not enquired whether or not the Church Commissioners pay the new bishop his stipend prior to his paying homage, but it is no secret that he is allowed to occupy the see house well before that.

10. Finally the new bishop is enthroned or installed in his cathedral church (Henry VIII's Act). This acts like a Coronation does for the monarch – in no sense changing his status or function, but giving it all a first public airing within the diocese at its focal point, and enabling him both publicly to relate to his cathedral and to preach to his diocese.† In certain cases monarchs have allowed the enthronement to precede the paying homage, presumably by stretching the words of the Act slightly – or by Royal Dispensation? Neither

---

*The text of this apparently varied slightly over the years (though its Henrician origins seem readily visible), and it was shortened at Queen Victoria's request in 1873 to the present length. It is set out in these lines to assist the drawing of breath. The text provided to me by the Home Office is in capitals throughout.

†There is no standard liturgy for this occasion, so no standard understanding of it. Unless an incoming bishop is prepared to throw his weight around hard before he arrives, he will as likely as not get caught with a 'dean-and-chapter' job which came out of the files from the time his predecessor was enthroned. These tend to lay too much emphasis upon defining the respective rights of the cathedral and the bishop in relation to each other, and not enough upon his taking up his ministry in the diocese.

enthronement nor paying homage affects the bishop's legal position – he *is* the bishop of the diocese from his confirmation onwards. On the other hand, it does not *feel* as though the man has started until he is enthroned and it is usual for him to wait for this till he has paid homage, and it is apparently impossible for him to pay homage except when the Queen is in London – and that has at times meant a delay of up to three months in the date of enthronement.

The 'conventions' have all appeared at the front end of the procedures, preceding the operation of the provisions of the Act. Prime Ministers nowadays have the constitutional task in the State of advising the monarch on virtually everything, and that obviously includes ecclesiastical appointments; Prime Ministers in turn have come to rely on the advice of their own Appointments Secretaries. These steps underly the conventions; and a crucial feature of the conventions (one with its roots long before the Reformation, no doubt) is that the monarch *publishes* the name of the bishop-designate (Stage 4). From that point on, the man concerned acts as Successor Apparent, including holding press conferences and meetings with diocesan staff, planning the enthronement at the cathedral, sending messages to the diocesan journal, and measuring floors and windows at the see house. This public role absolutely ensures that the proceedings thereafter of the cathedral chapter (Stages 5 and 6) are farcical.

Stages 5 to 10 in the above list are all included in detail or in principle in Henry VIII's Act, and would all require statutory authority to change them. With the exception of an oddity recorded below, all pressures for reform have had their outcome in a tinkering with the 'conventions', leaving the statutory framework as it was, and the powers unamended. A Church with the courage to say 'the people of God must choose their own chief pastors' would have gone for reform of the law years ago.

The Howick Changes
The Howick Commission reported in 1964, and it led to a new convention, tacked on before Stage 2 in the list above. This came through the creation of 'Vacancy in See Committees'. Without going into details, it is sufficient to record that these Committees, once formed (and they are always in existence,

even when there is no immediate vacancy) were empowered
from the late 1960s to submit a statement about the needs of
the diocese (without naming names); and this statement went
to the Prime Minister (and his Secretary for Appointments).
It did not preclude the other enquiries by the Secretary, whose
task in consulting interested parties and receiving advice was
stepped up by the conventions.* At the same time, there
was created a post of the Archbishop's Appointments Secretary.
The appointee to this latter post did not at that stage join in
the Downing Street consultations.

The Chadwick proposals and aftermath

The next step came with the Chadwick Commission in 1970.
Now the recommendations became bolder. The Commission
wanted to bring the major part of the decision-making process
across to the Church itself (the Commission was far from identifying Church and State), and around half the members proposed a Crown Appointments Commission (it was not called
that in the report) not unlike that which we now have – this
was known thereafter as Proposal A. Its Secretary was to
be the Archbishop's Appointments Secretary. This half of the
Commission proposed that two (or more) names should go
the Prime Minister and

> As the State came to have confidence in the representative
> organs in the Church, it might become customary, as it has
> become customary in the case of suffragan bishops, for Prime
> Ministers to submit [i.e. to the Crown] the first of a number
> of names submitted them by the Church.†

The other portion of the Commission discussed election of
bishops, and eventually proposed an 'electing' body virtually
identical with the nominating 'Commission' proposed by the

---

*There is a wonderfully mocking speech by Christopher Wansey in Gen-
eral Synod in March 1973, in which he ridicules the investigation by the
Prime Minister's Appointments Secretary of the needs of the diocese of
Chelmsford, which included the Southend Borough Council ('I will lift up
mine eyes to the Town Hall, from whence cometh my bishop').
†*Church and State 1970*, p. 36. It should be noted that the actual split of
numbers between the two proposals is not recorded, and by definition it
could not be a half for each, as three members dissented from both
alternatives and called for true autonomy for the Church of England itself
to choose its own bishops.

first portion! This was Proposal B. But the difference was that this body would have full power to nominate the new bishop, and would not be merely short-listing. There was a paragraph which said that many people in the Church want the sovereign still to be associated with the appointment of bishops 'in a symbolic continuance of the procedure at the ratification stage whereby the nomination is formally made by the Crown.'[2] They say that they recognize that it will not be easy to reconcile this 'with our recommendation that the effective choice should pass from ministerial hands', but they believe the constitution to be infinitely adaptable.

The Chadwick report made slow progress on this front through the General Synod, because the Standing Committee viewed the 'Worship and Doctrine' front as more urgent. Thus the first substantive debate on 'Crown Appointments' came in February 1973, and in that debate the Synod passed without division this motion:

> That this Synod, noting the view of the Archbishops' Commission on Church and State that some change is necessary in the method of appointment of bishops, instructs the Standing Committee to bring forward proposals to secure for the Church a more effective share in the making of these and other senior ecclesiastical appointments and to enable the Synod to decide whether or not in any new system of appointments the final choice should in its view rest with the Church.

The work was done, and the issue came back to General Synod in July 1974. Then Professor Norman Anderson moved on the initiative of the Standing Committee:

> That the General Synod
> (i) affirms the principle that the decisive voice in the appointment of diocesan bishops should be that of the Church;
> (ii) believes that, in arrangements to give effect to this, it would be desirable that a small body, representative of the vacant diocese and of the wider Church, should choose a suitable person for appointment to that diocese and for the name to be submitted to the Sovereign, and
> (iii) instructs the Standing Committee to arrange for

further considerations of these matters, including the administrative, legal and constitutional implications, and to report the results to the Synod at an early date.

In the course of debate amendments were handled that enabled the Synod to address a nuanced range of options, which included:

(a) a virtual standstill,

(b) a Church 'small body' submitting a short list from which the Prime Minister would choose at his (or her) discretion;

(c) a Church 'small body' submitting more than one name to the Prime Minister, but with the convention which applies in respect of the choice of suffragans that the first name on the list is always chosen;

(d) an affirmation of the principle of 'the decisive voice', but without paragraph (ii) in the motion above, stating *how* that voice was to be achieved.

In the debate the amendments were all swept away on a show of hands without a count, and the Anderson motion was then adopted by 270 votes to 70. It will be noted both that the Synod did not go into the middle or safe part of the range of options, but went overwhelmingly for the most radical proposal, and that the Synod viewed the principle of 'the decisive voice' as excluding any role for the Prime Minister. The Synod had also taken the point that the Prime Minister could not be turned into a 'mere postman' to forward the 'small body's' chosen name to the Sovereign, and preferred to believe that a direct submission of the name to the Sovereign gave logical expression to 'the decisive voice'.

The next stage was the Standing Committee's action in implementation of the resolution. There was delay, caused both by the need at the time for a General Election (it came in October 1974) and for the Worship and Doctrine Measure to go through Parliament in late 1974, and for Donald Coggan to succeed as Archbishop of Canterbury in December 1974, and to clear his diary. There were then discussions conducted by Professor Anderson and the Archbishop with the Prime Minister (who changed from being Harold Wilson to being Jim Callaghan during the discussions) and with the leaders of the two other main political parties (Margaret Thatcher, Conservative, and Jeremy Thorpe, Liberal, being the two consulted).

It broke surface by design on 8 June 1976 with a contrived
Parliamentary question from Margaret Thatcher to which Jim
Callaghan replied with a prepared statement. This included
the words:

> There are, in my view, cogent reasons why the State cannot
> divest itself from a concern with these appointments of the
> established Church. The Sovereign must be able to look for
> advice on a matter of this kind and that must mean, for a
> constitutional Sovereign, advice from Ministers. The arch-
> bishops and some of the bishops sit by right in the House of
> Lords, and their nomination must therefore remain a matter
> for the Prime Minister's concern. But I believe there is a
> case for making some changes in the present arrangements
> so that the Church should have, and be seen to have, a
> greater say in the process of choosing its leaders.

In passing, it is worth noting afresh that such an announcement came from the Prime Minister to the House of Commons.
The issue was one in the political arena, and the Church
leaders and decision-takers were left to pick it up from Parliamentary sources as they were able.

The public statement led to a report to Synod, and a debate,
again led by Norman Anderson, on that report. But it will be
seen that the pattern that was set before Parliament and then
before Synod was *not* what had been sought in 1974. In broad
terms the political leaders had held onto the following points
of principle:

(i) only the Prime Minister could advise the monarch, and
he (or she) was not to be short-circuited;

(ii) the Prime Minister was *not* to be put in the role of a
mere postman (or postwoman), forwarding to the monarch
the sole choice of a Church Commission;

(iii) because diocesan bishops in due course go to the Lords,
their appointment is in the strictest sense 'political' and
must therefore come from within the Prime Minister's rights
of patronage;

(iv) the prime ministerial rights in this matter could not
therefore be surrendered, and the absolute limits of con-
cessions that could be made were:

(a) any Church Commission must send at least *two* names
to No. 10, and the Prime Minister must have absolute

discretion as between the two; it was understood that the Church Commission would inform the Prime Minister of their order of preference of the two, and would notify precise voting figures in respect of that;

(b) even then the Prime Minister must also have the right to refuse both and to ask for further names;

(c) when the Archbishopric of Canterbury is vacant then the Prime Minister shall also have the power to nominate an Anglican lay communicant to chair the Church Commission; it was also part of the conversation that the Secretary-General of the Anglican Communion could participate, in a non-voting capacity, to represent the broader concerns of the Anglican Communion;

(d) the Prime Minister's Appointments Secretary should have a (non-voting) place on the Church Commission;

(e) it was assumed all along in the conversations that a 'Church Commission' would be roughly on the lines proposed in Chadwick, and that its proceedings should be absolutely confidential – it being crucial to the whole system of prime ministerial nomination that no other name was ever mentioned anywhere, save only that of the man who was both invited by the Prime Minister and then also accepted the nomination.

Norman Anderson had to work hard to get the Synod to accept this composition and role for what was not being called 'The Crown Appointments Commission'. However, he did so in broad terms in July 1976, and asked the Standing Committee to bring forward detailed proposals about the projected Commission. Then in November 1976 they decided, by an amendment from the floor, to hold the size down to 12 voting members: i.e. the two Archbishops (save when an archbrishopric is vacant), three elected clergy and three elected laity from General Synod for a five-year period of office, and four persons elected by the Vacancy-in-See Committee of the vacant diocese. Finally in February 1977 the Synod adopted the Standing Orders which controlled the membership of the Commission, the length of service (and the limit upon that, for Synod's own elected members, of ten years) and the method of election. The First Commission was duly formed in the early Summer of 1977 and tackled as its first assignment the vacancy in Birmingham to which, as a result of the two names they sent to

Jim Callaghan, Hugh Montefiore was appointed by the monarch.

In the procedure set out on page 82–5 above, no. 2 would now have to be re-written as follows:

2A. The Provincial Registrar notifies the Diocesan Registrar of the vacant diocese to convene the Vacancy-in-See Committee (which is always in existence, even when there no vacancy).

2B. The Vacancy-in-See Committee, attended by both the Prime Minister's Appointments Secretary and the Archbishop's Appointments Secretary, writes a description of the vacant see and a statement of its needs in its future diocesan, reports which will be going to the Crown Appointments Commission (it may need more than one meeting to do this, or the members may agree it by post).

2C. The Vacancy-in-See Committee also elects from itself four persons to represent the diocese on the Crown Appointments Commission (and may discuss names with those four so as to acquaint them of the mind of those who have chosen them).*

2D. The two Appointments Secretaries, subsequent to the main meeting under 2B (but without reference to any further meetings of the Vacancy-in-See Committee), visit the vacant diocese and interview every kind of churchperson, people from other denominations and other faiths, and leading citizens of the diocese, to ask them what advice or hopes they can proffer about the kind of man who should be bishop. They then do their own report to the Crown Appointments Commission.

2E. The Crown Appointments Commission meets for twenty-four hours. All its members have the right to propose names, sent in in advance, so that adequate profiles of the persons named can be provided by the two Appointments Secretaries. The Commission members share in prayer and worship, and genuinely address the needs and character of

---

*No method of electing these was built into the regulations originally, but General Synod in February 1993 laid down that these four, like the persons elected from General Synod, should be chosen by the Single Transferable Vote, the fairest form of 'proportional representation', a system much needed for filling an allocation of four places on the Commission with a true microcosm of the constituency.

the vacant diocese before considering names. When they come to names, it is no secret that they inevitably have to do much of their work by elimination. When they finally come down to two names (by whatever means), they have then to affirm to themselves that *both* are suitable to be bishop of the vacant diocese, and then vote definitively as to their personal preference between them. It is known that a 7–5 split does not count as an actual preference, which has to be 8–4 to be worth reporting. The matter is academic, in that the Prime Minister may quite properly exercise the discretion allowed under the convention and choose no. 2 – even a no. 2 who was outgunned by 12 votes to 0.

2F. The Prime Minister receives the names from the Crown Appointments Commission and, presumably, a report from the Downing Street Appointments Secretary, and stage 3 of the procedure on page 83 above follows and the requirements of Henry VIII's Act are then carried out in stages 4 to 10.

At the time of writing the fourth quinquennium of the Crown Appointments Commission is being served, and, unless something happens very quickly indeed, then it looks likely that in 1997 a fifth quinquennium will be begun. It is well nigh forgotten now that the system was a fudge, arising partly from the Synod's soft-headed desire to keep the Queen but lose the Prime Minister, partly from the desire (implicit or explicit) not to tangle with Henry VIII's Act, but to add another stage of convention onto the beginning of the process, and partly through the hard-headedness of the politicians involved who were not lightly to be trapped into giving away existing rights of patronage.*

---

*That is not to say that it has greatly preoccupied Prime Ministers. In the recent autobiographical accounts by Margaret Thatcher, *The Downing Street Years* (HarperCollins 1993), you will find no reference to bishops or the appointment of bishops in the index (the nearest approach is 'Bishop, Maurice – Prime Minister of Grenada'!). However careful research will being you to the following on p. 31:

[I saw Sir Richard O'Brien, chairman of the Manpower Services Commission, and also of the body appointed to advise me on the appoint-

A bold attempt at cosmetic surgery

There was one attempt made at reform in the early 1980s. For reasons which still elude me, the Standing Committee decided to address (by Measure) stages 5, 6 and 7 of the procedure set out on page 83 above. It will be recognized that these are the most useless – indeed the most cosmetic – features of the process. Well, in February 1982 Synod found itself addressing a proposal for a draft 'Appointment and Resignation of Bishops Measure'. The 'resignation' part of this was uncontroversial and in due course was enacted as a separate Measure. The 'appointment' part on the other hand addressed no issue of substance about the choice, nomination or actual appointment of bishops, but simply proposed to remove capitular elections (that is, 'election' by chapters) and confirmation ceremonies. In effect stages 5, 6 and 7 above were collapsed together into a simple 'ceremony of record' at which the Archbishop of the Province acting for the monarch was to swear the man in. (I tried myself to make something substantial of the concept of 'appointment of bishops' in the title, and tried to move an amendment to the draft measure to provide 'that it shall be lawful for the General Synod to provide by Canon for the appointment of diocesan bishops'. This was resisted on the very grounds that it would give substance to the intentionally cos-metic (but allegedly finance-saving) provisions of the Measure. There is a wonderful sense of being in a fantasy world when moving an amendment in Synod, only to have it defeated on the grounds that the Measure if so amended would actually

---

ment of a new Archbishop of Canterbury indicating] the extraordinary range of topics which crossed my desk in those first few days ... in view of my later relations with the hierarchy I could wish that Sir Richard had combined both his jobs and established a decent training scheme for bishops.

'Extraordinary' it may have been, but it was one of the few contributions she had been able to make to the future when she was leader of the Opposition, as the convention had the agreement of three political leaders (see pp. 88–9 above). The index reveals no further mention of Robert Runcie, whom she duly nominated, nor of other bishops. But the passage is worth noting not only for her sense of something 'extraordinary' about her range of duties as including appointing new bishops, but also for her (perhaps jocular?) sighing for 'a decent training scheme' (like the MSC ones!) which would have enabled existent or prospective bishops to see things her way.

change something! For my part, if the substance could not be changed, then I perversely thought that the cosmetic features – particularly the capitular election – ought to be *retained*, as it is the visible incredibility of the Henrician system in a twentieth-century Church which ought to lead to that system's total overthrow.)

The whole thing was then followed by a constitutional hollow laugh. After the Measure had completed its passage of General Synod in July 1983, it waited over a year to go to Parliament.* When it got there, it was defeated in one night (16 July 1984) in the Commons – by 32 votes to 17! There is some reason in *Hansard* to see objections about the (totally irrelevant!) appointment of the Bishop of Durham earlier that year as the main point of interest in the action of the Commons.† But it meant that capitular elections and ceremonies of confirmation remained in being *at the insistence of Parliament in 1984*. Part of the wonderful paradox was that it seems that the whole idea had had its origins in saving money; yet it was demonstrable that by Autumn 1984 there had now been many hours of committee work, not a few hours in full Synod, and the whole process of passing the Measure to Parliament – and after it all the expensive 'elections' and confirmations were still to continue. The Standing Committee took soundings at the November 1984 session of General Synod, and then brought back in February 1985 a proposal to have another go at Parliament with The Appointment of Bishops Measure. The Archbishop of York was amongst a minority on the Standing Committee opposed to this, and the debate in the Synod included not only his throwing his weight against the proposal

---

*The delay was in part due to a General Election in Summer 1983, after which a new Ecclestiastical Committee of Parliament had to be formed (see p. 123 below), and it in turn had to debate the draft Measure, deem it 'expedient' and find Parliamentary time for it. I attended a friend's confirmation ceremony in March 1984 on the assumption that it might be almost the last there would ever be, and I ought to get one look at it!
†The irrelevance of this line of reasoning is demonstrated in that the assuredly orthodox Dean and Chapter of Durham had shown no sign of acting as ecclesiastical watchdogs and declining the Queen's nominee when he had been nominated to them. They knew that the Queen's command over-rode such considerations! So for Parliament to preserve capitular elections seemed an extraordinary way of trying to protect the Church of England from reputed heresiarchs as its bishops.

but also the opposition of the three MPs who were there, and the Synod then defeated the proposal – which might *just* be interpreted as the Church of England accepting and endorsing the Parliamentary judgement that 'elections' and confirmations should continue.* And so they do, just as in Tudor times, to the present day.

The Commission and the Prime Ministers
We leave aside the cosmetic stuff on which the Synod has wasted so much time, and now consider how the Crown Appointments Commission system has worked. I set out some starting points to help evaluation.

1. The proceedings of the Commission are confidential, so that, although the Church at large loves to speculate about proceedings, in theory none of us knows anything about any proceedings at all. Anything I write below has been picked up informally or from known leaks.

2. It sounds as though the proceedings are very fairly conducted in the sense that all are given ample opportunity to speak their mind, and to occupy minority positions without coming under pressure.

3. It has been alleged in the church press recently, by a member of a particular Crown Appointments Commission, that full references are *not* supplied, and that in many cases summaries by the two secretaries have to suffice.

4. It is self-evident that many persons will be discussed who

---

*This was not quite the end of the story in respect of confirmations, as Brian McHenry moved a Private Member's Motion in General Synod on 12 November 1991 as follows:

That this Synod agree with the view that the ceremony of the confirmation of the election of a bishop is 'an expensive farrago of legal gobbledegook' (*Report of Proceedings* 1982 Vol. 13, No. 1, p. 249) and would welcome the introduction of a Canon modifying the ceremony.

Brian McHenry thought it could be done by Canon under powers derived from the Church of England (Miscellaneous Provisions) Measure 1976. There was doubt whether it could be done this way, and the motion was amended at the end to '. . . the introduction of modifications in the ceremony', a form of words which left the method open. It was then passed, in the pious hope that vicars-general could 'modify' the ceremony without legislation. Questions at later sessions of Synod elicited the information that the vicars-general were in July 1992 considering what modifications could be made, but in July 1993 had concluded that none could.

are quite unknown to the four who come from the vacant
diocese, and they will be reliant upon the summaries and/
or odd words of support or opposition from the central members of the Commission. (Sometimes too there may also be
names of people unknown to the Archbishops or the elected
six from General Synod, but that will be much rarer.) It is
obvious that a passing 'put-down' about a possible candidate
from an Archbishop might very well sink him on the spot.
(On the other hand, in those – no doubt rare – cases where
the four from the vacant diocese agree in advance about
wanting a particular person, and then stick to their guns, it
appears quite likely that they can get that person to the top
of the list. But if they do not agree with each other, then the
dynamics of the Commission mean that it will be other
people's choices which will dominate.)

5. There is no doubt that, despite the fond hopes of Proposal
A in the Chadwick Commission's report,[3] the political
leaders have viewed the two names as giving them a real
discretion. Whilst on balance it looks as though genial Jim
Callaghan did not ever go beyond no. 1 on the list in the
period of less than eighteen months in which he nominated
bishops to the Crown, yet it is clear that both Margaret
Thatcher and John Major have each been ready when they
saw fit to nominate no. 2 on the list, and to do so out of
personal preference and without regard to the voting on the
Commission. From this known fact a series of further evils
arise, and they now follow.

6. Because no. 1 is sometimes blocked by the Prime Minister
(even if the voting on the Commission is overwhelmingly or
unanimously in favour of him), that fact is bound to over-
shadow proceedings on the Commission itself. It is inevitable
that a soft word, or an angled report, by the Downing Street
Appointments Secretary will depress the chances of this
person as against that. Just as in Synod we are occasionally
told 'there would be no point in proceeding with that course
of action, because Parliament would not wear it', so on the
Commission it must be easy to say 'there would be no point
in submitting this name, because it is bound to be blocked'.
Perhaps we can illustrate this by a concrete example. It is
known from later statements that the then Bishop of Stepney was blocked by Margaret Thatcher in the appointment

to Birmingham in early 1987. The same Prime Minister had another three and three-quarter years in office still to run before her overthrow – was that same name ever submitted to her as no. 1 again? If not, why not? Was there no diocese for which he was natural choice in that period? And if so, then further blockings by Margaret Thatcher have to be recorded. Certainly it was noticeable that, very soon after the change of occupants in Downing Street, the same bishop went to almost the first vacant see, however unlike the Stepney area it was.

7. Because no. 2 is sometimes chosen, and proceedings are confidential, we actually have no way of knowing that *the whole Bench* is not in fact a set of no. 2's. The murk that attaches openly to a few known cases flows into all the cases. This was well illustrated by the hatchet attack on the present Archbishop of Canterbury by Clifford Longley, who could write in *The Times* just before the Archbishop's enthronement as follows:

> ... the Commission made Dr Habgood one of them and looked around for a plausible second name. He had to be not so lightweight that the Commission could be accused of not taking the exercise seriously, but weak enough to make it difficult for the Prime Minister to prefer him to the mighty Archbishop of York. If that is really how they played it, they misjudged Mrs Thatcher completely.[4]

Now this is mischievous (and unhelpfully follows in the article Clifford Longley's own discernment of 'the struggle which Dr Carey now faces, to have his leadership of the Church generally accepted' – a cause Clifford Longley was himself here obviously and deliberately undermining). It even raised the interesting question as to whether the Commission asked itself corporately what voting it should record ('shall we obtain our ends by having 8 for Habgood and 4 for Carey – or 4 for Habgood and 8 for Carey?') – and perhaps even asking its chairman (appointed by Margaret Thatcher) or the Prime Minister's Appointments Secretary how to achieve the right effect – and then being defeated by Thatcher's whim! The scenario is incredible – but the scope for speculation is undoubtedly there, and this is a pernicious instance of its outworking.*

But the parallel speculation could be made in the case of every single other appointment of a diocesan bishop. It is at least possible that in *every single diocese* to which a new bishop was appointed in the Thatcher and Major years there has been a unanimity on the Commission in favour of someone else and prime ministerial whim settled the issue, and promoted a man who in the Commission's judgement was a poor second. That is quite apart from the possibility that a Prime Minister ever exercised the further powers to reject both names submitted and to ask the Commission to provide two more. I do not believe that has ever happened – though it is logically possible that it has – but, if it has, it further strengthens the case against both the system and the actual appointees.

The possibility is well supported by what is known of relationships between Margaret Thatcher and the Church of England. Her policies for British society were highly controversial, and internationally (whether it were 'the bomb' or defence generally or immigration or Europe or the Falkland Islands or the Eastern bloc) they always admitted of strongly convinced opposition. The Church of England's leaders and potential leaders are not without views on these issues, and, to take but one instance, *Faith in the City* read as a sustained indictment of Tory policies. Furthermore, no Prime Minister will ever give any reason for passing over no.1 on the list (for it is not publicly known that the discretion has been exercised), so that the opportunity for sheer political prejudice – even unChristian political prejudice – sinking a particular man's chances is obvious. And who will say that a woman like Margaret Thatcher, whose interest was in power and whose conviction that she was right on all

---

*Curiously, the opposite speculation was also around – when George Carey's name was announced on 25 July 1990, the press hoardings contained statements that he was the 'unanimous' choice of the Commission. This surprised me (we are not supposed to know such things) and I tabled a synodical question in July 1991 which asked whether this stated unanimity could be demonstrated or trusted. Naturally I was told that it could not be, and was also told that the Synod Press Office had taken the view that it was unhelpful to say anything in public about it – which leaves us all open still to Longley-type speculations.

issues was overweening, restrained herself from exercising her prejudice?

There is a further knock-on corrupting effect. If at any point in the 1980s it became clear that the criteria the Commission would follow in choosing a man to be one of the two whose names went to the Prime Minister were the clean opposite of the criteria by which she would choose between the two, what was the Commission to do? And if any particular suffragan or other senior churchman were told his name was in the running for a particular see, would he not have to ask himself whether he would not be wise to soft-pedal criticism of the government for the next few months? A man might be very free to speak prophetically against government policies *once in office*, but clearly he would be well advised to curb his tongue in advance. Can such a pressure be justified theologically? But we have here a naked result of the still virulent remains of Erastianism; and we cannot know what other names – names perhaps of outspoken Churchmen who would have added distinction to the Bench – have topped the Commission's list and then been blocked by a Tory Prime Minister.

For the control retained by the Prime Minister is still enormous. The system itself cannot be altered without his consent; the confidentiality is part of the price paid for a church body having the chance to put forward two names; the Prime Minister's own Appointments Secretary is present in the discussions; and the ability to block either name of those put forward is a most potent lever. And even if the appointment is made in the fairest way, and the Commission's choice gets the PM's invitation, there remains something absurd, even something abhorrent, in a cleric opening a letter from the Prime Minister of the day, asking him if Downing Street may submit his name to the monarch, that he may become Bishop of Borchester. For there is nothing cosmetic about this – actual power of patronage resides in the Prime Minister and the letter not only implies it, but overtly operates and reinforces it.* (The recipient is usually too dazed or too overjoyed to

---

*This is perhaps the place to mention that the recent 'Episcopal Ministry Act of Synod 1993' includes the following assurance:

engage in either criticism or revulsion about how the invitation
has come to him. History would lead us to expect that there
will be little signs of revolution coming from the recipients –
even to the point where someone listed as no. 2 on the list
might accept such an appointment even though it were contrary to his earlier published principles.)

There is a historic tendency for Anglicans who sense the
power lying in hands of the State to play it down and try to
put a brave ecclesiastical face upon things. The classic,
indeed the OTT, form of this came in the Chadwick report,
where the 'Proposal A' group were defending the then current
situation, i.e. before the coming of the Crown Appointments
Commission:

> The Prime Minister is not a free agent in this matter. In his
> advice to the Sovereign he is subjected to six important
> safeguards:
> **(a)** public opinion is against any misuse of patronage ...
> **(b)** he can only recommend a ... priest ...
> **(c)** he does in fact recommend one person from a very small
> number ... approved by the Archbishops
> **(d)** the person ... must ... be acceptable to the majority of
> the dean and chapter ...
> **(e)** the person ... must after election be consecrated by
> other bishops.

> We find it difficult to understand how in face of all these
> safeguards the exercise of the present system *can be
> regarded as other than a choice by the Church.*[5]

This statement is the most blatant but most transparent win-

Ordinations and Appointments
Except as provided by the Measure and this Act no person or body
shall discriminate against candidates either for ordination *or for
appointment to senior office* in the Church of England on the grounds
of their views or positions about the ordination of women ...'

My italics here highlight another feature of the Church of England wish-
world. I made a passing point in the House of Bishops and then asked in
Synod whether we thought by this Act we were binding the Prime Minister not to discriminate – for, if he were to be bound by such an Act, that
would be a very surprising and even unconstitutional outcome of the
Synod vote, and, if he were not to be bound, then what 'senior office' did
we think we were including in the Act?

dow-dressing job ever. It remains slightly amusing in that it must once have had *six* 'safeguards' (at least it says there are six!), but when published it had only five. The mention of 'six' in the heading must be a footprint of something that once was, but by the time of publishing was not. Credulity is stretched to ponder on what could have been the now-deleted '(f)'. Perhaps it was the role of the Vacancy-in-See Committees, which were already in action, but do not appear to offer any shreds of 'safeguard'; or perhaps it was the shout of stage-managed welcome usual at an enthronement. But whatever it was, the Commission must have decided at a late stage that it was so threadbare a safeguard (even compared with the pathetic set given here) that it could not be included.

Take a look at what *is* included: there is no mileage at all in (a) unless nepotism or some such glaring scandal can be identified and documented and unmasked in a hostile press; (b) is taken for granted (fancy including it as a 'safeguard'!);* (c) was only a convention, was itself dependent upon the two Archbishops and *their* choices, and particularly did not apply in the appointments to Canterbury; (d) and (e) were totally vitiated by both the earlier announcement of the name of the selected person† and by the Queen's express command to the persons involved. The idea, for instance, that the Archbishops could decline to consecrate has been frequently thrown around, but Archbishops know that in such a case the Queen would (on the Prime Minister's advice) issue the Mandate to some other bishop – and the Church of England would be riven in two. If there were a case where a man's heretical views or unstable personality emerged after the 'conventions' (in which the Archbishops have already allowed the man's name to pass) had been completed, then the Archbishop of the Province might privately ask the man to withdraw, but if he insisted on his calling, then constitutionally the Archbishop would have no option but to proceed.

---

*One idly wonders how they failed to mention as a safeguard in this category that the person must be a baptized and confirmed male of thirty years of age, the husband of one wife, learned in the Latin tongue, certified as of sound mind, and holding a British passport ... Those safeguards would *really* have proved that the Church not the Prime Minister was controlling the choice.

†See p. 85 above.

The other wonderful feature of the 'Proposal A' extract above is the part I have italicized. This is a Humpty-Dumpty world indeed. When it has been established that the secular Prime Minister's choice is slightly trammelled by fringe operations by the Church, then it is concluded that all right-thinking people must view his (or her) choice as being in reality the Church's. It certainly was not the view of Jim Callaghan in the prepared answer in the Commons – he was confident that the powers were his, and *had to be his*, and he was giving away some small portion of them.* The truth would seem to be – under all systems known in England down to the present day – that ultimate power of choice is in the hands of the Prime Minister, that the Church (either by Archbishops or by Crown Appointments Commission) can do some short-listing, but that the Prime Minister has total power to block any candidate who is unwelcome to him. And in my experience persons who short-list for appointment to a post do *not* think they are choosing the successful candidate, but that they are creating a field for choice sometimes by a different body, always at a later date. Of course the Crown Appointments Commission in its early days must have thought it was actually selecting the bishop for a diocese, but at some point, probably soon after Margaret Thatcher's accession, they discovered they were in fact only short-listing. And the 'Proposal A' group could not have written as they did, had they not known that the only acceptable apologia for a system for appointing bishops must be one which unequivocally makes the Church of England itself responsible for its appointments. Their folly was the attempt to propose minimal changes on the fallacious grounds that the appointments *already* stem from the Church.

The broad range of Anglicans have always wanted to think this way: that is, in pretending that the Church of England is itself doing what is being visibly and nakedly done by the State. Anglicans have got so used to double-think in their apologias that it needs outsiders to blow the distorted thinking aside. The following quotations are worth pondering:

[The Principal of Ridley Hall went to Geneva in 1933.] Among other representatives of Continental Christianity he met some members of the Hitlerized Church of Germany.

---

*See the extract from the answer on p. 89 above.

He says that he was conscious of a certain embarrassment. 'When we press the religious independence of the Church,' he says, 'it is not always easy to answer satisfactorily their questions about "Who appoints your Bishops?" '[6]

The Howick Commission unanimously recommended that the place of the Prime Minister in the system ought (with modifications) to continue. Opinions from other Churches pressed us that it ought on the contrary, to cease. The witnesses who were not members of the Church of England were unanimous in pressing us to recommend that it ought to cease.

Previous Commissions suggested that the disquiet was the result of some measure of ignorance of the extent to which the Church is consulted under the present system . . .*

The Churches in Eastern Europe today which have retained their spiritual integrity more than any others are those where the state, before it became a Marxist/Leninist State, did not have the right to interfere in the internal affairs of the Church and still does not have that right. The Polish Catholic Church is free to conduct its own affairs and we see with what courage and effectiveness it does it. The Protestant Churches of East Germany are in the same position, and can give a marvellous prophetic witness to that society. The State, even a Marxist/Leninist State, has not dared to interfere with that state of affairs. In nearly all the rest of Eastern Europe where, under the old tradition of the Austro-

---

Church and State 1970, p. 29. When Margaret Thatcher was asked if her government had failed in any respect which she was prepared to mention, she replied, 'Yes, we have clearly failed to get our good policies across to the nation'. The policies were fine was her view: it was the communication of them that was the problem. So here – for the 'Proposal A' group a few pages later contribute the remarkable quotation set out above on page 100, suggesting that the Prime Minister's role is virtually non-existent, but presumably aware that not everybody else has yet noticed it. It is not however how the Commission as a whole proceeded on p. 29, for they continue ('Proposal A' group included):

. . . the impression we form today is that those who are disquieted and uneasy are usually aware of the main features of the present arrangements, and that more detailed information often tends not to diminish, but to increase their disquiet . . .

Hungarian empire and the Czarist empire, it was quite natural for the political community to be involved with the affairs of the Church, the Communist States took that over with pleasure and today control the appointments and the internal life of the Churches in the Soviet Union, in Hungary and Czechoslovakia.[7]

Abolishing the State participation

But the issue is not simply whether others can respect our appointments, nor simply whether in an extreme political case it would create a corrupt leadership; the issue is a simple one for us ourselves for today – how can the Church of England choose its own leaders freely, and know that each one was the one it wanted? And how can bishops be delivered from the haunting suspicion (in some cases the virtual knowledge) that they were the Prime Minister's own personal preference over against the man whom the Church truly wanted? When all the smokescreens have been cleared away, how can the live, active, visible Church of England by prayer, study and conference choose its bishops?

5. The Appointment of Diocesan Bishops: The Church's Own Task

The State's present process

The truth of the present process of appointing diocesan bishops runs like this: that we can make Canons on presbyters and deacons, on women presbyters and women deacons, but we cannot make rules for ourselves about a great central feature of church life in an episcopal Church. We are *forbidden* by law to make Canons on the appointment of bishops. We would think it horrific if the local vicar were appointed by the mayor, who is elected locally for one year at a time, but we allow the appointing of our chief pastors by nationally elected, short-term Prime Ministers.

I do not object only to the fact that the Prime Minister is seen as free to choose between two names submitted to her, or else send them back and ask for more. Nor do I object only to the fact that these arrangements are seen as a discretionary concession which can in principle be withdrawn. I object still more to the fact that the Church acquiesces in such a view. And I object most of all to the fact that the Crown has the last word. If – as we were told in 1976 when the present arrangements were agreed on – giving the Prime Minister the last word in episcopal appointments is the price we must pay for having bishops in the House of Lords, the price is too high. The Church must be free, and be seen to be free, to choose her own pastors. Otherwise their authority is seen to rest on foundations other than and additional to those of Christ and his apostles; and that, in effect, is a denial of the sufficiency of Christ as the only foundation and authority for our apostolic ministry.[1]

There remains one more conventional defence of Prime Ministerial appointment of bishops which used once to be deployed, namely the insistence that the sheer arbitrariness of such a method enabled men to be appointed who would never have been chosen by any church method – and certainly not by open election. The theory was that the Church thus gained great men as bishops, whereas church processes, where powers of blocking oddballs would exist, would only produce 'safe' men. Mervyn Stockwood (Bishop of Southwark 1958–82) was one frequently cited to illustrate the point. However, it is clear that judging by results alone is pernicious – a colonial power may make 'better' appointments (e.g. as chief judge or as district officer), but after decolonization it has no *right* to make appointments in the former colony however well it would do it. The Church of England is in the process of decolonization, and it is integral to the process that the State give up making the chief appointments. The idea that the Prime Minister was exercising such enormous independence of judgement also sits oddly with the evidence that in days before Howick and Chadwick No. 10 only took one out of three names submitted by the Archbishop of the Province.

Once we are clear, however, that the method of appointment is not going to be suspended upon the issue of 'results', it may be possible to review the 'results' again and see whether the alleged advantage does lie with the State appointments. For my money (as I have set out above) the State's ability to block is as weighty a matter as the State's power to appoint. And, when it comes to appointments, the last days before the coming of the Crown Appointments Commission were not only not distinguished by magnificent appointments, they were actually sullied by at least two drastically bad ones.* Nor has the

---

*Was Eric Kemp referring to these when he introduced the first debate in Synod on the appointment of bishops on 22 February 1973? He protected his flank thus: '. . . the views which I shall express this morning are views which I have held for a good many years, based upon considerations of principle and theology and not influenced by any particular recent appointment. Nothing that I say, therefore, should be taken as being in any way a reflection on any individual.' Was it that some appointments in 1971–2 might at first blush have been thought responsible for turning people against the independence of Prime Ministerial appointments? Eric Kemp appears to have thought that might have been alleged as the reason for his hostility. But he too was endeavouring to state *principles*, and it would have been absurd to develop principles in reaction against unwanted appointments.

Crown Appointments Commission itself done *too* badly, if we may judge on the one half of their nominees who have won successive Prime Ministers' favour, without knowing the other half who have not. So we say that those who appeal to results must be very sure of the results to which they appeal. Those who have always known that good ends may, in the providence of God, come out of evil means would never want the results to be used to justify the means – and nor should any Christian reflecting on the matter either.

Developing the Church's own process
My starting point here is that, without hesitation or equivocation, Henry's Act and the current conventions which have insulated it and kept it alive, must alike be swept aside or superseded. We are in great need of a church process which will not require sleight-of-hand defences, but will honour God and be clearly the Church's own process. I believe it to be easily attainable. It only requires a steadfast combined will by the Church of England, and particularly its General Synod, and the end will be achieved. It could come as a piecemeal contribution to disestablishment, or as part of a larger legislative package. On any reckoning it is the most urgent need of all in a programme to sever the Church of England from State control.

However, there is a preliminary question to be faced. Is it better to provide a complete alternative ready-made pattern for a churchly appointment of bishops, or is it better simply to aim now for the constitutional freedom to work out our own pattern as and when we wish? On principle, I have no doubt but that the latter is better, but there has always been around a wholly pragmatic defence of prime ministerial power of appointment which has taken this form: 'no one can show us a system which will work better [and therefore nothing must be changed]'. However, we can now 'see off' that stone-walling defensive tactic; at the very least, indeed simply as a debating tactic, we have only to answer the point thus: 'Why, we would have a workable and perfectly respectable churchly system if we retained for the moment the "Crown Appointments Commission", with its present composition save that of the Downing Street Appointments Secretary (and with a change for the appointing of an archbishop), and that Commission, omitting

the word "Crown" from its title, produced just one name, and
that one person were by the choice of the Commission thus
appointed to be the bishop of the vacant diocese.' It would of
course be possible to provide variants on this, but the well-
tried existence of a churchly system, the major snags in which
relate to the need to produce two names and to submit them
to the Prime Minister, gives the lie to the suggestion that no
workable churchly system can be found.

However, it is logically right to brush aside the question of
'what system?' and to concentrate on the need for freedom
to decide our own method. The amendment I moved to the
Appointment of Bishops Measure in February 1983 gives
the most succinct and transparent method.* The text was
simply 'that it shall be lawful for the General Synod to provide
by Canon for the appointment of diocesan bishops'. This first
of all recognizes the present dismal situation – that the
power of deciding how bishops should be appointed lies itself
with the State, i.e. with the Queen in Parliament. When Henry
VIII took over the powers, he did so not by a claim to a right
of patronage inherent in the monarch simply as monarch. No,
he got Parliament to pass the Ecclesiastical Appointments Act
of 1534, and bishops are still appointed under the Act. So the
proposal for a change is to amend the 1534 Act, and devolve
full powers upon the Church. A Measure which gives power to
the General Synod to pass a Canon is the accurate procedure
for superseding the present situation. It would also outflank
those who say 'you cannot find a better system' – for, in such
a case, there would be no change until the General Synod had
agreed a new Canon, and if they could not agree, then the
present situation would run on.

It would of course be possible to give alternative and much
more radical answers as to 'how' bishops should be appointed,
and it is such a scheme I suggest for exploration below.

A radical scheme for the appointment of diocesan bishops

I have made it clear above that I do not think it necessary to
have a scheme to hand for episcopal appointment by the
Church of England as a prerequisite for seeking our liberty to

*See p. 94 above.

find a system. I have also made it clear that the existing Crown Appointments Commission (and its base in the Vacancy-in-See Committees) would, if purged of its State connections and required to provide one name only, do perfectly well as a credible churchly system. It is not necessary, for the debating purpose of seeing off the notion 'you cannot find a credible system', to provide more than one. And I for one would be genuinely happy to see the (Crown) Appointments Commission basis continue for a while as shown. However, I am at times asked what I would *like*, and here I may indulge myself with a little more speculation. In order not any longer to be vague, I sketch a fairly full scheme in outline, but put on record that I have no vast stakes in any detail, that the whole is a *ballon d'essai*, and that I would be very ready to amend it in the light of comment and criticism. Equally I shall not mind if it is totally ignored – the points I have made in the main text and earlier in this paragraph are of much greater significance. And I would be very interested in alternative models.

Deep down, I think I believe in naked election by a wide popular franchise. In other words, I crave on behalf of a new bishop, coming into his diocese, the sense that he is actually wanted, and is seen by his people as the answer to their prayers and the outcome of their mutual deliberations. I would therefore want a diocesan electoral base at least the size of an existing Diocesan Synod, and preferably as large as a joint meeting of all the Deanery Synods (thus enabling all the parishes, including all the licensed clergy, to participate). I would service this electoral body with a Provincial Nominating Committee, chaired by the Archbishop, containing, say, five other diocesans (usually chosen by him from the sees neighbouring on the vacant diocese), and about a dozen persons from the vacant diocese, chosen in ways similar to the Vacancy-in-See Committee. These latter would have the task of describing the vacant diocese to the six bishops, but would not be expected to provide a blueprint of needs. The Nominating Committee would plan together to take not more than six and not less than three names to the electoral body. No name could go forward unless one of the representatives of the vacant diocese were ready to speak on behalf of that candidate. The Committee would have the task of providing written biographical information on each man within agreed limits, and should also add some commendatory paragraph as to the strengths the particular person would bring to the task.

Whilst the documentary material was being prepared, the actual names being nominated by the Committee would be released in the diocese, with a simple *Crockfords*-length detail of age and appointments held. At this stage, Deanery Synods would be meeting together on an archdeaconry basis. The purpose of this would be to see by informal discussion whether there were significant names which should be considered but had been overlooked. Opportunity would arise for new names to be nominated, provided that they attained a high threshold (e.g. 15 per cent of both the clergy and the laity of the electoral body). Such names, if validly nominated, would be circulated quickly by the Nominating Committee and action would be taken under its aegis to provide the basic data, and to find, presumably from those who nominated the person, the person best able to speak for him at the electoral body.

The electoral body would meet to elect. There would be a printed profile of each candidate. It would be possible to arrange for each nominated candidate to address the body, for, say five minutes. That is a possible, but not necessary, preliminary – but it would enable every voter to have had some real picture of persons who might otherwise seem very remote and insubstantial. Whether that happened or not, it would be integral to proceedings that there should be one proposer for each to commend each in turn. Ideally there would be no more than six candidates, though the fall-back provisions for local nomination *could* in theory take the numbers up to nine or even ten. Often it would be less than six. The length of time for speakers might have to be adjusted slightly to relate to the number of candidates. All forms of character assassination of others would be out of order. The crucial material about each would be in front of each voter in written form.

After this there would be a break-up of the body, and members would meet in sub-groups for informal clarification and digestion of what had been seen and heard – it might be alphabetical (i.e. random) redistribution, or it might be by deaneries, or two deaneries together. Some of the time might be given to prayer.

Then would come lunch and after it a solemn eucharist, with

a provincial president. Then there would be extended silence for prayer. Then would come the voting – and at this point the Church of England is able to inject into the procedure one of its glories (I almost said a theological glory) which is rarely connected with the election of bishops. The election would have to be done *by secret Single Transferable Vote.** It is as simple as that. Thus all the abuse that establishment people over the years have hurled at the supposed grinding rounds of voting, knifing and stalemates in overseas provinces would be short-circuited. There would be a single clean result, derived from a single transparent process, and all could hail the outcome as the true choice of the diocese.

A refinement that might be desired in the voting would be to ensure the proper support of both clergy and laity. This might be viewed as all the more necessary if the voting were done on a deanery synod basis, as there the clergy are outnumbered three or four to one. Counting them separately could lead to a situation of apparent stalemate, if the two 'houses' disagreed with each other. It is quite possible to propose ways of overcoming this difficulty, and I would be glad to propose them. In such a case the House of Bishops of the diocese ought also to have separate voting rights.

Adaptation for the appointment of Archbishops of Canterbury

The existing pattern for appointing Archbishops of Canterbury is highly unsatisfactory, not only because of the extra State weighting given to the Crown Appointments Commission in the chairing of the Commission by a State-appointed lay chairperson, but also because the four representatives of the Canterbury diocese are getting a voice in an appointment which is of ever less significance to them. Canterbury diocese is led in effect by two suffragans, both of them nominated by

---

*'STV' is the method of election used in electing to General Synod, and to its Committees. It gives the fairest form of 'Proportional Representation' in multi-seat constituencies and the most widely favoured candidate as the successful winner in a single-vacancy election. It is virtually proof against 'tactical voting', offers no incentive to one candidate to stand down in favour of another, and in principle does not offer a system which encourages candidates to try to 'beat the system'. It is used in civil elections in Northern Ireland and in Eire. It is the prime recommendation for fair elections of the Electoral Reform Society.

the Archbishop, with or without regard to the stated needs of
the diocese.

It is immediately clear that purging the State element from
the Crown Appointments Commission would not adequately
deal with the situation. There is much to be said for Christopher Wansey's proposal that the House of Bishops should
itself choose the Archbishop of Canterbury (which, again could
be done by secret 'STV'). Alternatively, an electoral body
could include the whole House of Bishops, suffragans of Canterbury Province, and representatives of Canterbury diocese.
If the international role were to be played up, then each Province of the Anglican Communion could also nominate its Pri-
mate (or someone else) to participate. I have no great stakes
in this. I simply outline a possibility – and it could be that
York should be done similarly. The process in the electoral
college could then unfold just as I have outlined it above for
the election of diocesan bishops.

The appointment of women bishops

The General Synod has recently provided for the ordination of
women as presbyters by sending a Measure to Parliament
and then promulging a Canon made in accordance with the
Measure. The Measure specifically excludes powers to ordain
a woman as a bishop. How then can this ever be attempted?
It will certainly be needed, perhaps ten years or so from now.

For this we need to set aside my proposals above for reforming the system, and in the first instance ask what would
happen if we continue to function under Henry VIII's Act. One
possibility is that the provision of women bishops *could* in
theory come by mere administrative action. In other words, if
a diocesan bishop sent the names of two women to the Prime
Minister when nominating for a suffragan appointment, it
would probably be within the powers of the Prime Minister to
forward one of the names to the Crown, and for the Royal
Mandate for consecration to be issued. Once that had happened, the Crown Appointments Commission could also presumably start to include the names of women in its short-list
of candidates, and Prime Ministers would have this factor to
weigh when choosing between two. Obviously, an archbishop
might advise a diocesan not to put up the names of women
presbyters when nominating for a suffragan, but a Stanley

Booth-Clibborn might very well persist in order to see what happened; he would at least make a point, and at most secure both the particular appointment and a determinative precedent. The Prime Minister could of course decline, but then the situation would be clear, that there was no progress on that front with that Prime Minister. If the diocesan or archbishop had to provide a legal basis, then he would simply say that all laws in the sixteenth century used male nouns and pronouns but that the general construction of, e.g. the criminal law, was that a woman was as guilty as a man for, say, theft, even if the law were couched in masculine language. This has always been a possible construction in relation to ordaining women as deacons and presbyters, and the enabling legislation has been passed in order to ensure that no doubt remained, and that bishops acted consistently. My guess is that, if the Prime Minister had the names of women sent him to be made suffragan bishops under the present system and he accepted them, that would become the standard interpretation of the law. The nomination would be made by Her Majesty, and an action against the monarch for acting unlawfully would be hard to bring and harder still to sustain.

Similarly it is of course also possible that the first move might come from the Crown Appointments Commission. The Commission could send the names of two women to the Prime Minister for nomination for a vacant see, and he would again have the task of advising the Crown. The arguments about the lawfulness or otherwise of nominating a woman as bishop would be the same as with a suffragan.

Failing such bold nominating by a diocesan or the Commission, it would appear likely that a Private Member's Motion in Synod, or a move by the Standing Committee on the basis of some working party report, could lead to the Synod deciding to proceed by a Measure, devolving to the Synod power to make a Canon on women bishops. But it appears very doubtful whether the Synod could proceed by such a Measure. To send a Measure to Parliament which at this point would amend Henry's Act (and arguably the Ordinal) would be to attempt what all other Commissions, debaters and expedients have been trying to avoid doing – that is, to amend Henry's Act. If there is a standstill on that front, then if a Measure to amend the Act were before Synod, would not other clauses start to

get added to it? And even if it could arrive at Parliament
pristine pure and with a single theme (perhaps part of one of
those pantechnicon 'Church of England (Miscellaneous
Provisions) Measures'?), what would it actually say? Would it
say 'Henry and the Ordinal notwithstanding, women can, by
statute law, be henceforth consecrated as bishops'? Or would
it say 'It shall be lawful for the General Synod to enact a
Canon providing for women to be nominated and consecrated
as bishops in the Church of God'? If so, it would be the only
Canon that said *anything* about the appointment of bishops –
thus far Henry's Act has kept a blank page in the Canons, and
this would be the oddest of first contributions to filling that
page. Or, wonderful to conjecture, would it say 'It shall be
lawful for the Prime Minister to nominate to the Crown a
woman presbyter to be made bishop' or 'It shall be lawful for
the Crown to nominate a woman as a bishop' or 'It shall be
lawful for an Archbishop, on receipt of the Royal Mandate,
to consecrate as bishop a woman presbyter duly elected and
confirmed under Henry VIII's Act'? All these look to be *ultra
vires* as far as Synod is concerned, and might well trespass
upon the Royal Prerogative.

Far and away the safest approach to this issue – and it is
an issue which might become genuinely emotive much earlier
than ten years from now – would be to get all powers over the
appointment of bishops into the hands of Synod as quickly as
possible. As Synod then makes provision by Canon for the
selecting, appointing and consecrating of bishops, so it can
include the permission for women to join the episcopate at the
right time. It is the sort of issue which should properly go to
dioceses – but not the sort which should go to Parliament.

Membership of the House of Lords
There remains one interesting element in any discussion of
the role of Prime Ministers in the appointment of bishops.
At the crucial point in the informal discussions between
Norman Anderson and Donald Coggan and the political
leaders of 1975–6 it appears that the House of Lords card was
played. The political leaders took the view that, as diocesan
bishops were, by appointment, joining a queue to sit in the
Lords, their appointment was by that very fact a political
appointment, and must be made by a free choice of the Prime

Minister of the day. This was used as the leverage to make the two churchmen agree to the provision of two names from the Crown Appointments Commission, when they had been mandated by the Synod to go for *'the* decisive voice'.

But ought the two to have settled so easily for that answer? A contrary pattern would have gone like this: 'If you yourselves wish to reform the House of Lords, so as to deny the five stated bishops and twenty-one others by seniority from having seats in the Lords as "Lords Spiritual", we will not object nor fight it. We value our own potential freedom to appoint our own bishops by our own decision-taking machinery very highly, and we are prepared to pay what you might deem a political price to get it.' Had our two answered that way, the political leaders would have been over a barrel. In the 1970s it was commonly thought that the House of Lords was unlikely to be reformed by either major party – the Tories not wanting to rock the boat because they had an inbuilt majority in the Lords and might lose it, and Labour equally hesitant because they valued the relative toothlessness of the Lords, and a reformed House of Lords might have more bite. It would have been almost impossible in the 1970s to have simply excised the bishops from the Lords without opening the door to wider reform; in effect our negotiators would have been able to say: 'We are ready for the reform of the House of Lords, and even the exclusion of Anglican bishops; but if *you* are not ready, then do not threaten us with the consequences as though you would start such a reform: simply give us the freedom we request, and then decide among yourselves by whatever means you wish *either* to settle for us appointing Lords Spiritual *or* to go for that reform.'

There was, in any case, an element of the confidence trick built into the premise that the Prime Minister of the day *must* appoint to the House of Lords, and must do so by clear choice or discretion. Consider the following cases:

1. In hereditary peerages, the House of Lords receives a totally random set of members, injected there by accident of death and birth, and without any participation by any Prime Minister (save the grantor, long dead, of the peerage). It would not be impossible to view Lords Spiritual as entering the House of Lords by a kind of parallel process – a Lords

Spiritual Corporate peerage of twenty-six persons with the office passed on by succession within the forty-two sees.*

2. It would be possible to say that the argument is currently an overkill, as some diocesans will never reach the House of Lords anyway; in the five or so years it usually takes to get there, some will die or retire early, and at the point of appointment therefore, save with the five senior sees, the Prime Minister does not actually *know* that that particular appointment is creating a peer, and therefore cannot insist that it must be viewed as political. It would be entirely appropriate, if the House of Lords is not otherwise reformed, to insist that *no* original appointment of a bishop to his see is political, but that, when a vacancy occurs among the twenty-one who currently take their place by seniority, then the Prime Minister of the day *chooses* a diocesan bishop from those still outside the Lords to become a Lord Spiritual. The Prime Minister's hand would then be shown at exactly the point the political leaders insisted it should be – i.e., in sending men to the Lords. At each vacancy there would be around fifteen bishops-in-waiting from whom he or she could choose, and a clear political choice could be exercised. The Prime Minister could have regard to seniority, but would not be bound by it. (There might of course be a certain *cachet* in having been overlooked by some Prime Ministers.) The only time that the Prime Minister's hands would be bound would be when a senior see went to a man not already a peer. And that would be a very small price for Prime Ministers to pay for the far greater range of selection open to them.†

3. The above are two expedients by which the political leaders could get themselves off the hook if they did not want to reform the House of Lords. However, it appears that the situation has changed. The Liberal Democrat Party has reform of the House of Lords in its policy, and so now also does the Labour Party. The report of the Labour Party 'Policy Review Group on Democracy for the Individual and the Com-

---

*Forty-two because neither Sodor and Man nor Gibraltar in Europe qualifies.

†In the last fifteen years, the only appointments there have been to the senior sees of those who were not already peers were David Jenkins to Durham in 1984, George Carey to Canterbury in 1991 and Michael Turnbull to Durham in 1994.

munity' entitled *Meet the Challenge: Make the Change – A New Agenda for Britain* includes the following: 'We propose the abolition of the House of Lords and its replacement with an elected second chamber with a specific and precisely defined constitutional role.' In the light of these policy indicators, the negotiators might now be in a position to say to political leaders, 'Let us help you: let the removal of the Lords Spiritual be the trigger for a proper overhaul of our Upper unelected House.'

4. It must not be viewed as sheer gain for the Church of England that we have these twenty-six places at the moment. Bishops have relatively short time there, and relatively little chance to engage with the House and its business on a day-to-day basis. There is a convention (of a very recent sort) that archbishops who retire are made life peers. But that is not extended to other bishops – and the House of Lords could well have done with retaining Hugh Montefiore, for instance, when he retired from the see of Birmingham in 1987. If it were possible to remove the existing, nearly *ex officio*, Lords Spiritual without otherwise damaging the existing composition of the Lords, then to have a generous creation of life peerages amongst all religious denominations (following Donald Soper, George MacLeod and Rabbi Jacobowitz) would be visible benefit.

We must not be trapped as it seems Donald Coggan and Norman Anderson were trapped. The Commons are free to initiate an overhaul of the House of Lords, and to take what action they wish in relation to the bishops who sit there. But the politicians should never ever be able to manoeuvre us out of getting our freedom on the grounds that the seats in the Lords would be at stake and we, the Church, dare not let them go.

The upshot
If the reform never got beyond the existing Crown Appointments Commission way of doing things, with a single name coming from a wholly church process, then we should have crossed the line from an Erastian to a godly form of appointment, and would be far far better off as a result. Bishops in particular would know they had been the choice of the Commission and were not under any suspicion of being

favoured by the Prime Minister for political or other prejudiced reasons. That would be gain indeed.

But if my 'radical' package set out above were adopted then bishops would come into their dioceses knowing *how* they had been chosen. They would know their dioceses wanted them. They would be entirely free in relation to the State. They would have a charter from God, through his people, to exercise their episcopal ministry fearlessly.

Similarly, the people of the diocese would know they had put their confidence openly and transparently in the man (or woman) chosen.

We need action.

6. Parliament

Parliamentary control

The traditional theory of Parliamentary control of the Church of England, at least until the nineteenth century, was that by this means the layman was governed by his elected (lay) representatives in his religious life as well as in the rest of his personal and civic life.* If there was any tendency for the bishops and clergy to lord it over God's flock, then Parliament had the right checking powers to keep the matter in balance.[1] However, Parliament was totally secularized by the end of the nineteenth century, and its theological competence to take counsel for the institutional life of the Church of England rapidly dwindled to vanishing point. Whilst a good slice of its powers of legislating for the Church have been devolved to the Church Assembly (since 1970 the General Synod), so that the Church largely governs itself by 'Measure', even so a Measure is Parliamentary legislation. As a Measure needs Parliamentary approval, final control of legislation rests still with the Palace of Westminster. My main interest below will lie in the House of Commons. I offer therefore a fairly astringent view of its suitability as a court of final decision on spiritual issues and church government.

The nature of the Commons

At the General Election in 1992, 651 seats were fought, 524 in England, 72 in Scotland, 38 in Wales and 17 in Northern Ireland. The Members returned for these seats showed a small overall majority of Tories, an opposition which was largely Labour, a perceptible number of Liberal Democrats (twenty), a sprinkling of Welsh and Scottish Nationalists, and representatives from different sides of the Northern Ireland divide. They were all elected on a 'first-past-the-post' basis, and many of them, because of a three-way or four-way split of the main

---

*The masculine pronouns and adjectives here are accurate. Women had no vote in Britain till after the First World War.

contenders, were elected on a minority vote.* Because of the
possibility of the 'tactical' voting which is precipitated by
the 'first-past-the-post' system, no candidate can be sure that
all who voted for her or him actually *wanted* her or him. The
electors may have been engaged in voting to stop someone else
being elected, rather than positively to elect the one who got
their vote. As an advocate of electoral reform, I cannot but
draw attention to the unrepresentative and actually random
character of the elected 651 persons. Certainly the votes that
were cast, when counted up nationally according to the party
support indicated, gave a distribution of voting in nothing like
the proportions in which the seats were distributed in the
Commons.

There are of course no religious tests for being a voter – we
have universal adult suffrage for those over eighteen, the only
non-voters being lunatics, criminals and peers.

The candidates were usually selected by a party 'caucus'.
They may have mentioned their religious beliefs, and, if so,
that may have been welcomed by some and discounted by
others. The important issues were loyalty to the party and
credibility to the electorate, and 'does his/her face fit?'.

The Members were of course elected on a 'ticket' – a party
manifesto. Whilst these may or may not have had ideologies
approximating to Christian ethical concerns in them at odd
points, there was no grounding of any policies upon the Christian revelation, the truth of God, or the establishment of the
Church of England. There may have been rare members
elected who, in their own persons, went beyond their parties
and expressed a personal moral or even religious concern on
some issue that might have arisen.

The Members actually elected include some practising Anglicans, but that is a wholly freak result of the election. The
persons returned could include Roman Catholics, Jews, Muslims and so on – and clearly could and do include large numbers who openly abjure all religious beliefs. Furthermore, at
the time I write there is evidence that some Members are not
personally concerned with acting morally. One further point

---

*The most extraordinary instance of this was Sir Russell Johnston
(Liberal Democrat), who, in a four-way battle in Inverness, was elected
with slightly over 26 per cent of the votes cast – and the three others all
got more than 22.5 per cent.

worth noting is that whilst it is possible for a practising Anglican to be elected, it is not possible for a Church of England
clergyman ordained in this country to sit in Parliament as an
elected Member. I deal with this odd banning more fully in
Appendix C.

The Prime Minister is the leader of the majority party. He
or she is nowadays elected by that party. Neither in national
nor in party regulations are there any religious tests or
requirements (save perhaps among the Ulster Democratic
Unionists!) for such election.

There are no religious tests for being sworn in as a Member
of the Commons.

Prayers are said by the Speaker's Chaplain, an Anglican,
every day at the beginning of business. An antique Anglican
form is used. The proceedings are not open to the public, so
no count of numbers is available. I am told by the Chaplain
that there are always *some* present, a number occasionally
swelled by the presence of a Member coming early to be absolutely sure he or she has a seat in order to raise certain points of
order when public business begins; standing orders, it appears,
limit the raising of such a point to those who have seats (and
there are not enough seats to go round if everyone comes, so
the early bird, believing or unbelieving, arrives for prayers
before business starts and thus secures the valued seat, at the
cost of a little outward piety).

In the conduct of business there is no ideological basis agreed
across the House, no appeal to the revelation of God as binding
anyone other than a speaker who cares to invoke it (few do).
The processes of decision-taking are that the government side
determines policy in Cabinet, turns it into motions and then
into legislation, and gets it through by sheer dint of its overall
majority and the requisite forms of 'Whipping'. This is not to
deny that backbenchers may influence policy through pressure
behind the scene, nor is it to assert that governments can
totally ignore the attitudes of their supporters in the country
– but in general governments are there to govern, and they do
so by taking their majority through the lobbies time after time
after time.

This also means that making speeches is, for most speakers
(and particularly opposition ones), an exceptionally frustrating
process. An important issue is to be decided; the opening

speeches are made; the House empties; Members with an
interest address empty benches; they make absolutely no
impact on the few who are there; it does not seem to matter
where the truth of the matter lies, for nothing that is said in
debate can change anyone's mind; but the debate rolls on;
the numbers reappear towards the end; the closing speakers
deliver their perorations; and the numbers dutifully troop
through the lobbies in their predetermined proportions. The
legislative and decision-taking role of the Commons is an exercise in sheer number-power. There may be theoretical accountability to the country, but it is poorly exercised. And the power
in the House is the power of a majority to get their way – it is
impossible to represent it as a conscious exercise of a stewardship on behalf of God, except in the almost trivial way in which
everything we do is in God's hands, and 'the powers that be
are ordained of God'.

I set these processes out in this way because they justify our
conclusion that both the formation of the House of Commons
and its way of business once formed, are, in the strictest and
most objectively descriptive way possible, 'godless'.* There is
thus *no* basis in theology for Parliament controlling the
ground-rules of the Church of England or for the leader of
the majority party having a decisive (and, for all we know,
politically angled) say in the choice of bishops. These powers
may derive from history, but that does not make them sacro-
sanct. If Parliament is, in formal terms, godless, then there is
something blasphemous in its control of the Church of
England.

Parliament and the Church of England

It is against this background that I want to examine the role
Parliament has played, and is free to play, in the life of the
Church of England. It devolved powers, as we have seen, in
1919 under the Church of England Assembly (Powers) Act. It
appears that that Act has itself been at times amended by
Measure, including most notably the Synodical Government
Measure in 1969. The Church Assembly (till 1970) and the
General Synod (since 1970) have had powers to draft Mea-
sures, and send them to Parliament for single readings in

---

*See the extended note at Appendix B.

each House. A measure is considered by the Ecclesiastical Committee of Parliament, and, if that deems it 'expedient' that it should be introduced to the two Houses, then it is debated. Finally, if accepted in both Houses, it gains the Royal Assent and becomes law.* There is a convention that a 'free' vote is allowed by party whips on church legislation – members can make up their own minds, and be present or not, and vote whichever way they wish.

There have been some notable upsets in Parliament. The first famous one came in 1926 and was the defeat in the Lords by one vote of proposals for a see of Shrewsbury. But the most famous of all were the two defeats by the Commons of the revised Prayer Books of 1927 and 1928. These defeats haunted the leadership of the Church of England thereafter for nearly fifty years, and thus led to the Church of England (Worship and Doctrine) Measure 1974. Even then the Synod only asked for the more 'limited' powers over liturgy, and left the 1662 Book of Common Prayer in the custody of Parliament. Under the present arrangements, if any part of the text of 1662 is ever to be rescinded or abolished, then that will require a Measure to Parliament – and it might surprise many Parliamentarians to receive such a Measure in, say, 2015. It is not a wholly cosmetic matter either, as its continued existence as our authoritative basis affects what happens in parish

---

*Curiously, until a late stage, it was intended in 1919, as recommended by the Selborne Committee in 1916, that the 'Enabling Act' should take the assent of Lords and Commons to Measures for granted by a form of 'inertia' tabling, and Measures deemed 'expedient' by the Ecclesiastical Committee would then have received the Royal Assent without debate, 'unless within forty days either House of Parliament direct to the contrary'. But Archbishop Davidson accepted in the Lords an amendment by the Lord Chancellor which states 'on address from each House of Parliament, asking that such Measures be presented to His Majesty, such Measure shall be presented to His Majesty'. (See G. K. A. Bell, *Randall Davidson, Archbishop of Canterbury* (Oxford, 3rd edn 1952), pp. 978–9.) That is the procedure now followed. It is arguable, as a matter of historical judgement, that Davidson should have resisted the amendment. On the other hand, even the 'inertia' tabling vests full powers in Parliament still, and they would certainly have been exercised in respect of every controversial matter which has been contained in a Measure. The only difference is that controversy would have been flagged up at an earlier point, and 'ambushes' would have been avoided. But if the powers should not be there anyway, it makes little difference.

churches on Sundays, and affects the occasional offices too. And we cannot make any other service other than an 'alternative' service, as long the BCP itself is there. That in turn may affect how we converse with other Churches, as it affects how we see ourselves, and how we appear to them.

However, the most remarkable recent intrusion of Parliament into the liturgical matters of the Church of England came in a different way. In 1981 and again in 1984 there were attempts to initiate in the Lords 'Prayer Book Protection Bills'. The basis of these was that, where a certain number of persons signed a form, the incumbent would have to provide 1662 forms at the main service of the Sunday once a month. This reactionary move, originating in Parliament, would have overridden the Worship and Doctrine Measure, and amended it by unilateral action. It would not of itself have compelled the Synod to revise the Canons on liturgy (which enshrine the details of the Worship and Doctrine Measure), and the clergy would actually have found themselves unsure whether to obey the Canons to which they have sworn allegiance, or the law of the land, which has highest claims upon them. In the first case a 'ten-minute bill' accepted in the Commons reinforced the Bill being introduced in the Lords. However, neither Bill made progress and that particular Erastian aggression quietly died away.

But it is not the wayward ventures of antediluvian peers which have been the main problem. It is rather that recent years have seen deliberate Parliamentary blockages being put upon the Measures desired by the Church of England. One was the infamous rejection of the (useless!) Appointment of Bishops Measure in 1984 by 32 votes to 17.* Another was the rejection of the Clergy (Ordination) measure in July 1989 by 51 votes to 45.† It does not matter whether the Synod was right or wrong in what it had sent to Parliament; and it does not matter whether Parliament was right or wrong in the decisions it took. The only issue is whether Parliament has

---

*See pp. 46, 67, 93–5 above.
†This made lawful the ordination of a candidate who had either been divorced and re-married or had a marriage partner who had previously been divorced and was now in the second marriage. Very special safeguards were built in – and the Measure did duly gain the support of the Lords and Commons when it was returned to them seven months later.

any right in theology to make the overruling decision. The
issue is almost one as to whether the General Synod is a child
who cannot be allowed to take full responsibility for his or her
life. A heavy parental hand exists, and at intervals it will come
in and block the child's decision – and the fact that it can do
that affects all sort of other decisions the child might want to
make. There was a very good instance of this in connection
with the famous Church of England (Worship and Doctrine)
Measure mentioned earlier. It was clear that the soundings
taken in the Church after the publication of *Church and State
1970* meant that General Synod should have asked Parliament
for what were called the 'larger powers'. These would have not
only given Synod control over 'alternative' services, but would
also have given it responsibility for the 1662 Book of Common
Prayer as well. However, the Standing Committee of Synod
came to believe that the Parliamentarians saw the entrenched
character of the BCP as one of the foundational features of
the establishment – perhaps even of Christianity itself. So
they advised the Synod not to provoke Parliament by asking
for the larger powers, and the Measure went through providing
only the narrower powers. The judgement may well have been
correct as a matter of sheer prudence – Parliament was not
enchanted with the Measure anyway, and it was treated as
controversial and was approved in the Commons by 145 votes
to 45.

Children indeed cannot take full responsibility for their own
lives. But we are not children – or at least not children of
Parliament. We should have the same right to determine our
own rules as any voluntary society in the land.

To be fair, there have been many areas of church life, apart
from Worship and Doctrine, where over the years powers have
been devolved from Parliament to Synod or to other church
procedures. The Pastoral Measures from 1969 to 1983 and the
Dioceses Measure of 1978 are good instances – large flexibility
in joining, dividing, adjusting, suspending and so on (both of
parishes and of dioceses respectively) are vested now in church
procedures. And, of course, we hear little about it when these
devolutionary moves go well. The process has been such as to
enable the leaders of the Church of England to take the view
that a direction was firmly set and it would lead in the process
of time to something like total disestablishment. The com-

plaint here is that the process has got slower and slower; no
actual programme with a clear point of arrival has ever been
issued; the House of Bishops or General Synod tends only to
further the process in a reactive way when some logjam or
practical difficulty arises; Parliament has actually defied the
Synod on occasion, and is obviously ready to do so again; and
when disestablishment is suggested the tendency is to say 'it'll
come of its own accord' – which in the legislative field is mani-
fest nonsense. No legislation yet ever wrote itself, amended
itself, steered itself or enacted itself.

The ordination of women as presbyters

At the time of writing we have just gone through the Parliamentary stages of taking the final decision on the ordination
of women as presbyters. In fact, Parliament approved; and by
the time this book is in print the first women will have been
made presbyters.

Yet the Parliamentary veto has had bad effects, and might
possibly have had much worse ones. For the sake of this argument, I need to paint a particular political scenario, as it quite
plausibly appeared might occur prior to the General Election
in April 1992. The hypothesis, none too remote, went like this:

> The final vote in Synod on the ordination of women as pres-
> byters was due in July or November 1992; in the event the
> 'separate reference' device was used in July, to give each or
> any of five separate Houses the chance to defeat it; if they did
> not defeat it, then the final vote would come in November.
>
> Meanwhile in April 1992 there was a general election.
> Labour thought in advance they had won it and were prepar-
> ing their victory speeches and parties. More cautious
> observers expected a 'hung' House of Commons – and this
> was a genuinely likely outcome. Clearly the 1987 Tory
> majority of over 100 was going to be drastically cut. Equally
> clearly, third parties, whether Liberal Democrats or Welsh
> or Scottish Nationalists or Northern Ireland parties, were
> going to have a far-from-negligible swatch of seats. If they
> could, for instance, muster forty seats between them, then,
> of the two main parties, one would have to get more than
> forty seats more than the other to have an overall majority.
> A 'hung' House was only too likely.

What would have happened to church legislation in such a case? Well, a Prime Minister leading a minority government – or possibly one in a coalition – has many higher preoccupying priorities than forming an Ecclesiastical Committee, and all administrations take up to six months to have such a Committee in action (we have seen that the fateful vote on the Appointment of Bishops Measure in July 1984 had taken over twelve months to come to the Commons because there had been a General Election just before it went through General Synod). So, we are to suppose that in a 'hung' Commons an Ecclesiastical Committee may well be formed at a slightly slower rate than the usual – but, for the sake of the argument, it might have been in action early in the New Year in 1993. The Committee recognizes that it must hear witnesses, and starts to compile a list of people it must see. It even starts to fix dates for their hearings. But then the coalition breaks up and the government either resigns or loses a vote of 'no confidence'. There is a new General Election, fixed for May 1993. The Ecclesiastical Committee is disbanded before it has gone far on its business. A new election is held. This time one party does get a narrow majority. The Ecclesiastical Committee is formed by Christmas 1993; it starts its hearings early in 1994; it finally deems the Measure 'expedient' in June 1994 and it gets Parliamentary time in late October 1994. General Synod has a special meeting in February 1995 to promulge the Canon, and the women are finally ordained *two and a half years after* the General Synod 'Final (sic!) Approval'.

Well, in the event we were slightly more fortunate than that in April 1992 – against the odds John Major *did* get his overall majority, and so governmental life has been able to proceed in its normal adversarial and non-coalitional way (which, paradoxically, is thought by the larger parties to be the way of stability). So Parliament did not reject the Measure. It simply took a mere twelve months to get round to debating it, a delay caused partly by the Ecclesiastical Committee making such heavy weather of it (and there was reason to think the Ecclesiastical Committee had somehow got itself packed with opponents of the Measure, and their nitpicking was a concern to find it 'not expedient' on any grounds available, rather than a true picking over the issues of whether citizens' rights were imperilled by the Measure). It could, as we have seen above, have found itself using twenty-four months. And the Church of England at large, and up to 1,000 women deacons in particular, have had to wait upon the timetable as well as the decision, both of which Parliament had entirely within its own constitutional rights to determine. We have been the hapless victims of their timetable.

A half-hidden agony was also going on in many people's minds all that time. Bishops could not fix dates for ordinations, lest they appear to take Parliament for granted. Proponents seethed as the Ecclesiastical Committee went its Macchiavellian way. Opponents asked themselves whether they really wanted a defeat for the Measure *in Parliament (non tali auxilio)*. Even the keenest Erastians could see that if Parliament did exercise its powers of veto, then an horrific Church–State confrontation would ensue – with a serious possibility either that bishops would ordain without the Measure, or that the women deacons would do a Greenham Common on the Palace of Westminster itself – either of which consummations would, in the view of one observer, have been greatly to be desired.*

The actual debate on the ordination of women in the Commons on 29 October 1993 mirrors those agonies, and the *Hansard* that reports it makes fascinating reading. Some vignettes of our Parliamentarians at work on theology will here help my case.

The turnout of 236 Members voting (215 in favour; 21

---

*It is actually quite difficult nowadays to imagine the bishops defying a Parliamentary veto. Yet they did in 1929. In 1984–5 they declined to go back to Parliament about the *congé d'élire* etc. – and they allowed the previous pattern to continue. In 1989–90, on the other hand, where they thought a certain outcome to be pastorally necessary, they went back again to Parliament after seven months. This was a procedure almost identical to the 1927–8 repeat try with the Prayer Book. The difference was that this time the bishops got their Parliamentary approval on the second attempt, and were saved from the cleft stick of a double defeat by Parliament. If they had lost again, would they have lain down under the decision, or gone back for a *third* time, or defied it and ordained the people concerned? Perhaps reflection on the 'emergency' policies of the bishops after the 1927–8 Prayer Book debacles would have nerved up their courage. Or perhaps not.

against) was viewed on all sides as very high and very satisfactory. It was, of course 36 per cent of the Commons, so the absentee rate was also very high.

Before the debate was opened, a communicant Anglican, Andrew Bowden, raised as a point of order whether it was proper for 'Members . . . who hold other religious beliefs or who are agnostics, atheists or feminists [!]' to vote. The Speaker predictably replied that the House was proceeding 'pursuant to an Act of Parliament' (i.e. the Enabling Act), and therefore all members could take part. One wonders what kind of Parliamentary role Andrew Bowden had in mind for his mini-synod of Parliamentary Anglican Christians to exercise. And was he trying to get something on record, or did he actually not know who was empowered to vote?

Nineteen members spoke in the debate. Of these at least six indicated that they thought it wrong for Parliament to be debating the matter at all. They were: Tony Benn, Simon Hughes, Clare Short, Andrew Mackinlay, Emma Nicholson (known as a disestablishmentarian from other speeches rather than this one), and Jean Corston. If they were typical of those present but silent, let alone those absent, it is clear that it is embarrassing to large numbers of Parliamentarians to take such decisions.* Some other Members in effect said, 'This is the business before us; I will address it responsibly without raising questions about why it is before us' – a stance which was pragmatic and efficient, but did not reveal how happily or unhappily they exercised their powers.

The five who spoke against the ordination of women were *very* sure of their powers. The first was John Gummer, who concentrated on theology. The next was Ann Widdecombe, *who had already left the Church of England and joined the Church of Rome on this very issue*: one wonders, if she was reckoning to exercise power over the Synod's decision in the Commons, how she had earlier thought that the Church of England had already made a decision and was going to ordain women as presbyters – when clearly she spoke in Parliament

---

*A survey by the Westminster-based opinion polling company, Access Opinions, in 1992 concluded that a majority of MPs favour disestablishment – a majority secured, no doubt, by the Celtic fringe, but with considerable strength in MPs for English constituencies (*CEN* 4 September 1992).

as though the decision was still to be taken – and taken there.
If she were able in the Commons to save the Church of England
from the ordination of women, why had she earlier left it? The
third opponent was Patrick Cormack – very sure of his powers.
The fourth was the member for Antrim, North, one Ian Paisley.
He, it proved, had even put it in his election address to the
voters in Antrim that the Church of England would be trying
to ordain women and he would oppose it in Parliament – no
doubts about theology or powers in *that* Parliamentarian. The
final opponent to speak was David Atkinson, another Roman
Catholic, who said he had been hesitant but was encouraged
by Ian Paisley's intervention!

That count left another eight in favour of the ordination of
women, and at least not opposed to having a controlling vote
on the issue. These were (in order of speaking): Michael Alison
(Second Estates Commissioner, the Church of England's
spokesman in the Commons); Frank Field (a devotee Anglican
establishmentarian); Peggy Fenner (worried about male
chauvinism); Michael Stern (a 'lapsed Jew', defending his right
to vote); Peter Hardy (a non-conformist member of the Ecclesiastical Committee (!), who might be a broken reed for the
establishment, as he thought Parliament should not oppose the
Synod – which is almost saying that the powers are wrongly located); Roger Sims (mainstream Anglican, accepting that
de facto powers are in Parliament); Glenda Jackson (an agnos-
tic, with a weighting in favour of women); and Michael Bates
(Anglican, ex-Free Church, 'honoured' to be able to contribute).

Perhaps the nineteen speakers were not a typical cross-
section (but then a cross-section would reveal the 400 plus
members who were not there, and the 200 plus further ones
who were there to vote in favour – on whatever ground). However, the actual debate raises *a posteriori* what I have tried to
raise in this book as an *a priori* issue: whether the Commons
is formally competent to take theological decisions for the
Church of England, and also raises the issue of informal competence – that is, as to whether even the nineteen who caught
the Speaker's eye and made speeches revealed as a group a
sufficient grasp of Christian theology to engage responsibly
(and Christianly!) with the issue.

Cut the connection

Whilst it is difficult to visualize how good a steward of the Church of England's resources any pre-Reform Parliament would have been, I suspect that John Keble in 1833 was, in formal terms, correct about what had happened to Parliament. Whether it had chosen to lay its secular hands upon Irish bishoprics or not, it was already ceasing to be a recognizably Christian assembly, and constitutionally was now not an Anglican one. When we come to the present day, the Commons has greatly changed since 1833 through universal suffrage, secret ballots, votes for women, enfranchisement at eighteen, boundary commissions, abolition of University and City seats, and the disappearance of seats from what is now Eire. But it has gained little or nothing in terms of the Christian faith, and, even if it had, a mere happy coincidence (it can be no more than that) of MPs and the Christian faith is no basis for formal State control through Parliament of a branch of the Church of God, a Christian society accountable supremely to God for its organization and patterns of corporate life.

Ways of severing

How could the severance be done? Well, a continued series of Measures like the Synodical Government Measure, the Pastoral Measures, the Worship and Doctrine Measure, and the Dioceses Measure could be sent to Parliament until every area of church life had been devolved. It looks at the moment as though this will only happen when particular difficulties arise in particular fields. Furthermore, these very Measures themselves (and most notably the Pastoral Measure) have at intervals to be amended, for they do not give full powers, but instead demarcate areas within which powers can be exercised. So we need, as part of the granting of full independence to the Church of England, a comprehensive devolving Measure which not only gives full powers over its life to the Church of England and its Synod or other governing bodies, but also gives the Church full power to alter the constitution which thus 'enables' them. There is fuller discussion of this in Chapter 11 below.

General Synod

One of the last-ditch defences of State control is constituted by a counter-attack upon General Synod, and so a word in defence of General Synod is in order here. The Synod has been called unrepresentative in various pro-establishment writings, and also in the Ecclesiastical Committee of Parliament and in the Commons, and in that quintessentially representative chamber, the House of Lords. But the Church of England must *have* a central corporate and representative organ of church government, and the only issue is: what kind should we have? There are good reasons for having a separated 'House of Bishops'; there are good reasons for electing on a diocesan basis; there are then good reasons for ensuring that both Clergy and Laity are distinctly represented; and there are constraints upon the total size and costs of the resultant body. Furthermore, there are interesting questions, recently aired in Synod itself, as to whether the electoral base for the Laity should be all those persons whose names are on the parish electoral rolls, or whether the present system, of an 'indirectly' elected Synod (with the electoral base all the Licensed Clergy of the diocese and the Lay members of the Deanery Synods), should be preserved. But there is no way we can go back on our tracks and remove the centre from the Church of England: quite the reverse, if decolonized, we shall need it all the more. The work of General Synod and particularly of its secretariat would be considerably and very helpfully reduced if nothing had to be got through the Ecclesiastical Committee of Parliament, and then through the Lords and Commons themselves: but the necessity of a central organ of management and policy-forming is unquestionable.

I would go further. Over the years I have slipped at intervals into the Strangers' Gallery of the House of Commons (and have also been in the Visitors' Gallery of the Lords). Without prejudice to the issues of political or theological orthodoxy, and with every allowance for my own prejudices, I report that General Synod debates are far more satisfactory as debates than are those in Parliament. The everyday experience of members of Synod is that each speech is made with a view to changing the minds of opponents or doubters (little chance of that in the Palace of Westminster), each amendment is tabled in the hope that it will either collapse or gather widespread support (little chance of that sort of activity in the Commons), and, although there are all sorts of groupings and loyalties, there are no whips, and no pressure on anyone to vote in defiance of his or her conscience.

In summary I submit that, whatever changes our synodical structures may need, in principle they *are* representative, and the colony needs independence, the child is grown up. Let Erastianism perish, and true responsibility before God for our corporate life in Christ flourish.

My own synodical ha'porth

The Private Member's Motion I tabled in Synod in early 1992 included this severance of our bondage to Parliament as part of its intent. It would have been called in November 1993, when it was second on the 'PMM' list, but the Synod ran out of time. It may now be debated in July 1994. It runs as follows:

That this Synod request the Standing Committee to bring forward proposals for the lifting of direct State control upon:
(a) the appointment of diocesan bishops;
(b) legislation coming from this Synod.

Amendments have come in to appoint a Church and State Commission, a matter on which I have commented in considering the appointment of bishops in Chapter 5 above. Unless the debate is again delayed, I fear most readers will know the upshot of that debate before they read this chapter.

7. The Monarchy

The Crown of England

Anglicanism as a separate ecclesiastical entity in Christendom was from the start highly monarchist. Henry VIII's own supremacy over the Church was no theoretical paper power – it was crushingly actual. If this title 'Supreme Head on Earth of the Church of England' was marginally modified by Elizabeth to 'Supreme Governor', there was still no doubt that the Old Testament models were ruling unchallenged. When James VI of Scotland arrived in London to be also James I of England, it was with evident joy that the Presbyterian-bred monarch then embraced Anglicanism – and did his best to export it lock, stock and barrel back to Scotland. Charles I arguably lost his own head rather than lose episcopacy, because in his view he would have lost everything worth having in monarchy if he lost the bishops. Charles II came in in 1660 claiming liberty of conscience to use the Prayer Book, and quickly deprived everybody else of the liberty not to. The Royal Supremacy ran supreme until 1688 – and then in practice it came apart.* The incredibility of a Roman Catholic as Supreme Governor of the Church of England was part of the decline; the acquittal of the seven bishops on trial for high treason contributed to it; the flight of James compounded the case; the necessity for Parliament to declare the throne vacant and invite William and Mary to occupy it virtually clinched it; and the stark requirement of law that those clergy who had solemnly sworn allegiance to James should now equally solemnly, while James was still alive, swear that same allegiance to William and Mary, completed the sorry story.

But even then the legal position of the Crown in relation to the Church of England was the same. The monarch embodied the State, and ruled through Parliament. Bishops swearing allegiance to the Crown were being appointed to

*See Chapter 1 above, pp. 18–20.

their sees by the State in the person of the monarch. In Hanoverian times Prime Ministers emerged, and quickly became part of the unwritten constitution, claiming the right to give all advice to the monarch. This in turn was entrenched by the constitutional lawyers of the nineteenth century, being consolidated into a theory which gave monarchs virtually no personal power or discretion at all. By this means, the Crown as a 'constitutional monarchy' rides high above all political quarrels or squabbles, is never on the 'wrong side' of a political question, and can never be blamed for anything that goes wrong. No doubt the effect of this was greatly heightened by the simultaneous spread of the British Empire throughout the world, and the fascination of Victoria's imperial throne exercising mighty jurisdiction over something like one-fifth of the earth's surface. In its latter stages the effects of this have been stupendous – a kind of semi-religious mystic awe has surrounded the whole institution, and has evoked something near to worship not only through what is now the Commonwealth, but also in the United States and other plainly 'foreign' countries.

Supreme Governorship and Church

What role has the Crown possessed in relation to the Church? Some of this emerges in the set forms used to inaugurate a new monarch – forms which have to be drawn from the archives, so long is it since they were in use. As the personification of the State, the new monarch makes an 'Accession Declaration' (which in the present monarch's case was apparently made when she first opened Parliament) as follows:

> I ... do solemnly and sincerely in the presence of God profess, testify, and declare that I am a faithful Protestant, and that I will, according to the true intent of the enactments which secure the Protestant succession to the Throne of my Realm, uphold and maintain the said enactments to the best of my powers according to law.

The next stage is the taking of the Coronation Oath, the relevant parts of which at the present Queen's coronation were as follows:

Archbishop: Will you to the utmost of your power maintain the Laws of God and the true profession of the Gospel? Will you to the utmost of your power maintain in the United Kingdom the Protestant Reformed Religion established by law? Will you maintain and preserve inviolably the settlement of the Church of England, and the doctrine, worship, discipline and government thereof, as by law established in England? And will you preserve unto the Bishops and Clergy of England, and to the Churches there committed to their charge, all such rights and privileges, as by law do or shall appertain to them or any of them?

Queen: All this I promise to do.

Then the Queen ... shall ... make her Solemn Oath ... laying her right hand upon the Holy Gospel in the great Bible ... and saying these words:

The things which I have here before promised, I will perform and keep. So help me God.

Then the Queen shall kiss the Book and sign the Oath.

The requiring of the Declaration and Oath set out above is integral to the whole principle of Supreme Governorship. The events are objectively inaugurating, recognizing and then honouring a constitutional monarch who is Supreme Governor both of the State – i.e. the United Kingdom – and of the Church of England, and of the latter because it is an organic part of the former. (It is of course a moot point, part of the very point at issue in this book, as to whether the State so *needs* to have the Church of England as organically part of its life, that the governorship of the civic realm of England would be diminished or weakened if the Church part were not mentioned: but then it seems Wales, Scotland and Northern Ireland are going to have to manage without, as far as monarchical oaths are concerned.)

The monarch's personal involvement
However, the principle of Supreme Governorship (and establishment) is not the only weighty issue in view when a new monarch makes the Declaration and the Oath. For at this point something personal is occurring in the monarch's own person. It is no stuffed dummy or stringed puppet who has to put her (or his) person behind the words; and they are far

from empty words. There is a personal commitment to the Crown's role in relation to the Church of England which, though it does not include so many and varied tasks as the governorship of the United Kingdom does, the new monarch undertakes just as personally, just as seriously. True, the process, being in the context of worship, enables the monarch and people together to pray for the fulfilment of all the weighty burdens of office, and to seek God's grace in so fulfilling them. But, whilst the liturgical text (including vows) sets out an objective theological understanding of what is being inaugurated – in this case the relationship of monarch to people – which would be the same whosoever came as true successor to the throne, the response of the actual person coming to the throne is inevitably and movingly personal. We are entitled and encouraged at that point to believe that the new monarch *means* the Declaration and Oath and, for instance, not only is not an agent of a foreign power (let alone of an alien prelate!), but comes with single-minded understanding and enthusiasm into the role cast in principle by the succession and explicitly in the rites. The personal commitment is further expressed in the monarch's very personal reception of communion.

The monarch embodying the State

From accession, as expressed in these rites of inauguration, onwards, the monarch's person and her or his State role become merged. Thus the Queen has 'governed' the Church of England for forty-two years largely by giving the Royal Assent to legislation which touches the Church, and by nominating as bishops those whose names have been provided to her by the Prime Minister. To the extent that her Supreme Governorship is bound up with issues treated here in other chapters (i.e. in relation to the appointment of bishops and the enactment of legislation), she cannot in these roles be viewed as separable from the system. If the Church of England is run by the State, then the monarch of England gives the final touch at each point where the State impinges on the Church. That 'final touch' is not simply a ceremonial flourish, an attractive *accoutrement* of a process which could be pursued without her – as, for example, if the Olympic Games were to be held in England, when the Queen might have some stage-managed ceremonial role in opening the Games, but they could equally

be opened without her. Such is not the case with her role as
the consummator of State action. She herself will have no
discretion in relation to that action; she may be personally
hostile to it; but her personal sentiments can only be conveyed
privately in advance to a Prime Minister ('to encourage, to
warn, and to advise'); and, once her assent is needed, it must
inevitably be given. Events are then far past the point where
her private opinions have any standing, and she must necessarily keep them to herself, even to controlling her non-verbal
communication when under the eye of the press and the
camera. She is the ultimate fount of authority in the State,
and her signature or Royal Assent consummates State action.
It is almost impossible to conceive of Supreme Governorship
in any other way.

However, the Church of England has rarely been very exact
in its thinking about this. There has, until very recently (of
which more below), been a tremendous sentiment of romanticized affection towards the Crown. This has been in no sense
distinctive to the Church of England, but the general existence
of the affection has meant that Anglicans have felt both privileged and possessive in respect of their chances to indulge
their romanticism. From one standpoint, this is witnessed at,
for example, royal weddings at St Paul's, the Maundy Money
rite somewhere in the country every Maundy Thursday, and
the Royal Family's attendance at Sandringham parish church,
and similar places. 'We' – the Church of England – host these
events, and we walk tall when they are on. From a different
angle, we have the Queen visiting the Synod at the inauguration of each quinquennium, and the Queen both issuing Royal
Mandates for the consecration of new bishops and then sum-
monsing diocesans to the Palace to pay homage, a very moving
ceremony which cannot fail to impress the new bishop. The
Church of England has simply conceived of itself, whether by
native right, royal favour, or divine grace, as having a personal
stake in the royal person who is constitutionally our Supreme
Governor.*

---

*There is, of course, another side to this. Monarchs are forbidden to marry
Roman Catholics, and members of the Royal Family who do marry Roman
Catholics lose their own right of succession. These penalties, which are
designed to preserve the Church of England from another James II, would
presumably be abandoned by legal process upon disestablishment.

Supreme Governorship as personal?

That is all very well. But the very romanticism of it has often
tipped even senior churchpeople over the line into believing
that her Supreme Governorship is itself personal. This has
produced a quite widespread, if woolly-headed, notion that her
person can be separated from the apparatus of State – which
allows the intermittent growth of the notion that distrust of
the role of Prime Ministers in the appointment of bishops can
be indulged without it affecting the Church's relationship with
the Crown. Palace good, Downing Street dubious: that has
been our *Animal Farm* slogan. As a result of this unwarranted
polarizing of the two, expedients are regularly devised to allow
bishops to be appointed by direct nomination from some church
body to the Crown. It was found in this shape in Proposal B
in the Chadwick Commission report.* It was still being held
out as a hope in the General Synod debate of July 1974. It
was completely demolished, as far as diocesan bishops were
concerned, in the Parliamentary Answer of Jim Callaghan in
June 1976 (See Chapter 4, p.89). It has never thereafter been
seriously explored again in respect of diocesans. However, it
has continued to be much treasured as a notion, and it got
another more or less official airing in the report of the Van
Straubenzee Commission, *Senior Church Appointments*, in
1993.[1] This Commission went into some detail of *how* such a
direct access to the monarch could operate; and, of course, it
involved a tooth-combing search for constitutional precedents,
and then arguments by analogy with them. There is 'Counsel's
Opinion' from Sir David Calcutt, which finds that there might
possibly be just enough room in the constitution for direct
access to the Crown by the two Archbishops. It was reckoned
that the Archbishops, in their role as Privy Councillors, enjoy

---

*"Many members of the Church would feel it fitting that the Sovereign
should continue to be associated with the process of election in a symbolic
continuance of the procedure at the ratification stage whereby the nomination is formally made by the Crown. We acknowledge that it would not
be easy, from the constitutional standpoint, to reconcile this with our
recommendation that the effective choice should pass from ministerial
hands. But the British constitution has proved remarkably adaptable . . .
We are confident that here . . . a solution acceptable to all could, with
goodwill, be achieved.

'We therefore recommend that the part of the Prime Minister ought to
cease . . .' (*Church and State 1970*, p.42).

some existing direct contact with the Crown, and could properly employ that channel of communication on the Church's
behalf. Sir William expounded on this when he spoke as an
invited guest at the first Synod debate on his report in February 1993; and he gave us a picture of the Archbishops as Privy
Councillors, in which role 'both have a right of audience with
the Sovereign'.[2] It almost sounded as though they would surprise the Queen with their errands!

John Habgood dealt magisterially with the proposal in this
first debate on the report, as follows:

> ... to demonstrate that Sovereigns can make, and some-
> times have made, decisions on their own account is not at
> all the same thing as saying that they can act on advice
> from someone other than a Minister of the Crown. In fact
> there is no precedent for such action ... The Prime Minister
> may be acting alone, but he is not simply acting in a personal
> capacity. He is acting as the chief Minister of State to advise
> the Head of State.
>
> That is the crucial issue. The Queen is not Supreme Gover-
> nor simply in a personal capacity, although we greatly value
> the personal qualities that she brings to the task. She is
> Supreme Governor by virtue of being Head of State. To
> suggest, therefore, that she might act as Supreme Governor
> in a way that deliberately bypassed her normal consti-
> tutional relationship with the State would be to undermine
> its basis. I do not believe that Sir David's Opinion helps us
> to face this key issue ...
>
> The fact is that if we want as a Church to retain a relation-
> ship with the State as symbolized by the Head of State,
> there is no way of avoiding the constitutional machinery of
> State. It is as simple as that. I therefore urge the Synod
> to stop wandering round this particular minefield and to
> concentrate instead on some of the helpful remarks made
> elsewhere ...[3]

Now it is admittedly true that the issue to which Jim Callaghan had referred – that is, that diocesan bishops are on
their way to the House of Lords – obviously did not figure in
the discussion of other senior church appointments. But the
Callaghan statement was invoking that outcome in order to
make the case for the projected nominating body sending two

names to Downing Street rather than one; and it does not seem to have been part of his intent to do other than take for granted the constitutional route for such nominations, i.e. through his office. He seems to have been saying that in all appointments which the Crown makes the Prime Minister's advice is requisite.*

There is also one other conceivable field where the Church of England has at first sight a direct relationship with the monarch. This is in the field of making Canon Law. Without entering here into the detail of the long history of the Convocations, we should simply note that today when the General Synod has received permission to make a Canon (which usually derives from powers conferred by Measure – as, for example, with the Canons on Worship and Doctrine), the Synod petitions the Crown for permission to 'execute' the Canon – i.e. to put it into effect. Synod then duly receives Her Majesty's Licence to 'promulge' the Canon, and duly does so. It all sounds like a cosy direct relationship. But in fact it is not – the route to the Crown is through the Home Office, and the Home Office advises the monarch as to the advisability of executing the Canon. Valerie Pitt, in her memorandum dissenting from the Chadwick Report, wrote:

> ... as long as it [the Crown's veto] exists it is possible for the State to use it. Indeed this has happened and not only in 1928 and not only in Parliament ... Two Canons, that on the marriage of the unbaptized and that on the seal of the confessional were discreetly withdrawn from the Code presented for the Royal Assent because it was intimated that they were unlikely to get it ...[4]

The Home Office is virtually never mentioned when Canons are before the Synod, but it and its officials (under a beady government eye) are there in the background just the same.†

---

*See p. 89 above.

†Another very minor (but typically establishment Anglican) evidence of governmental involvement is that, even when the monarch has assented to a Canon, it cannot be promulged until the Licence to promulge has been forwarded to the Synod by the Home Office. Rumour also has it that this is not done until it has been 'engrossed' – an arcane Home Office procedure whereby the text of the Canon is inscribed on parchment. The need of the Licence means that an extra three-month period has to be allowed after a Canon has been passed before it can be promulged.

What the various attempts to bypass the Prime Minister
have been saying is: 'We love the Queen – we don't love the
Prime Minister – we like the thought of the Queen being in a
symbolic way our Supreme Governor – we don't like the
thought that the Prime Minister pulls the strings, and then
the Queen dances – so we will cut out Downing Street.' This
sentiment has clearly been mother to the policy of finding
direct access, but it is an insufficient parentage. Its formal
illogic and its practical ill consequences are well spelled out
by the three would-be-disestablishing dissentients from the
Chadwick Report.[5] I met its last gasp myself in April 1991,
when being interviewed by Norman Tebbit for the TV programme on disestablishment which he compiled and presented
in May that year. After I had dealt with the issue of where
powers of appointment should lie, and he had agreed with the
need to locate them in the Church itself, he then added:

> What about a wholly powerless symbolic role for the mon-
> arch – perhaps like her being 'Head of the Commonwealth'
> in the political sphere, a 'headship' which leaves republics
> in the Commonwealth with total autonomy, and yet says
> something about affection and loyalty – could not the Queen
> become 'Head' of the Church of England in that sense? Would
> that not meet the sentiment which is around?

I replied at the time that it would not do as far as I was
concerned – we would then be open to all the partisan criticism
to which an established Church is exposed, without having the
apparent benefits. In particular, I was concerned not to be on
an apparently different footing in relation to the Crown from
that of other Churches.

The decline of royalism
That route of sentimental royalism leads nowhere. However, I
suspect that fewer and fewer people now think it is a path
worth pursuing in any case. For something very serious has
been happening to 'monarcholatry', and was quite visible
slightly before the Habgood *coup de grâce* (though possibly not
at the point where the Van Straubenzee report was sent to the
printers). The serious effect is simply this: the Royal Family
has been de-divinized. So I suspect we shall not be seeing
again this curious 'monarch alone' concept.

It virtually all happened in 1992. In the spring Andrew Morton published his book, *Diana*, suggesting that the Prince of Wales had been a woodenly uncomprehending husband to a wife who could not cope with the pressures on her – and that she had succumbed not only to bulimia, but also to at least one attempt at suicide. Every incentive was given to the great British public to believe that the Princess of Wales had personally sanctioned the account. The Princess Royal quietly got a divorce from Mark Phillips, and in the autumn married again, in Scotland. No great shaking of thrones in that – probably most of us just wished her well. But during the summer the Duke and Duchess of York had also separated – and the Duchess had some fairly compromising, or at least suggestive, photos of her taken by zoom lens during a holiday when she was with her American press adviser. Then came the transcribing and replaying of a telephone call between the Prince of Wales and one Camilla P-B. This went a long way to suggest a sustained guilty relationship between the two of them, perhaps stretching quite some way into the past. Then the Prince and Princess of Wales formally separated too – and by November 1992, they appeared irreconcilable.

At this point I encountered suddenly a complete mood change in both press and public, and it is my belief that this was not merely a subjective personal impression but reflected an actual shift in the nation's outlook. It is, however, easiest to report it from a personal point of view, as it is likely that only a known opponent of the establishment would have experienced the change in quite the way I did. It went like this. Until mid-November 1992, whenever I got involved in discussions or disputes (formal or informal) about disestablishment, I knew that I could be as confrontational as I wished with most present features of the links between Church and State, but that the Queen's position – for reasons set out broadly in this chapter – was not only inviolable, but even unquestionable. If the logic of any change in, say, Prime Ministerial appointments was that the Queen was to cease as Supreme Governor, then there was almost total market resistance to the notion. If a change would not touch the Crown – it could be looked at. But if it would touch the Crown – then it was virtual treason to propose it, and only the imbecilic or b-minded or bomb-throwing anarchist could persevere with it.

And it was that kind of thinking which led to the romanticized notions explored above, notions of sustaining the Crown whilst ditching all the political *accoutrements*.

But overnight this changed. Suddenly I began to get calls from the daily tabloids and even the quality Sundays, and occasionally the radio and television, and the questions now all took the same form: 'Do not the troubles of the Palace, and particularly of the Prince of Wales, mean that the Church of England will have to be disestablished?' The place which had had a thicket-fence round it until that mid-November, and was thus impenetrable for disestablishmentarians, had suddenly exposed a weakness *within* the thicket-fence; and Palace-watchers, instead of protecting the Crown in its establishment role, were themselves asking whether, as a matter of public confidence, the Crown could sustain the responsibility which the Supreme Governorship of the Church of England placed upon it. And it has to be said that the fascination of that question has run on and on, and fifteen months later shows little sign of abating. I was in the studio audience of a Sky TV production in February 1993, and George Austin, the Archdeacon of York, who was a protagonist in the discussion, said words to this effect: 'I have never agreed with Colin Buchanan on establishment issues, but I find now that the prospect of having a man who has cheated on his wife since soon after they were married as Supreme Governor of the Church of England fills me with alarm.' George Austin might be viewed as having read the worst possible interpretation into the tapped 'Camilla-tapes'; but it has to be realized that the Palace had taken no steps to deny the authenticity of the tapes, and this omission had certainly charged the ominous interpretation with total believability. Whilst the press did not pick up George Austin's comment on that original occasion, there came a point just before Christmas 1993 when he repeated it in a sermon – using the actual word 'adulterer' – and that led to a tremendous flurry in the media.

It is arguable that the whole news interest, both before George Austin's comments and in relation to them, was based on a wrong understanding of the Supreme Governorship. It should be clear from the arguments above that the role of Supreme Governor of the Church of England goes constitutionally with the Crown, and its exercise is a constitutional one which is in no way dependent upon the personal character or habits of the actual monarch who has the role. George Austin at one point got near to how the role might relate to the monarch's person; that was when he asked how someone who broke his marriage vows could be trusted to keep his Coronation ones. However, in view of the way in which a constitutional monarch is a prisoner of the constitutional machinery, it is a little difficult to see how the monarch in his or her own person *could* manage to break the vows, save perhaps by becoming a Roman Catholic – which would certainly require Abdication in such a way that it would not then be a monarch who joined the Church of Rome!

The constitutionalists were able to defend the Prince of Wales in his role as Heir Apparent. There were three lines of defence:

(a) his succession is, we hope, a long time off (and perhaps in that time he'll do better, and/or put this behind him);

(b) he has only engaged in a peccadillo, and many of his ancestors did much worse things (and cheerfully enjoyed our trust as Supreme Governors);

(c) because his role is constitutional and not personal, his personal behaviour is in the strictest sense irrelevant.

These are all right as far as they go – his behaviour is either (a) forgettable, or (b) forgivable, or (c) separable, as far as becoming Supreme Governor is concerned. But (a) is dependent upon the Queen having many years ahead (and none of us knows how long we actually have – and she is sixty-eight); (b) is dependent upon a comparison where no comparison is admissible – the world of today's media no longer has the restraint from which Edward VII (and even Edward VIII) benefited; and (c) is formally true, but clearly could not survive truly outrageous behaviour – the Christian Church expects some kind of role models in its leaders, and to argue that a Supreme Governor does not fall into that category can start to look like casuistry. The present Queen's forty-two year reign has – rightly or wrongly – written into the national sub-conscious *some* expectation that the Crown, to be credible, will be free of suggestions of personal scandal.

All this kind of argument is, of course, doubly necessary to those who wish to *defend* the establishment, and they are liable to be pushed into artificial or bizarre forms of defence.

But the situation since mid-November 1992 also stretches
those who wish to dismantle the establishment. The point of
principle for which we strive is that the Church should take
responsibility for its own life, and that the machinery of
government, including the actual office of Head of State, should
formally and theologically be divorced and distanced from any
interference with that life. The principle of establishment is
not dependent narrowly upon the personal virtues of successive monarchs – though it might have difficulty surviving too
many publicized vices. But the principle of disestablishment
is not connected one whit with the personal virtues of the
monarch, and I have had to explain frequently in recent
months that, as I never wanted respect for the throne to hinder
disestablishment, so I cannot wish for any disrespect to further
it. To that extent, the private life of any member of the Royal
Family is absolutely irrelevant to any matter on the disestablishment agenda. In those agenda the issues are quite different, are to be handled on a wholly different plane, and can
even be complicated by the prospective co-belligerence of the
Archdeacon of York or of others disappointed with the heir to
the throne. Jaundiced establishmentarians are likely to be
poor allies for principled disestablishmentarians!

What happens at the Accession?

It may be helpful, to round up the survey, to spell out what
would happen if the Queen died suddenly and the succession
became an actuality.* Of course I hope for long life for her –
and I have been telling the media, as my normal response,
that no one will be praying for her health and long life more
ardently than the Archbishop of Canterbury, who will have to
unravel a great jumble of sensitive issues very fast indeed if
the succession occurs.

The first basic point to grasp is that the Heir Apparent
becomes monarch, Head of State, *and* Supreme Governor all
at once at the moment the ruling monarch dies. He can (like
his great-uncle) choose to abdicate – and he can, presumably,
forswear his claims in advance. But what he cannot do is, on
his mother's death, decline or delay to become king. It has

---

*It is, I think, formal treason to desire the monarch's death. But it must
be possible somehow to hypothesize it.

already happened to him before he can open his mouth. And, to labour the point, he is also simultaneously and *ipso facto* Supreme Governor of the Church of England. The United Kingdom is never without a monarch, and the Church of England is never without a Supreme Governor. Some of the press have talked and written as though the Church of England would somehow confer the role on a new king – not a bit of it, as king he has the role.

Secondly, the tricky issues would largely relate to the Coronation. The death of a monarch means that a Coronation has to be arranged at fairly short notice – in 1952–3 the planning time was sixteen months and, so a reading of the biography of Geoffrey Fisher would suggest, it was not enough. If the present establishment remained, then the following questions, posed quite neutrally, would obviously need answers:

(i) Is the Coronation held, as traditionally, in the context of an Anglican Communion service? (If the answer is 'yes', then it is logical to ask 'which rite?', but that would be a very small problem.)

(ii) Are there ecumenical components to the rite? Or does establishment mean that it remains a distinctively C. of E. event? (Of course, traditionally the Moderator of the Church of Scotland had a walk-on part, but the question goes further than that.)

(iii) How far *is* the heir to the throne able to make the personal commitment required?

(iv) Is the heir to the throne a communicant, such as to be able with integrity to receive the sacrament personally?

(v) Would the Princess of Wales be Queen? And, if so, would she be crowned? Or would a divorce have taken effect before any Coronation?

(vi) Quite apart from the Christian religion, how are other religions to be represented – if at all?

That pillar of the establishment, John Habgood, when asked last year whether the Coronation Oath might be revised, himself said:

Well, I would think it would have to be, because the religious make-up of the country has changed so much, and if the Coronation service is going to unify the nation, as it must do, then it must recognize that we now live in an ecumenical and multi-faith society.[6]

Does the Coronation Oath exclude disestablishment?

There is one other question about the Coronation Oath which Hugh Montefiore posed in his column in *Church Times* in 1990. He propounded the notion that the Oath means that the monarch cannot consent to any disestablishment of the Church of England because he or she has sworn to 'maintain and preserve inviolably the settlement of the Church of England, and the doctrine, worship, discipline and government thereof, as by law established in England'. He further propounded the idea that this means that the only time the Church of England *can* be disestablished is after a monarch succeeds to the throne, but before that monarch has taken the Coronation Oath. Any time thereafter, a Measure or a Bill for disestablishment would have to be denied the Royal Assent! And *that* would certainly be a constitutional crisis.

However, I am clear that no such sensational scenario is sustainable. If the Oath meant that the 'settlement' could not even be amended, then every piece of church legislation – Act or Measure – for at least 150 years would have had to be resisted by the monarch. If, on the other hand, the Montefiore interpretation meant that every thread of connection between Church and State could be severed, *save only the last*, then disestablishment would be perfectly easily achieved with some mere token thread of connection left in place (as, e.g. that titles of sees established by law should not be changed save by recourse to Parliament), and the substantial separation could still be achieved. But in fact no such token is needed, as there is ample precedent. Queen Victoria in 1838 took the Oath to uphold the settlement of 'the United Church of England and Ireland' as 'by law established' and was perfectly ready (with constitutional advisers at her elbow) to give the Royal Assent to the Irish Church Act in 1869; and by this she disunited the two Churches, disestablishing the Church of Ireland and wrenching it from its (Parliamentary) union with the Church of England. Similarly George V in 1911 took the Oath to uphold the settlement of the Church of England, when the Province of Canterbury included the whole principality of Wales. Yet he too was ready to give the Royal Assent to the Welsh Church

Act in 1914, and by that Act the dioceses in Wales were in 1920 disestablished, and (as with the Church of Ireland) wrenched from their ecclesiastical union with the Church of England.

We conclude therefore that the only restriction laid upon the monarch by the Coronation Oath is that he or she will not act *unlawfully* contrary to the settlement of the Church of England – a force to the Oath which exactly reflects the concern in 1689, in the wake of the illegalities of James II, when the Oaths were first re-shaped to protect the Protestantism of the Church of England. Suppose then that legislation providing for partial or total disestablishment passes Lords and Commons and comes to the monarch for the Royal Assent; the monarch of the time is as free (and as bound) after taking the Coronation Oath to give the Royal Assent as he or she would have been before taking the Oath.

Disestablishment and the Crown

Where would disestablishment leave the Crown? The answer is simple – it would leave it in England in exactly the same position as it is currently in in Wales. I am myself as a citizen very happy to belong to a nation where the headship of state is vested in a dynastic constitutional monarchy, and I would not expect people at large to change their minds much at the point of disestablishment – whether they are still in a condition of pre-de-divinization semi-religious awe, or whether somewhat more realistic about the human shortcomings of the Royal Family. For every normal constitutional purpose, let alone every other royal occasion (such as Ascot or the Opening of Parliament or a visit to a home for the blind), the monarchy would fulfil exactly the same functions, even though shorn of its special church role. It is, after all, not far to seek a nation which is quite used to it – Wales.* And, as far as I can see,

*There are of course other Commonwealth countries under the British Crown (and none of them of course with that quaint anachronism, an established Anglican Church), but there is reason to think the Crown is very slowly losing its hold in people's affections in them for reasons which have nothing to do with Christianity. And within the United Kingdom there are the six counties of Northern Ireland, but there, although there is no religious establishment, the local divided views on both Christianity and monarchy are so wildly unlike anything anywhere else on earth that it is impossible to use it as a test case. Wales would appear a safe instance.

opinions about the monarchy are little different in Wales from what they are in England, and loyalty to the Crown is surely no less?

However, it has to be admitted that there is a concealed snag in this reasoning. It is at least possible that loyalty to the throne in Wales is mysteriously sustained because of the position of the throne in relation to the Church of England *in England*! It may well be that the whole cluster of church matters related to the Crown – Coronations, Royal Peculiars, Chaplains to the Queen, Maundy Money, Bishops paying homage, the title *Fidei Defensor*, and the visible worshipping presence of the Queen in church – have both heightened and preserved the mystique of the monarchy, and have tinged the semi-religious awe with a further tinge of religious ceremonial. Again, I am not convinced that this cluster of associations, if it actually has helped preserve respect and awe, is of itself a reason for preserving the establishment of the Church of England. But we do have some duty to our State, and should give thought to what for the monarch should follow after the demise of the establishment.

Far and away the simplest answer would be that the monarch would be free, in his or her own person, and not by dynastic succession or by statute, to follow the religion of his or her own choice. It would be possible to enshrine State duties within that, except insofar as they then became exclusive, at which point they should be secularized. (It would be up to the State to decide whether, for instance, it still wished to debar a Roman Catholic from wearing the Crown, or whether, with the right constitutional safeguards, a Roman Catholic heir could both succeed to the throne and practise his or her own religion as monarch.) It would also be possible (and desirable) to invite all religious groups in the country to pray for the monarch, and, without necessarily lapsing into a multi-faith syncretistic event, it would equally be possible to devise inaugural ceremonies, such as a Coronation, which both drew upon the loyalties of all the religious groups in the country and also allowed the monarch some special place for the public engagement of the rites of his or her own faith. It could well be in this context that there came the taking of vows to serve all the countries where the monarch of England is Head of State to the limit of his or her abilities.

Anglicans might well regret the outcome, for strong traditionalist and sentimental reasons. However, it is not only that the monarch *is* Head of State in various countries, none of which but England have a state-controlled Church (this is leaving the Scottish pattern of establishment aside); it is not only that we owe it to an incoming monarch to be allowed to express with integrity his or her own religious position; it is also that in England itself we have a plurality of Christian denominations *and* a plurality of faith communities, and in the freedom for the monarch all these, whether of the monarch's persuasion or not, should detect freedom also for themselves.

I find it possible to be not only an Anglican Christian, but an Anglican Christian with a strong sense both that the Christian Churches should be united and that we have genuine good news which we ought to want to offer to other religions, *and* to believe it right to sit on no apparent advantage that might come our way through the slightly forced adherence of the Crown to the Church of England, and through the resultant Supreme Governorship, which actually binds us to the government in power as much as to the monarch's own person.

8. Parish Concerns

There is a hatful of concerns which the present State control of the Church of England brings to the surface in the parishes of the land. In each case I try to describe the present situation and then indicate how the area concerned could operate or be developed in separation from the State.

Membership

Membership of the Christian Church universal is by baptism. There is nothing denominational about baptism, but it is baptism into Christ in the worldwide or catholic Church. In the early Church, whether apostolic or post-apostolic, to be baptized was to belong. And the injunctions of Paul in his Letters – as, e.g. in 1 Corinthians – are injunctions to a visible community (it would be difficult even to identify the leaders, so corporate is the address to them). In that kind of model of the local Christian community, to be baptized was to be participant in the decisions of the local church.

There was of course a condition. The condition was that the people continued as worshippers – indeed that they were participant in the Lord's Supper ('we who are many are one body, for we all share in common in the one bread' (1 Cor. 10:17)). It is clear in general that the New Testament churches had both a concept of disciplinary excommunication (1 Cor. 5:2), and also a concept of lapsing self-excommunication (as, e.g. in 1 John 2:19). Continuing in the fellowship was vital to being viewed as a 'member' of the body.

It is hard to relate this to an inherited Christendom. In England all were supposed to be baptized in infancy according to the Reformation formularies, the 1604 Canons, and the 1662 Book of Common Prayer. In the late seventeenth century they were inevitably 'C. of E.' unless they managed to persuade themselves, or a local vicar, or even a magistrate, that they were not. They were supposed under the rubrics of the BCP to receive communion three times a year.* And thus, simply as ordinary parishioners, they were members of the Church, almost without trying. As there were no other representative tasks for lay people to fulfil, save the office of churchwarden, most parishioners would in, say, the eighteenth century have viewed themselves as 'belonging' to the C. of E., in much the same way that they viewed themselves as belonging to their village. But equally, within the eighteenth century, there was a decline in faith, a decline in church attendance, and some real signs of alienation from the institution. Thus baptism and worshipping membership were slowly diverging from each other. And yet in this situation infant baptism continued, with the clergy actively seeking out infants for baptism, as the Canons and rubrics required of them.

The situation was further complicated by the sharp rise in nonconformity in the second half of the eighteenth century, and its full flowering in the nineteenth. Now other Churches had to define denominational membership as well as membership of the Church catholic or worldwide. On the whole bap-

---

*A strict rubricist would no doubt say they could not receive communion without being confirmed (see the 'confirmation rubric' in the BCP). But the evidence is that from 1662 till around the 1860s large numbers did *not* get confirmed, simply because bishops did not get round their large dioceses in days when travelling was often difficult. See the S. L. Ollard essay 'Confirmation in the post-Reformation Church of England' in the SPCK symposium, *Confirmation: Historical and Doctrinal* (1924). A tacit witness to this lies also in the Occasional Conformity Act of 1711, for this accepted that dissenters (who would certainly not be confirmed) might receive communion in the Church of England on an 'occasional' basis, but provided that, if they wished to retain public office (for which 'conforming' was the legal qualification) then they must not return to their dissenting house. If it had been possible to insist on the 'confirmation rubric' that would probably have ruled them out nicely, which was the probable intention of the law, but it would also have ruled out a high percentage of ordinary conforming Anglicans. The confirmation rubric provided an ideal of catechizing before admission to communion, but never acquired a legalist force until bishops started getting round their dioceses more regularly from the middle of the nineteenth century onwards – and soon afterwards an Anglican exclusiveness was built round episcopal confirmation by the new sacramentalist school of thought, and strict rubricism in relation to it came into fashion (see my *Anglican Confirmation* (Grove Liturgical Study no. 48, Grove Books, Bramcote, 1986), p. 31, and my essay 'Confirmation' in David Holeton (ed.) *Grow In Newness of Life* (Anglican Book Centre, Toronto, 1993), p. 106 ff.).

tism – even infant baptism – was accepted, but some affiliation
to the denomination, whether at age twelve or twenty-two,
became necessary. So rites such as 'being received into membership', 'receiving the right hand of fellowship' or even (rarely
in the nineteenth century) 'being confirmed' were developed in
the Free Church denominations. But the Church of England
had nothing comparable. From the 1860s onwards there may
have been clergy, and perhaps even bishops, who began to
explain confirmation as conferring 'membership' or 'full membership' of the Church of England upon recipients; but this
was self-evidently impossible, not only because all knew deep
down that baptism was the sacrament of membership, but also
because no actual duties or rights – such as Free Churchmen
obtained when they took out membership – were conferred in
confirmation. The pressure downwards upon the age of confirmation has also made the kind of membership the Free
Churches practise an impossible implication of the rite – in
the twentieth century the desire to get choirboys, servers, and
children at the top of primary schools through confirmation
has often meant it is administered to ten-year-olds.

The point at which the Church of England had to start
clarifying its mind was with the creation of the electoral rolls
to provide a local church electoral base for choosing Parochial
Church Councillors in 1920. After some debate, the electoral
rolls were based upon a baptismal franchise, as well as residence in the parish. However, entering the electoral roll of a
parish did not *make* people members of the Church of England.
The application form began by the applicant stating 'I am
baptized' and 'I am a member of the Church of England'. Nor
was being confirmed, being communicant, or even attending
worship, needed. In days when all or nearly all infants born
in this country received baptism, as was the case between the
Wars, almost all parishioners would qualify for 'membership
of the Church of England'. Only those who would have claimed
membership of another Christian denomination (and any
unbaptized) would have been unable to join the roll. (The
declaration that one was not a member of a Church 'not in
communion with the Church of England' ran for the first fifty
years; but it was removed in 1973, and some rewriting of the
application form to give clearer scope for applicants from other

denominations to declare themselves also members of the
Church of England is under way as I write.)

The Church of England went on claiming all 'unattributable
baptized' persons as 'members', whether they were on electoral
rolls or not till 1979 (when the figure concerned was around
thirty million!). Realism about the kind of 'membership'
involved, along with the virtual impossibility of providing an
accurate count, has led to that figure being dropped. On the
other hand, there is no other way in which 'membership' can
be registered, and so dropping the figure has led to a declining
to refer to 'membership'. We nowadays in each parish may
need to record the numbers of parishioners, the numbers of
the electoral roll, the numbers of 'usual Sunday attendance',
and a variety of other figures. But we are not keeping a record
of members! That figure is not even attempted – for all that
popular parlance still says 'I am a member of the Church of
England' or 'I am a member of St Peter's'. One of the difficulties
is that those forms of words spring equally naturally to the
lips of attenders and of non-attenders.

If we separate from the State, what options are open to us?
I set out a scale of possibilities.

1. We could continue as we are, claiming to be the historic
national Church of the land, and on those grounds treating
baptized parishioners as members.

2. We could refine the matter a little, and treat entry on the
electoral roll as 'registering' membership. We would then
have a definable 'registered membership'. This would clarify
the situation without substantially changing it.

3. We could step up the requirements for entry on the roll
– as, e.g. requiring regular attendance at worship and/or
being a communicant. This would certainly tally with the
New Testament material from which I started – and baptismal membership could then be defined as 'lapsed' unless it
were 'registered' (or perhaps 'active').

4. If we are able to secure much-needed reforms on another
front, i.e. that of admission to communion, then we could
deliver the roll from looking largely bureaucratic and almost
an afterthought to church life; instead we could incorporate
it more fully into the worshipping life of the Church. The
fully developed pattern would look like this:

  (a) Infant baptism would be given to the children of active

members, and they would thereafter be communicant with their parents (or with one parent in many cases). They would be recorded as 'child-members' or some equivalent description.

(b) If they continued faithful and communicant, then, at an age for entry to the roll (currently sixteen), they would have a rite of 'confirmation', in which they both ratified publicly their baptismal faith and were registered and enfranchised as adult members of both that congregation and the Church of England nationwide (and the Anglican Communion worldwide). Their instruction and preparation would be orientated towards responsible adult membership – and the rite would quite properly be conducted by the bishop, and include the laying on of hands, prayer, and communion.[1]

(c) For those who lapsed (whether through parental decline in faith, say in their early childhood, or through personal giving up of Christian discipleship, perhaps during their early teens) then the rite would await their return to the faith, at any age of adulthood. It would not be unlike the confirmation of adults that now exists, save that its 'registered (active) membership' element would be explicit both in word in the rite and through our actually registering them on the roll at the same time.

(d) For the unbaptized who were converted to Christ, adult baptism would not need confirmation attached to it (though the present clumsy and theologically odd practice logically *could* continue and would not absolutely *have* to be reformed at the moment the above patterns were introduced).[2] In such cases, baptism itself would spell out and confer 'active membership', thus relating very closely to New Testament norms.

(e) At the moment the rolls are cleansed and re-created once every six years. Whilst this could be done by informal administrative action, as it is now, it could also be done by great eucharistic services of re-affirmation, re-commitment and re-enrolment once every six years. It would be appropriate to 'sustain' or 'continue' membership in such a liturgy, even whilst it was necessary to 're-register'.

The upshot of this developed pattern would be that, without any disturbing or improper hassling of the 'fringe', there would be a clear point of decision and distinction which would enable the Church to be the Church, membership to be membership, and baptismal commitment to Jesus Christ to be the characteristic feature of that Church. But, I say again, it is not an absolutely necessary concomitant of breaking with the State that we have to clarify our minds on membership. It is simply that the opportunity would arise at that point, and unless we still insist on theological woolliness as the distinguishing feature of Anglicanism, we would be wise to go for biblical clarity.

The parish
The Church of England is accustomed to thinking in terms of geographical parishes, and of global numbers of parishioners. At Institutions the new incumbent receives from the bishop 'the cure of souls, which is both mine and yours'. There is no doubt that this 'cure' (or, in contemporary English, 'care') implies all the parishioners.

The revised Communications Unit publication, *The Church of England A-Z: A Glossary of Terms* (CHP 1994), which is a simple guide for the sake of journalists and press officers (often of secular institutions), includes under its entry 'Established Church' the following:

Incumbents have a pastoral responsibility towards all residents in their parishes and not just to church members.

If we leave aside the question-begging reference to members, we are again faced with the issue of the exact relationship to 'parishioners'. Clearly, they are not being viewed as all being 'C. of E.' (though perhaps in an established Church they should be!). The issue is therefore what kind of *distinctive* responsibility in relation to, say, 8,500 parishioners (including 500 Muslims, and 150 Sikhs, and not a few Satanists and Astrologers) the incumbent has. What are his 'pastoral responsibilities' which are *not* those of an incumbent in the Church in Wales, or of the Methodist minister in his parish?

Clearly parish boundaries, however absurdly drawn in history, have certain positive values. I know, in a way that my local Methodist minister or a local 'House church' pastor does not know, *where*, geographically speaking, my evangelistic responsibilities lie. A parish system does that. I would want a disestablished Church to keep that concept. The whole Church of England does conceive itself as having a mission to every man and woman in the land, but that is a function of our national spread on the one hand, and is neither an inbuilt feature of establishment, nor imperilled by disestablishment, on the other.

So does 'pastoral responsibility towards all residents' mean that I am concerned for their social welfare? Yes, I am. But that arises from my 'earthed' gospel, in which salvation must touch people's lives as lived in society. My Methodist neighbour shares the same concern – the only difference again being that I have a defined area and he has not.

Or does 'pastoral responsibility' mean that my doors are open to parishioners who come to ask for occasional ministrations? They are open, and I am glad to have enquiries, some of them from superstition, some from true Christianity. I may get more such than my Methodist neighbour, but his door is equally open, and the only difference is the way that folklore (not the statute law) influences people's thinking. But in any case, to be available to all who come is nothing like exercising 'pastoral responsibility' for all 8,500.

Or does someone somewhere still think that, if an incumbent of the 'established Church' knocks on the door of any old parishioner in any urban parish, that incumbent will somehow *both* have more right of entry, or right to a hearing, than the Methodist minister will have – *and* will have it on the grounds that the C. of E. is 'by law established'? There *may* be a differentiated run-on of goodwill towards one Church rather than another, and that is likely to be more widespread towards a larger or better known Church than towards a smaller one; but it is hardly attributable to the present position in law of the Church of England. Furthermore, when a door is being closed against a caller, the representative of the established Church has no more clout with which to resist it than has a Free Church or Roman Catholic caller.

Or does the 'cure' of souls, and the 'pastoral responsibility towards all residents' actually mean that we are *super-established*, i.e. that all parishioners, without distinction of faith-community, baptism, or belief, are actually 'ours', part of 'our' flock? To claim this would be not only to go further in make-believe than even most establishmentarians – it would also be a complete abandonment of mission, a rejection of the Scriptures, and an assertion of sixteenth-century Christendom. No doubt again, it has its romantic appeal. But it will not withstand the cold light of reality.

So, I repeat, is there *anything* which gives me or the parish of which I am incumbent by law, by the very fact of my incumbency, a special or distinctive *actual* relationship with the parishioners? Potentials are all very well – but any Church, any religion, may have those – and changing our position in law will not affect them.

Churchwardens

The two churchwardens are the ancient lay office-holders within the parish, and in most cases were the *only* lay officers until the formation of a Parochial Church Council, elected from the electoral roll, in 1920 or 1921. Because the parish from which they were traditionally selected was constituted of all the parishioners, the vestry meeting, which was the traditional annual meeting of all the parishioners, continued alongside the creation of the electoral rolls and the inauguration of the Annual Church Meeting at which the members of the electoral roll elected the PCC. Usually the 'vestry' meeting (its name is changed nowadays) has been held first, and the two churchwardens have been chosen by agreement between parishioners and incumbent. They have then become *ex officio* members of the PCC, already in office when the Annual Church Meeting has been convened.

The qualifications to hold office as churchwarden were, anciently, simply to be twenty-one (i.e. to have reached one's majority), lay and male, though in fact all parishioners, with remarkably few exceptions, would also have been baptized as a matter of course until the time of the Civil War and the Commonwealth. There was then a growth of Baptists, Independents and Quakers, and universal infant baptism could not be taken for granted.* But it is likely that most persons who were nominated to be churchwardens would have been duly baptized. Beyond that there were no requirements. The Prayer

---

*'We include an office for the baptism of those of riper years, which, although not so necessary in the time of the former book, hath now, through the wicked growth of anabaptism in these late licentious times, become the more necessary . . .' (Preface to 1662 Prayer Book).

Book required parishioners to receive communion three times a year, but there is plenty of evidence that churchwardens were appointed who never attended church, got confirmed, or received communion. There were even suggestions at times (as with Hook when he was at Leeds parish church) that churchwardens might be appointed as a kind of official opposition to the incumbent. They were *parish* officers (for all their churchly duties) rather than church ones – it simply was that caring for the church finance, fabric and charities was part of the task of conscientious parish wardens. In later days the churchly duties have become the only ones remaining.

When the Churchwardens (Appointment and Resignation) Measure received the Royal Assent in 1964, qualifications for the office were established. In new parishes for some time previously, churchwardens had had to be confirmed and actually communicant; now the same qualification was established for all parishes, unless the bishop gave permission otherwise. This was a cautious recognition that the office is an ecclesiastical one, and that the senior lay members of the Parochial Church Council should be at least as visibly qualified to hold office in the Church as the other PCC members.[3] On the other hand, no substantial change was made in the choosing by the 'vestry' meeting, rather than by a church meeting. The only difference is that those who are parishioners of one parish, but on the electoral roll of another, may join the resident parishioners of the latter parish to constitute with them what the Measure calls 'a meeting of the parishioners', with the task and powers of choosing the churchwardens. And it has to be recognized that 'parishioners' nowadays means a confused jumble of all religions and none, of baptized and unbaptized, of the superstitious, the feeble-minded, the advanced secularist, and the positively evil. This is the sweeping enfranchisement which the successor to the ancient 'vestry' meeting gives for the 'parishioners' to choose the churchwardens. It is, admittedly, the case that they are supposed to do it jointly with the incumbent; yet the fall-back proviso still exists that, if people and incumbent cannot agree, then the people choose one and the incumbent chooses the other. Thus the enfranchisement is still very real.

This amazing anachronism has not been without challenge. In November 1992, David Hammond, a lay representative of

Birmingham diocese, brought to General Synod on behalf of his
Diocesan Synod the motion that:

> This Synod instruct the Standing Committee to introduce
> legislation to amend the Churchwardens (Appointment and
> Resignation) Measure 1964 so that Section 3(1) read, 'A
> meeting of the persons whose names are entered on the
> church electoral roll of the parish shall be deemed to be a
> meeting of the parishioners for the purposes of this
> Measure', thereby repealing Section 3(1)(b) which gives the
> franchise to other residents of the parish.

One would have thought that in 1992 this would have gone
through on the nod – but far from it. The mover raised one or
two spectres – he hoped we would not think that this tidying-
up was a retreat from our mission to the world; and he also
challenged those who were in favour of the existing 'meeting
of the parishioners' as to whether in fact they were prepared
to go out and urge the neighbourhood to come to the meeting.
But after he had spoken, then we got into the truly bizarre.

Two main speakers urged the rural situation upon us.
Although the village communities do not turn out in force to
choose churchwardens, somehow it is important to our mission
that they can. One otherwise highly responsible synodsman
said: 'Having a wider electorate means that churchwardens do
have to take into account the views of those who may not
actually have voted for them but who nevertheless had the
right to vote for them.' But this sort of sentiment, if it has *any*
force at all, which I greatly doubt, would also imply that the
PCC should be elected on the same basis. And the various
speakers against the motion, including two bishops and an
archdeacon, said simultaneously that the world outside the
Church was not going to invade the meetings of the parishioners and run in unworthy specimens (and therefore we
could relax about the present inclusive franchise), but on the
other hand that it was vitally important that the world *could*
do so, as that is how the world outside knows that we are open
and accessible for all. Gordon Bates, the Bishop of Whitby,
even said: 'If we want access to the community and if we want
access to its structures, then the community must have free
access to us and to our structures.' Of course, he and others
were simultaneously assuring us it would not happen, and so

we should not fear it. A personal response would be to say: (a) I do not wish to *elect officers* in institutions of which I am not a member, and I do not conceive of the Church's 'access to the community' that way; (b) the community around is wholly unaware of this trade-off which we are so generously offering them in order to get 'access' to them; and (c) to insist that powers remain in a certain form, on the grounds that virtually no one will ever exercise them, gives dreadful hostages to fortune.* In other words, the potential for desperate disruption is actually there – an unpopular vicar, for instance, confronted by a local community angry over some action he had taken (or was alleged to have taken) could in extreme cases find himself facing a 'meeting of the parishioners' packed with opponents who would have the power to force in at least one hostile churchwarden. A rare event? Well, maybe – but actually more likely to happen than that the world will ever turn up in force to back the regime! And if the options are that 99.8 per cent of the time the world will not be there, and the other 0.2 per cent of the time a hostile world will be there, it is difficult to see what benefit the inclusive basis of the electorate can be.

Well, the General Synod, in this passion for keeping wholly unreal doors open to a wholly unaware world, swept away the Birmingham motion. It remains on record as an example of the bizarre persuasion that our structures, simply as structures, have to mesh with society around us for us to be truly missionary. It is not only wild self-deceit; it is not only unique in the world as a rationale for the Church's formal captivity to the State; it is almost certainly also an evasion of the true witness to the gospel that we should make – for, if it says anything to the world (which one must realistically doubt), then it tells unbelievers, unbaptized and members of other faiths that they are at least honorary members of the Christian

---

*If I may illustrate this from recent experience, I found a lay synodsman in my own diocese in 1993 complaining furiously that opponents of women's ordination *were trying to get MPs to vote against the Measure*. He had somehow assumed that the location of powers of veto with Parliament had to be matched by a tacit understanding that they would not be used. Powers in the wrong place that are never going to be used can well be dispensed with – and powers in the wrong place that *are* even occasionally going to be used need to be removed quickly.

Church, without repentance, faith, baptism or commitment.
Could a more ambiguous message be given?

The Parochial Church Council

There would be little change in this if the legal position of the
Church of England in the land changed. However, if we want
the Church to be the Church, then it is obvious that not only
the members of the PCC should be communicant Christians,
but that the electorate also should be. My proposed reform of
the listing of names on the electoral roll is set out above under
'membership'. It is obvious sense that it is 'the members' who
should elect the PCC, just as it is 'the members' who should,
jointly with the incumbent, appoint the churchwardens.

It is not too far beyond the brief of this book to recommend
that Annual Church Meetings adopt the Single Transferable
Vote for elections to the PCC, thus giving the fairest possible
microcosm on the Church Council of the range of interests,
ages and emphases to be found amongst the membership.*
Powers for such a use of justice in representation already exist.

Baptism

One of the supposed ancient rights of parishioners, one
reinforced by generations of folklore (and bad practice by the
parish churches), is that parents can bring babies for baptism
'on demand'. In the wake of the Industrial Revolution the habit
grew in town parishes of giving baptism at 4 p.m. on a Sunday
afternoon, accepting all babies brought, and often receiving
them therefore from other parishes. This was contrary to the
rubrics of the 1662 Book of Common Prayer, insofar as they
required baptism to be administered after the second lesson
at Morning or Evening Prayer. On the other hand, it was, in
its inclusiveness, in line with both the BCP rubrics and the
1604 Canons, both of which require the clergy to warn and
admonish all their parishioners to bring their newborn infants
quickly to baptism. The provisions for emergency baptism
(with a folklore memory from Augustine of Hippo that if a

---

*I am of course aware that in many places there is little or no competition
for election to the PCC – and incumbents are likely then to treat a change
of system of election as irrelevant and complicating. To this we have to
reply that, if no election is needed, then it makes no difference which
system it is which is not used.

child died it absolutely *had* to have been baptized) reinforced
this further – and the rise of the anglo-catholic movement in
step with the urbanization of England meant that positive
teaching about a dollop of grace automatically being given in
baptism was being injected into the folklore.

I have traced in an earlier book how all this institutionalized
'indiscriminate baptism' was step-by-step phased out in the
revision of our formularies in the last half-century.[4] At the
heart of the changes lies the simple fact that there is *no right
in statute law* for parents to have baptism for their infants on
demand. There is careful provision in the Canons that parents
who ask for baptism should have 'preparation' in advance, and
there is even a possibility that this should 'delay' the baptism
– with further provision that parents who think themselves
unduly 'delayed' should have recourse to the bishop of the
diocese. But it is clear that his ruling is final, and there is no
appeal in statute law. There is a deep, silent, but often painful,
struggle going on in the Church of England as to how we
should be most faithful to the gospel of Jesus Christ: is it by
giving an unquestioning welcome to all who ask for baptism,
or is it by asking questions in turn to see if there is any (or
perhaps enough) commitment to the faith of Jesus Christ in
the parents or parent for infant baptism in such a case to be
credible? I do not stay here on how to resolve such issues, but
refer readers to my book, mentioned in footnote 4 above, and
to the Movement for the Reform of Infant Baptism which
exists to press us into a missionary future.

The latest statistics at the time of writing (those of 1991)
indicate that 27.5 per cent of live births in England lead to
infant baptism in the Church of England. (Another 5.5 per
cent are baptized at an age over one year and under twelve.)
The drop of around 1 per cent year by year is steady and
apparently relentless. Thus it is less and less true to view the
country as largely baptized (though it may be true of those
born in England prior to 1950, which is when the figure began
to fall). There are of course other faith communities affecting
the statistics. There may be a few who ask for baptism but do
not proceed to it. But clearly there are also very large numbers
of secularized persons who have children without any awareness of Christian rites, any connection with the Christian
Church, or any looking beyond themselves and their own

parenting for the future of their children. This is particularly an urban phenomenon.

The implication is that, once we have grasped that English infants do not have automatic rights to baptism simply through being born in England, infant baptism is to be administered in conformity with the gospel, and the gospel as it affects the parents. Baptism is not 'a dollop of grace' to be given like immunization to newborn babies for their later good – the evidence from results (which is not formally the way to argue) is that the merely baptized do not appear to be immunized from anything very much in later years. Unless they are going to grow in grace within the worshipping life of the Church through the parental model of discipleship and patterns of life, then it would be more honest, and therefore more desirable, if they were not baptized in infancy.

This is a field in which the Church of England has already gone some way in separation from the civil community, and clearly no longer identifies that civil community as being Christ's Church without remainder. No change in law is necessary for separation of Church and State, and the issue has to be handled on theological (including both sacramental and missionary) grounds.

Marriage

Marriage is in a very different category from baptism. It is not only that the essence of the rite is a couple taking each other in matrimony (to which the cleric is a responsible witness), rather than the Church itself administering a sacrament on gospel terms. It is also, through historic forces, that every parishioner has in principle the *right* in law to get married in his or her parish church (and in any parish where he or she is on the electoral roll). This even applies, as I understand the law, to those previously divorced; they still have a right in law to get married in their parish churches, and the difference is that no cleric has a duty in law to officiate at that solemnization. But a couple, of whom one was divorced (and the previous partner was still living), could, if they could find a cleric to officiate, approach the incumbent of their parish church and insist on both their banns being read and the building being available for the service and the books being provided for the marriage's registration. I do not know whether or not this ever

happens, but I believe it to be the law.* There is a total right
of those who have not been married before to be married in
their parish church, *and* to have the incumbent (or other minister in charge) to officiate; and a diminished right of couples
where one has been married and divorced before to get married
in the building, but not to require any particular minister to
officiate.

Some doubt has arisen in recent years about the marriage
of the unbaptized; but as, historically, baptism was taken for
granted, the requirement of it is not written into the law –
and the doubts have been theologically driven, on the grounds
that parties to marriage should not (and perhaps cannot) be
required to take vows in the presence of God, and actually to
name the Trinity themselves, if they are, as unbaptized, in
formal terms unbelievers. However, this does not appear to
have any legal force, and if the alternative is a wholly nominal
and even farcical adult baptism, the general view has been
that the unbaptized should be allowed to be married in church,
and it is probably as well that it has not been tried in the
courts!

From a theological standpoint, whilst it is important for
many reasons that the Church should know in each society
what constitutes a monogamous marriage covenant in that
society, it is not crucial to that definition that a Christian
liturgy accomplished or surrounded the covenant. In England,
because civil ceremonies in Register Offices are relatively new,
and are an alternative to church weddings, there is still a
strong instinct towards church weddings even amongst overt

---

*I have combed Timothy Briden and Brian Hanson *Moore's Introduction
to English Canon Law (Third Edition)* (Mowbray 1992), without getting
the point wholly clear. The authors are in a realm where Canon Law does
not exist. They are sure that the Church of England holds something like
a Roman Catholic view of the *vinculum* which binds husband and wife
together for life, and therefore (so it seems) they are quite silent about
any role for the Church of England or its clergy in the solemnization of
such marriages – it is simply assumed that these are 'civil' marriages,
though the Church has to recognize them *de facto*. Once civil marriages
and civil divorce came into being in the last century there was bound to
be a tension – and this tension has prevented a Church *which is bound
in the first instance by statute law* from making Canons on the subject,
as any rules more restrictive than statute law would be deemed 'inexpedi-
ent' by the Ecclesiastical Committee of Parliament, and could not therefore in our Erastian situation be formed into Canons.

unbelievers. There is a complicating problem at the moment, in that Register Office weddings are so unceremonious, so without glamour, colour, sparkle or ornamentation, that a simple desire for a wedding 'with all the trimmings' will inevitably predispose a couple (or their families) towards a church wedding. There is some hope that legal alternatives will allow for greater enrichment (including choice of premises) in the future.

The issue for the future of a Church of England separated from the State is where the 'rights' should lie. It is in formal terms absurd that unbelievers should have 'rights' over the clergy or the parish churches. There may even be occasions where a minister may wish not to officiate, either because the couple appear to be under outside pressure or to be totally and visibly incompatible (ministers must be very cautious about taking a stance on these issues), or because the existing lifestyle (as, e.g., in a partner-swapping group arrangement or in prostitution) makes it more than doubtful whether monogamy or the fidelity basic to it has registered with either or both of the applicants.

On the other hand, the State will not lightly grant rights to officiate, if it is thought the institution will be selective or discriminatory in its exercise of those rights. It would seem that, the moment the Church of England is free to pass its own Canon Laws about candidates for matrimony as solemnized in church, then it would have to be in consultation with the Crown lawyers that its provisions were made. This is comparable to the steps, in which I was myself involved, in which the Liturgical Commission created and the General Synod amended and approved an 'alternative service' for marriage; in this, the Synod could in theory have approved any form it liked, but in fact we were closely advised by the State as to the limits of variation possible in the vows, in which the 'taking' of each other in marriage is encapsulated. In fact, the text had to have State approval, as correctly enshrining the State's understanding of marriage, and no doubt a Canon Law on the situations in which Church of England clergy should or should not officiate at marriages would be similarly vetted. That does not mean for a moment that any Canons should be unduly restrictive, or that the parish church should not be open to outsiders; but it is a simple plea that we should be free to create our own rules, and enshrine them in our Canons, and take our own decisions in the light of theological truth, our concept of a mission to the nation, and the pastoral position arising from requests for marriage.

There could be situations beyond this. If we reach the point of licensed 'marriage celebrants', then it is likely that the present provisions would be overtaken by that innovation. Then the clergy could apply to be such 'celebrants' and could, if the law so provided, then officiate in church – as also anywhere else – but would not be *bound* to accept all who applied to them. That would certainly enable the Church of England to make its own rules, simply to regulate and guide its own clergy – though it might also find its readers and even pastoral assistants and others were getting licensed . . .

Another alternative would be where all marriages were civil, and were done by a simple registration ceremony at the Register Office. A church service could then follow almost according to taste, technically of the form of 'prayers after a civil marriage', though as like as not incorporating almost all of what is currently in a liturgy for solemnization. In such a case, all Churches would be free to determine the terms on which they would offer the liturgical service.

Funerals

It appears that the next of kin of dead parishioners have the right in law to have the coffin containing the corpse buried in the churchyard of the deceased's parish church, and in such a case (with small exceptions) to have the burial service used. There is no need for a parishioner to be in any visible or known sense an 'Anglican' for this right in statute law to apply to him or her. One of the exceptions is where the person has died unbaptized, and that is likely to be a larger and larger category in the future – though the question about baptism is rarely asked, and the Church of England gave (church-based, rather than statute-based) guidance in the ASB that parents of infants who are dying 'should be assured that questions of ultimate salvation or of the provision of a Christian funeral for an infant who dies do not depend upon whether or not *he* had been baptized'.[5]

If the above are the limit of parishioners' rights in law, then all other existing funeral customs would seem not to be granted of right, but to be purchased! There are on sale a plot in a corporation or other cemetery, or a place in a crematorium oven. There may be requested – and purchased or granted free – the services of a minister, but Canon B38(4a) makes it fairly clear that there is no obligation in law for any specific minister to accede to any particular request, and the response of the Church of England's minister in these cases derives from pastoral concern, not from statutory duties.

As with marriage, the Church of England will have to be obedient to the general law (i.e. in this case in relation to the disposal of dead bodies), even if it is freed from direct State control in other respects. Thus the rights of parishioners, not in respect of church services, but in respect of having their bodies, on decease, interred in a church graveyard still in use, would seem an appropriate continuance of a right that is related to local community life, and to the reverent remembrance of the dead and the record of where at the heart of a village or small town (which are the usual cases) particular persons' bodies were buried. The Church of England ought to have no problem about that right, though, if church graveyards remain otherwise under church control, then some control about the services held (or deliberately not held) for different categories of persons and about the monuments and inscriptions raised, must remain with the Church, and would be part of the powers devolved by Parliament. One assumes that burial in church graveyards is an ever-decreasing activity, not only because cremation seems ever more popular, but also because, as church graveyards fill up, there are not necessarily new church lands to hand into which to extend the graveyard.

The continuance of Christian ministries in conjunction with the disposal of remains runs on in a secularized nation through two persistent factors. The first is obvious – it is that funerals come at death, and deaths come at the end of lives, and lives come to an end most frequently in old age, and the elderly may well have had more Christian involvement than their middle-aged children, young adult grandchildren, or toddler great-grand-children betray. Where this Christian involvement, often long in the past, is known to the next of kin, then a Christian service seems appropriate. The second factor is the sheer readiness of undertakers to offer to the bereaved the services of a Christian minister, and then to negotiate those services when the offer has been accepted. Often, one suspects, not only the shock of bereavement but also the lack of any alternative idea, means that the next of kin settle quickly for a Christian minister and Christian service. In these circumstances, unless some other denominational allegiance is known, then on present patterns it will almost certainly be an Anglican minister (and in most places, on the evidence to hand, the clergy of the parish within which the deceased had been a parishioner) who officiate. Dioceses have become very dependent upon funeral fees, and this in turn means that ministers are unlikely to be grudging about accepting funerals.

Of course, in the process, a shrieking anomaly is exposed. Whilst the elderly may have more overt Christian practice in their background than the young usually have, and even sometimes have had some understanding of the biblical faith in their lives, yet there are many for whom this has not been the case – and there is always too a proportion of funerals of the young and middle-aged. In urban crematoria thousands of corpses go to the flames each year, with Christian words spoken by ministers who had never met the deceased during their lives and quite possibly had met none of the living either until the death was notified. There is often no evidence at all that either the deceased or the mourners entertain a 'sure and certain hope of the resurrection to eternal life through our Lord Jesus Christ'. Sometimes hymns are chosen at the gentle instigation of the undertakers, but, quite apart from the inhibiting effect of tears and grief, it proves that no one present has sung anything in a Christian service for many years, or at all, and the hymn that is announced is sung by the minister alone. What the Church of England does not see, of course, is the slow deliberate rise of wholly secular funerals – as Christian folklore gradually departs from people's conscious and subconscious ways of thought and behaviour, so a small, but growing, proportion of the bereaved ask for a wholly secular terminal rite. In any urban context, this can be verified by simple enquiry of an undertaker.

Already ministers tend to speak of 'fully Christian funerals' (the sort that often have a genuine church service) and 'a service at the crem.'. It may well be that, if in years ahead we get a more defined concept of active membership, we may officially offer a two-tier provision. That is in no sense to urge that we should turn our backs on 'services at the crem.', but a recognition that liturgically and pastorally there may be profound differences between funerals for believers, and funerals for those in apparent unbelief. Whilst the most persistent run-on of the 'occasional offices' is, for reasons shown, in the category of funerals, yet it is also here that some of the greatest contrasts between the words of the rite and the visible facts of the persons present (and departed) stand out.

Patronage

A very simple wisdom is appropriate. It is this: that the existing system only survives because there has been no agreement on how to override it. Abolition of it did get to within a whisker of being accepted in the debate on patronage in the early 1980s, and its days are doomed. It is unthinkable in a genuinely disestablished Church that patronage of the parish churches should continue, with power exercised by a remote third party.

Summary

If we return to the model of the apostolic Church, set as a slightly alien institution in both the Roman Empire and, at times, the Jewish Quarter in the Roman cities, it is clear that our context locally is quite unlike that of the first generation Christians. The post-Christendom conditions do not replicate the pre-Constantinian ones. Yet, if we want a model, this Church in an alien context provides us with a more plausible model than any of the last five centuries in our own civilization. We need a credible way of ceasing to pretend that the state is Christian, and with that a realistic way of recognizing that society around us is not Christian. Once that is clear, then a committed basis for membership and a willingness to call unbelief unbelief give the right springboard for mission. How to pursue *that* is not the theme of this book, but getting the local springboard right will greatly assist.

9. Other National Considerations

Finance

The finances of the Church of England are held in 12,000 or so parishes, forty-four dioceses, one Central Board of Finance, a myriad of trusts, societies, and charitable funds – and the Church Commissioners. Of these, it is the position of the Commissioners which is of special concern in any change of relationship between the Church of England and the State. It is the major point at which the Church of England does not really control its own finances. The Commissioners were created by The Church Commissioners Measure 1947, and came into being on 1 April 1948, thus uniting the old Ecclesiastical Commissioners and Queen Anne's Bounty. They are in effect a Parliamentary Trust. They hold a large part of the 'historic resources' of the Church of England and, with a disposable income of around £140 million per annum, are probably functioning *on a scale twenty times as large* as the next largest unit of finance in, or connected with, the Church of England. In the last analysis, they are not a Church board of finance, they are a Parliamentary trust.

They are currently suffering from a great loss of confidence in them throughout the dioceses and parishes of the Church of England, because of both their reported loss of £800 million worth of assets in the last five or six years and their perceived unaccountability and even complacency in the face of such losses. When I first drafted this chapter in January 1994, I had just come from a House of Bishops meeting at which the bishops had had to absorb the forecast that the existing cut of £5.5 million per annum from the grants to dioceses for augmentation of stipends would in 1995 have to be much more than doubled, and in the event in February it has turned out, instead of £5.5 million, to be £12 million. In 1996 it is scheduled to be a further £16 million. That is the stipends of around eight hundred clergy in 1995, and of over a thousand more in 1996! Furthermore, because of previous principles of grant-making, cuts from the Commissioners are now likely to fall

most heavily where the heaviest subventions have been hitherto paid. This in turn is a very serious threat to the urban
dioceses. However, I write it not to address policy about clergy
stipends but to illustrate the sinking heart with which the
bishops contemplate the Commissioners' future grant-making.

I am making no attempt here to give a full account of the
Commissioners. I simply note that the various stages of slow
disestablishing of the last forty years have never touched upon
the Commissioners. The Chadwick Commission coolly, and
with a minimum of discussion, recommended no change in
1970:

> The government element in this constitution does not pres-
> ent any special problem for us. No one suggests that the
> Church Commissioners are influenced in the performance of
> their functions by anything other than the interests of the
> Church.[1]

Valerie Pitt, in her 'Memorandum of Dissent' (with which Peter
Cornwell and Denis Coe concurred), wrote on the tenth page
of that Memorandum:

> Even if we made no progress at all with any of our other
> proposals, it would be right that the Church should give
> some attention to its financial institutions and responsi-
> bilities, and I therefore propose:
>
> *That the Church should ask the Government to join it in
> a review of the present structure and responsibilities of
> the Church Commissioners for England, and that such
> an enquiry should consider among other things ways and
> means of making the corporation more clearly and directly
> answerable to the General Synod of the Church of England.*
>
> For the powers which have accrued to the Commissioners
> in the development of their original mandate give them an
> influence in society which must make their near-autonomy
> a matter of concern both to the Church and to the State.[2]

I do not think this proposal was ever even debated in General
Synod (in which Valerie Pitt never came to sit), but it has a
highly contemporary ring to it.

In all the slow disestablishing steps since 1948, there has
been a deft and determined skirting round doing anything

about the finances. Indeed it is likely that the step-by-step
process (which at its present pace bids fair to bring complete
freedom to the Church of England about a century from now),
has been deliberately pursued in a way that will avoid confronting the financial factors. We can look in one decade at
freeing elections to Convocation from being forced upon us
whenever there is a Parliamentary election; then we can look
in the next decade at making provision for alternative services;
then in the decade after that we can revise the Pastoral
Measure; and so on. Of course the process has contained
slightly more items each decade than my cartoon sketch indicates, but it has never touched upon the place of accountability
of the Church Commissioners. One suspects that many of our
leaders have hoped that other issues would go forward without
Parliament ever noticing the financial question. And it is at
least possible that there was a strong folk-memory that the
Acts by which the Church of Ireland and the Church in Wales
were disestablished had disendowment as the major bone of
contention within them.

There is probably little jealousy among the other Churches
about the Church of England's assets today. But a hint of how
we have appeared to them in the past should at least prevent
our taking our inheritance for granted. Thus the 'orthodox
dissenter', Bernard Lord Manning, could write in the 1930s:

When in the sixteenth century Englishmen ceased to be of
one mind about religion, it was – we always said so and we
must go on saying so – a monstrous piece of impudence and
an injustice that kings, parliaments, courtiers, and politicians should decide which part of the flock of Christ in
these islands should enjoy what hitherto all had enjoyed. It
was perhaps defensible . . . [that Anglicans] should tempor-
arily receive some social, financial and architectural compen-
sation in the form of prestige, ancient endowments, and
buildings. But when the episcopalian sect rids itself of State
bonds and ceases to be a national institution the position
changes. They cannot have it both ways; and yet, so oddly
is the Anglican mind constructed, that they will not even
see that they are asking for it both ways unless someone
points it out to them.

As things now are, let me remind you, we all have a

status in parish churches and cathedrals, as citizens if not as churchmen. . . . But if any form of disestablishment were to take place, and what has been the property of the Anglican Body as a national institution were to become its property as a private, self-governing episcopal sect, with power to exclude whom it will, to pull down and alter at will, our position would be completely altered . . . [3]

Whilst it is unlikely to be Dissenters endeavouring to sequestrate our assets in the 1990s, this diatribe does remind us of the basis on which the Commissioners hold those assets, and does remind us that Parliament can wholly legitimately lay hands upon it. Much of the step-by-step approach seems to have been designed to keep the issue of finance from arising.

On the other hand, at this very moment of writing all is not well with the Commissioners. The glad rush of spending in the 1980s is over. The colossal loss of assets has taken our breath away. The malpractices pinpointed by 'the Lambeth Group', the body appointed in 1993 by the Archbishop of Canterbury to investigate the Church Commissioners' losses, rankle with the Church of England. And even the forthcoming swingeing cuts seem to be reported to us from an alien grant-making body which, far from being 'ours', tells us from a great distance what money will or will not be sent us in which year. The Commissioners are not answerable to General Synod, but in the last analysis to Parliament, and are being experienced by the Church of England, and even by the leaders of the Church of England, as a body aloof from the impact its own policies make upon the life of the Church. I hesitate to go further on this point – and that is not only because I have no inside knowledge of the Commissioners' structures, but also because I am aware that here of all points in this book we are in the most fast-moving situation, and what I have written in February 1994 may have moved on far by June, let alone by mid-1995. What is obvious to all is that such a powerful grant-making body is, by definition, an alternative seat of power. Its 'near-autonomy' (to quote Valerie Pitt) is a worldly distorting force playing upon the life of the Church of England. Where the money is, there the power is. We are ill-served by a structure which holds comparatively vast sums in trust for us, but is, in terms of power, almost inaccessible to us.

I believe the Church of England should, in seeking its freedom, look Parliament in the face, and ask boldly for the Commissioners' assets, and for direct control of the structures,
policy (including of course investment policy) and decision-
taking of the Commissioners – with the whole being answerable to the General Synod. If the Parliamentary reply were to
be that, by a historical fiction, some proportion of the assets
from Tudor times now belonged to the 'State' rather than
the 'Church' (a difficult distinction to make in post-Henrician
England), then Parliament certainly has the power to confis-
cate them. There might be some negotiation. Probably at the
end Parliament, noting that over 50 per cent of the outgoings
fund the pensions of the clergy, would cede the bulk or even
the total to the new Central Church Fund. But whether all
were ceded or part were confiscated, the deed should be done.

As this volume goes to press, there is an announcement
of a new 'Commission on the Organization of the Church of
England'. The press release on 16 February 1994 says:

> The review will include the relationship between the execu-
> tive functions of the General Synod, the Church Com-
> missioners, the Church of England's Pensions Board, and
> the staff of the Archbishops ... It will not, however, go into
> the detail of the internal organization of each constituent
> body.

When the chairman, Bishop Michael Turnbull, was asked at
the press conference whether those terms of reference included
issues touching on the establishment of the Church of England,
he apparently replied that, although establishment issues
were not explicit in his terms of reference, he could see that
they might well arise. Indeed, we may expect that any treatment of the relationship between the Commissioners and the
Church of England will reveal establishment issues very
clearly. So perhaps there may be a facing up to them yet.

Ecumenism
There is a simple tale to tell under this heading – the establishment of the Church of England is one of the biggest barriers
to healthy reunion of the Christian Churches in England. The
post-War story goes back to Fisher's famous Cambridge
Sermon on 3 November 1946. There, as he re-opened issues

about the quest for unity, he deliberately turned people's eyes away from 'constitutional schemes' – a pattern which had had an innings before the War, and was then only ten months from inauguration in South India. His train of thought went as follows:

> In this country I think there are three special reasons which make the constitutional method the most difficult of all ways to reunion.
>
> In the first place the Church of England is an established Church; it has a very complicated legal nexus with the State, which enters deeply into its machinery of government.
>
> The Free Churches would certainly not accept the establishment as it is. And while they might agree that a reunited Church could valuably retain some measure of State connection, the process of extricating the Church of England from what it was not desired to retain and of accomplishing its transference to a newly devised constitution would be a work of even greater magnitude and difficulty than the scheme of reunion itself.
>
> Secondly [we cannot sabotage the Anglican Communion by sinking Canterbury];
>
> Thirdly [internal tensions need resolving first].[4]

The predilection of Geoffrey Fisher for the existing establishment is well known, so that we may well surmise that the problem to him was not that the establishment might hinder reunion, but that a plan of union might sink the establishment. Certainly the other reasons he gave for not tackling reunion properly read like excuses. In the harsh light of reality they have to be confronted head on in reunion negotiations or they will postpone all attempts at reunion *sine die*.

The direction he set was faithfully followed. The step he was suggesting was that the Free Churches should try out episcopacy 'by taking it into their own system'. There was to be no scheme, no goal of organic union, but an assimilation of the Free Churches to the pattern of an episcopal Church modelled by the Church of England: 'My longing is, not yet that we should be *united* with other Churches in this country, but that we should grow to *full communion* with them.' The establishment issue was clearly determinative. It raises the question as to whether the New Testament would rank establishment above reunion.

This notion went around the Free Churches, was not welcomed by most of them, but finally was adopted by the Methodist Conference of 1953. After asking some questions, the Conference appointed a team to begin 'Conversations' with the Church of England. The Church of England in turn appointed their team, and the 'Conversations' proceeded. The 'parallel episcopates' which were built into Fisher's suggestion caused problems, and by the time the final report was produced in February 1963 the majority of the participants accepted that the two Churches would have to move on at some point from being two Churches to being one. This was duly labelled 'Stage 2'. About it the 'Conversationalists' wrote:

> At ... [Stage 2] ... there will be very extensive legal and constitutional changes for the Church of England, which are likely to be the equivalent of the granting of complete self-government. It is to be assumed that the united Church will be free to settle its own forms of doctrine, worship and discipline, to appoint its own officers, and to settle disputes in its own courts with the same degree of freedom from State control as is now possessed by the Church of Scotland. This will involve a radical revision and repeal of the Acts of Parliament by which the Church of England is now governed ...[5]

Geoffrey Fisher had tried to avoid raising the disestablishment issue, and he went into opposition in his retirement and tried to hold the undertakings down to a Stage 1 of adjusted relationships only.

In one sense the idea of Stage 2 was a proper conclusion of the unsatisfactory Stage 1 of parallel episcopates. The setting out of its requirements also enabled an outlining of what virtual disestablishment would entail. These in turn were bravely stated in the extract above. But it has to be confessed that for practical purposes Stage 1 was the only change in sight, that this involved far more cost for Methodism than for the Church of England, and that the Church of England 'Conversationalists' could cheerfully describe what a theoretical Stage 2 would be like, even whilst privately reckoning that it was a long time off. Even a mutual pledge to proceed to Stage 2 had little content to it, for two disagreed bodies can only undertake to *try* to unite – they cannot 'agree to agree' when the terms of agreement are still unknown.

Nevertheless, the placing down of a marker called 'Stage 2' not only kept the goal of full organic union in sight, it also kept the Church–State relationship in sight. Thus, when the more detailed treatment of 'The Scheme' came in the 1968 report, there was a survey of establishment issues:

> ... From the Church's standpoint ... there is need to watch lest the pastoral advantages which Establishment brings should be bought at too high a price ...
>
> Its dissolution would be a tragic loss, but this is not to say that it does not need reconsideration in the light of present needs.
>
> ... the Methodist Church is unambiguously self-governing in all matters of practice and policy within the limits set by the Methodist Church Union Act of 1929, and subsequent amending Acts, and Methodists expect the future united Church will be no less clearly seen to govern itself than the Methodist Church is seen to do now.[6]

Despite these cautions about establishment they are sugared over with sentimental hope at the end of the chapter. Now the Commission starts to write about 'new links with the national community' and, as the climax, 'the strengthening of the relationship between the national Church and the Sovereign'.[7]

It was right to do some adumbrating of the Church–State issues in these documents, but the harsh reality of the Scheme was that Stage 1 *had* to happen, whereas Stage 2 remained far off and indistinct in minds concentrating on Stage 1. To put it another way, the big changes for the Church of England were to arise at Stage 2, whereas the big ones for Methodism arose immediately. And when it comes to the establishment, the Church of England likes to have its problems somewhere in the middle distance, to be addressed at some blessedly unknown date.

As the issue dragged on through the 1960s and was revived briefly in 1971–2, it was easy for Anglicans to forget the reason for its genesis – simply that Geoffrey Fisher had declined to face up to the problem of the establishment, and had proposed

a clumsy procedure to evade it. The result was that we found
ourselves in 1968–9, and again in 1971–2, voting on a scheme
for adjusting relationships (well, yes, with an indistinct union
on the horizon), and not a scheme for union. It is exactly
the kind of pattern which can produce negative passion in
opponents, but is hardly calculated to induce positive passion
in proponents. And it duly went down through successive
defeats on the Anglican side.

The Chadwick Commission was sitting whilst the penultimate stages of the Anglican-Methodist debacle were being
worked through. It is largely forgotten today that the Commission was supposed to be addressing ecumenical implications. Its terms of reference were:

> To make recommendations as to modifications in the consti-
> tutional relationship between Church and State which are
> desirable and practical and in so doing *to take account of
> current and future steps to promote greater unity between
> the Churches.*[8]

It cannot be said that the Commission took much notice of
other Churches' views. The members were engaged in reor-
ganizing the Church of England's own peculiar glory, and
apparently were not to be rushed into serious disestablishing
moves. So they record that the other Churches think the place
of the Prime Minister in appointments ought to cease, but in
part go on to retain it – and they record that the other
Churches want Parliament to have no control of worship, but
then neither does the Chadwick Commission itself. But these
are tiny points in passing, for it is certain that the Chadwick
Commission really only nods twice briefly in the direction of
ecumenism, and the report gives little hint of the prominent
place unity with other Churches plays in the terms of reference. In the report the matter was handled in a wholly cosmetic
way. The Church of England has always been good at voting
for unity when unity is on the agenda (apart from final
approval, of course), but forgetting about it altogether when
anything else is on the agenda.

After this we all went back to the ecumenical drawing-board,
with 'talks about talks', Ten Propositions, and a draft 'Covenant for Unity'. In the process, the 'Covenant' became a multilat-
eral process; the 'service of reconciliation' was made honest

and acceptable; and 'Stage 2' faded further into the mists of the future. The Covenant also went down, almost exactly ten years after the Anglican–Methodist Scheme. Once again, we had a pattern in which other Churches would 'take episcopacy into their system' at a Stage 1, and the main gain was adjusted relationships between denominations. But again we faced the question: who would go to the stake for 'adjusted relation-ships'? And the zeal of the opponents (who were worried about the Church of England taking on women ministers through the ecumenical back-door) outstripped the half-hearted support of the majority.

It stands out a mile that no Church can unite with an established Church. It follows by the same logic that a Church which professes a commitment to visible unity, but clings to an establishment in preference to taking unity seriously, is a proud and purblind body, in open breach of its own avowed principles. Indeed, if the Church of England were a 'free' Church, part of the very reason for dissent by the existing Free Churches would have disappeared. Unless we have some demonstrable and categorical biblical imperative for our colon-ized status, we owe it to other Christians, if not to God and to ourselves, to rid ourselves of it.

The simple truth is this: there may be some harmless and secondary features of the Church of England's establishment which could be carried forward into a united Church with serious claims to a 'national role'. But the Prime Ministerial nomination of bishops, and the legislative veto in Parliament, are not such features. Whilst they remain, all Churches which would like to explore uniting with us are bound to turn away in sorrow. Until we have reformed ourselves unilaterally, and shed these most substantial of our chains, we cannot be taken seriously as wanting to merge with any other denomination.

And if we view the ecumenical imperative as a scriptural and God-given duty laid upon us, then, if we delay to reform ourselves, we are in breach of that command; indeed we are disdainful and untrustworthy partners. Our sister denomi-nations do not always complain, sometimes because they wish to remain institutionally separate themselves, sometimes because they think that being established is an article of faith to us – and they can be pardoned for so thinking, for such appears to be our stance.

What can we do? We can dismantle the most offensive features of the establishment unilaterally and soon; then we can open talks with the major non-Roman denominations in England; and we can talk about how to unite with them in a one-stage healthy union. They for their part could hardly have a stronger sign of our seriousness. The time is overdue.

Mission

The 1662 Book of Common Prayer has no mission – or, to be accurate, no evangelistic mission – for the Church. The most it has got is the post-communion prayer that we should 'do all such good works as thou hast prepared for us to walk in'. There is, on the Prayer Book theory, no one outside the Church. So there is no mission out from the Church. Schmemann, the well-known Eastern Orthodox theologian, says somewhere that Justinian united State and Church by abolishing the Church – but it is just as true to say that 1662 united the two by abolishing the State, for there is no 'civic' world out beyond the Church. Both stretch together to the horizon.

Now it is possible to conceive of mission in a non-directional 'presence' way. It is possible to think of a Church of England which simply exists across a wide swathe of people – the whole of a parish – and it exists in them because they are really members of it; and it is the only place it exists, not only because they are an exhaustive statement of the parish in human terms, but also because we are not going to give any extra weighting in our account of the existence of the Church to those who actually come. If we mark up those who come, we shall inevitably mark down those who don't – and we don't want to discriminate.

I say 'it is *possible* to conceive of mission' in that way. But it is wildly absurd to do so. There is no dynamic, no 'going out', no service to the local community, not even the service of the saints. At no point are there two parties – so there is no one group to give service to another group, for all are the Church, all are the Church without distinction. There are no insiders and no outsiders. When all are Church, in effect none are. The famous Temple aphorism that the Church is the only society which exists for the benefit of those who are not its members is fatuous as far as the Church in which he was an

Archbishop is concerned – for, on a classic establishment view, the English who are not members are nowhere to be found.

But the New Testament *has* a boundary to the Church. It is called baptism, and its role within the New Testament Church is relatively easy to discern. We still have baptism, but until very recently it was given automatically at birth. This reflected presuppositions of 1662, and accordingly it put the baptismal boundary round the whole nation. It thus demarcated precisely nothing ecclesiastically, and lost much of its New Testament role in the process. For unless baptism marks the Church off from the world, it says nothing or worse than nothing. We have a great need in England today to find the Church – and mark it off; and we have an equal need to find the world, and chart where it is also. In the process, we may get our boundaries wrong, but unless we can attempt to establish boundaries, we shall find we have, as noted, no Church and no world!

As we then gird ourselves for mission, we need to know whether the baptized are with us or against us. Ideally, even in the twilight hours of Christendom, we should be prepared to de-register people and to tell them that they are self-excommunicate. Then the corollary will also appear, that a Church with a membership of Christ, a motivation, and a mission will emerge. It is a consummation devoutly to be sought.

Prophecy

Whilst 'mission' properly includes social action, and involves any task which comes to hand which may promote the reign of God, there is a function over and above it – that of prophecy.

The prophetic task of the Church is to proclaim God's righteousness to the nation, and to do so fearlessly and cleanly and, with due allowance for human sinfulness, from as uncompromised a position as possible. Here our Old Testament models have more place. The individual prophets, as, e.g. those of the eighth century, were called of God and sent to confront monarchs and rulers and the religious 'establishment' (in its metaphorical sense) of their own day. Certainly, they had at intervals to polarize from the authorities of their time, and in the name of God rebuke them. They were always uncomfortable people to have around.

Now the Church of England is capable of playing such a role

in the country today. Instances to which earlier reference has
been made include the report on nuclear bomb in 1982 and
Faith in the City in 1985. No one doubts the actual courage of
individuals who chair such working parties or lead deputations
to government departments. Nor are there lacking people to
tell us that the existing establishment gives a smooth passage
into the corridors of power for memoranda from chairmen of
Boards and Councils of the General Synod of the Church
of England. If this is true, it is yet not self-evidently right –
and as so many people approach the establishment simply on
an opportunist basis, such access needs critical examination.

Was it Lenin or Stalin who said 'The Pope! How many divi-
sions has he?'? The point here is simply that the card-vote or
at least the shop-front of the Christian Churches is important
politically. It is quite arguable that the kind of Church House
staff that exists enables more detailed work to be done by
Boards and Councils than is true in most other Churches.
There may be entrenched lines of communication; there may
be open doors in some departments. But, whilst true opportunism will continue to take advantage of such bridges (if they do
exist), no argument for the current Church–State relationship
should be based upon opportunism. This exactly mirrors the
issue of the presence of bishops in the House of Lords.

In forming a reasoned response, we must make certain broad
points:

1. It must be recalled that, whatever courtesies or open-
nesses are displayed to us from the Palace of Westminster
or from Whitehall, that does not mean that the State is
confessing Christ or the standards of Christ or the biblical
revelation of God.

2. Christians are not the only religious group with advice,
fears or visions to present to the government – Jews, Muslims, Hindus and Sikhs have policies for which they wish to
bend the government's ear. The government itself is strictly
'non-religious'.

3. The proper way for Christians to confront the government
is ecumenically. The new 'ecumenical instruments' are supposed to be the channels by which the Churches approach
the government or make public statements on Christian
issues. It is part of the understanding of them that at intervals one Church will do some work and lead the advocacy

on behalf of all the others, but in such cases the adherence of the others should be well indicated, and the ecumenical dimension to the thrust well advertised.

4. Where major statements have to be made at short notice, then the presidents of the 'ecumenical instruments', the Council of Churches of Britain and Ireland and the Churches Together in England, should be brought into concert to make them.

5. At each point, whilst Church of England persons – and particularly bishops – will judge themselves to be free of any compromising motivation and thus free to prophesy fearlessly, yet the process would be greatly enhanced if all suggestion could be shed that we are lackeys of the State.

6. A very high priority in proclaiming the kingdom of God in our present circumstances is that we should cut the connection with the State. Would that our Roman Catholic and Free Church partners in ecumenism and sharers in a vision of the kingdom would not tip-toe delicately round our existing establishmentarian sensibilities, but instead urge us to sever the chains, and get ourselves free also.

Broad points may be all that we can make at this moment. But the hour is no doubt coming when we shall need to be free to be the prophetic voice God would call us to be.

10. Some International Perspectives

Any of us who have talked with Ulster Unionists will know the maxim 'You cannot understand us unless you have lived in Northern Ireland'. On the other hand, those of us who have had to listen to Unionists, even when they are falling over themselves to sound moderate, have tended to pull back and say, 'Even if I did live in Northern Ireland, I hope I would never get caught in the peculiar distorted mould of thought that is yours'. It is my experience that English Anglicans give the same impression not only to English non-conformists, but also to our brothers and sisters from Anglican Churches overseas (and beyond Offa's Dike and Hadrian's Wall). We have the only established Church in the whole Anglican Communion; we are in all sorts of ways not only the point of historical origin of Anglicans elsewhere; but we are also, through the position of the Archbishop of Canterbury, the hub of the present day Anglican Communion. Yet we alone believe we are responsible for ourselves alone; we alone believe everyone else to be out of step but us; and we alone can understand why it is important and valuable – nay, indispensable – that we should be the established Church of the nation. We alone would become a sect if we were disestablished – for the others, totally free of State connections in a hundred different nations, their standing as part of the one holy Catholic and apostolic Church is not only *not* bound up with being owned by the States they are in, it is almost as it were bound up with *not* being enmeshed with the government of their particular countries.

The degree of self-deceit to which this can lead was well brought out in the Radio 4 debate in February 1992. Michael Alison, who spoke second for those opposing the motion for disestablishment, said:

How different can you get from the secular trend which has

followed secularization in the United States? What do our people want, which would they prefer? Are they halted between two opinions in this? I doubt it... 90 per cent, according to the MORI poll on 4 July 1990, 90 per cent of the respondents reckoned that they were Christian in outlook and loyalty. The Church is the gift of God to the nation as Christ our head is the gift of God to all the nations. And to withdraw from our obligation, our moral responsibility and our potential before them is unimaginable.[1]

Now Michael Alison is the most deeply imbued establishmentarian of them all. We have seen above that he believes the country desperately needs to have this intangible force at work in every part of the country's life, and that establishment is the way to provide it. We have also seen his readiness to equate the Tory government with the special providence of God;* and we have seen that he believes that the proper way for the Church of England to play the role he outlines is for the God-given government to own it. All this appears to be the fruit of peculiar English thinking (for we know it will not stretch as far as Wales). But in this broadcast speech, he set up the United States as the fall guy, in order to etch a contrast between our enlightened position and their benighted one. He got his reply – Elaine Storkey, a prominent lay member of General Synod, made the following contribution to the debate:

I want particularly to take exception to dear Michael Alison, whose national fervour I appreciate no end – I think it's wonderful. On the point that he made, where he was talking about an example from 'secularized' America and particularly from religious education in America, that there be a good reason why we don't go down that road: I have a huge problem with this because, if you actually look at 'secularized' America, children go to church. If you look at the 'National Church'-ed Britain, children are falling away from churches at a rate, we are told, of 25,000 a year. If you look at 'secularized' America, the population as a whole goes to church at about 42 per cent – if you look at 'National Church'-ed Britain between 9 and 10 per cent go to church.

---

*See Chapter 3, fn on p. 75.

If you look at 'secularized' America and drive through it, churches are going up in every state at the rate of knots. If you drive through 'National Church'-ed Britain churches are closing or being pulled down in every county. If you look at 'secularized' America, children get their Christian education from the churches that they attend. If you look at 'Christian' Britain, you'll find that children get a great garbaged view of Christian education from the schools, which is usually taught to the lowest common denominator. So I think if you are going to found your argument on *that*, we need a much rounder position, please.

In one sense, the 'dear Michael Alison' says it all. Elaine Storkey is expressing that affectionate distancing which we employ towards members of our own families who have a bee in their bonnet about Russian soldiers marching through the Channel Tunnel to take possession of our land, or, more positively, the efficacy of a stated herbal remedy to keep you going as an active cyclist until you are 101. We listen politely and even affectionately, but are slightly embarrassed when the member of the family starts telling the deluded story to visitors. You can hear Elaine Storkey taking us all gently to one side and saying: 'Yes, I know his point has little to do with reality, and I think I had better make it clear that I do actually know the real situation.' Of course, one can try facts upon the actual deluded persons. The member of the family can be told actual statistics about the size and length and safety precautions of the Channel Tunnel – or even about the disposition of Russian troops on the French side – or about the mortality and decrepitude rates of those who have faithfully taken the particular herbal remedy all their lives, but none of this gets through. So all we can do is say 'dear Aunt Agatha', and show the rest of the world we personally can see the facts.

If Elaine Storkey could make the informal comparison, then there are also those who can make the formal. One of the most penetrating studies of the Church of England's establishment came twenty-eight years ago from Peter Hinchliff, then Professor of Ecclesiastical History at Grahamstown, South Africa, and an Anglican presbyter. His book, *The One-Sided Reciprocity: A Study in the Modification of the Establishment*[2] brought a fair-minded and judicious analysis to bear upon our establishment. But he wrote from the vantage-point of a disestablished Church, in which tangles with the fact of the establishment of the Church of England were part of the history of the present-day Church, and a need to be distanced from the then government of the Republic and its policies of *apartheid* was crucial to its witness. Peter Hinchliff has since spent a quarter of a century ministering in the Church of England and is now Professor of Ecclesiastical History at Oxford, but his mind, like his book, stands unchanged by his ministering in an established context.

The same capacity for Anglican self-deceit is delightfully focused in the treatment given it by the Scottish journalist, Stewart Lamont. His journalistic book, *Church and State: Uneasy Alliances*[3] has a quick look round the world to see how Church and State relate in different climates and political contexts. Base communities and liberation theology in South America rub shoulders with underground Churches in communist Eastern Europe (the Berlin Wall came down just as his book was published). But when he comes to England, his chapter title is 'The naked Empress' – she is a once-grand, now ridiculously fallen, old lady, whose self-worth amidst her nakedness is preserved by self-delusion. The little boy may have said 'The Emperor has no clothes on', and the word got through to the crowds. But the Emperor himself, or in this case the naked Empress, gets the message last of all.

So it is so often with our own Anglican Communion. The other Provinces recognize our relative longevity, and are not without respect. But they know (and tell each other) that in conversation with us, they keep bumping into this area of private battiness, this delusion of grandeur, this total parting of company from reality. Usually they are deferential towards us, but every now and again something slips out.

The classic case of this came in 1981 when the Church of England had a 'Partners in Mission Consultation'. The pattern of reporting came in two stages: the 'external partners' produced their report separately from the home team, the 'internal partners', then consulted with them and assisted in

a re-writing. A mischievous script-writer could almost have foreseen what would happen on the Church and State front.
The external partners initially reported as follows:

Church and State
87. We believe it is better for the Church to speak as an independent one. From this position the Church can say all things in all spheres (for instance, social questions, re-armament, pollution and so on) – agreeable and not agreeable facts which are necessary for the welfare of the congregations and the world population. We know that the Church of England is standing in a specific tradition. We propose that it try a slow separation – step-by-step – of Church and State. We prove our assertion with the following examples:

(a)   leaders of the Church are appointed by the State;
(b)   priests can baptize, marry or conduct a funeral of people who are not baptized. What is the Church in this part – a ceremony master?
(c)   the finances of the Church are controlled by the Church Commissioners, whose leaders are appointed by the Crown, so that the Church has no freedom to decide alone what it can do with the money.

Structures
88. The external partners are of the view that the Church of England must examine and take action regarding the following points which concern its structures in view of the mission of the Church today.
89. The establishment of the Church is a hindrance to the mission of the Church and the Church is unable to perform its prophetic ministry freely. It is noted that the Church in its present set-up is not free to appoint its spiritual leaders, which inhibits its witness.
90. [Dealing with voluntary societies]
91. The Church of England must be prepared to break away from its historic past in the interest of new life and witness in the world . . . [4]

That is half the script. It is courteous, it is restrained. It is at points only half-focused. But centrally it is very clear – people from other denominations in England, and from Anglican Provinces and other parts of the world simply cannot see how the present Church and State relationship can be defended. It is obvious, almost at sight, that it is an anachronistic and indefensible run-on from a past in which it may have been acceptable and even inevitable. And their great concern surrounds the properly prophetic role of the Church, cleanly polarizing from the governing power in a State, and then confronting it in the name of the Lord. How, you can hear them saying, can someone clasped to the bosom of a powerful partner, simultaneously stand back and cleanly confront the other's errors?

The second half of the script would be equally easy for any English Anglican to construct from prior knowledge. The internal and external partners met up at Scargill, and hammered out a common report, 'The Message of Scargill'. The actual script describes what then happened . . . :

Disestablishment

134. The external partners faced the Consultation with the sharp statement that the Church of England is hindered in its mission by its Establishment.

135. In discussing this we have come to see that the real issue is not so much the precise organizational arrangements (with regard to the monarchy, the selection of bishops, etc.) as the impression so often given that the Church of England is a church of the privileged which fails to address itself to where things actually hurt, where the good news of the Gospel can be discovered and proclaimed. So we do not propose any effort to re-structure the Establishment; it is the attitude so often dominant in the Church of England that must be transformed . . . [5]

So we get the wonderful and wholly predictable result. The external partners propose a step-by-step disestablishment. The internal partners read it with alarm, explain to the external partners that they cannot come in and in three weeks understand such a unique structure as the Church of England or such a delicately poised partnership of Church and State – but that, of course – and here you can hear the paternalistic patience with which the internal partners explained it to their oh-so-slow-to-understand brothers and sisters – they *have* nevertheless discerned something very important, something

the Church of England needs to learn, and it is this: that our
attitude needs to change – and it would be a serious distraction
down a side-road to get too worried about our structures.*

The external partners may have argued their corner, or they
may have simply lain down under it. But the internal partners
prevailed, and must have sighed with relief as they smoothly
eased the spotlight off their compromised structural relationship with the machinery of the State.

The end of the report was a 'Postscript: the Heart of the
Message'. Here the establishment issue crept back in:

> 192. What then was the heart of PIM(E) 81's challenge to
> the Church of England? We are shackled, it said, by an
> accumulation of traditions, customs and archaic structures.
> We believe, wrongly, that we can respond to God's call to
> mission without disturbing our inherited structures. In fact
> substantial changes are needed in forms of ministry, in our
> pattern of voluntary societies, in synodical structures, in
> state relations, in methods of finance, and in inter-diocesan
> relations . . . [6]

Well, if we really cannot respond to God's call to mission without disturbing structures, how was it that 'The Message of
Scargill' quoted above proposed exactly that? Or what bright
scribe slipped 'state relations' back in? Or was it agreed as a
weasel word which did not have to mean changing anything
whenever we do not want it to? And do the home Anglicans
really think that all structures are up for review except 'State
relations'? That would be paradoxical indeed.

The last stage came when the Archbishop of York of the
time, Stuart Blanch, was preaching in York Minster at a time
when the General Synod was considering the Partners in Mission report in July 1981. He was chairman of the Consultation,
but he was also an entrenched anti-disestablishmentarian. He
simply told us from the pulpit, almost as an axiom to stand
behind all further discussion: 'Let us get this clear – the ques-

---

*This is described from the point of view of a convinced establishment-
arian, who obviously thinks the squeezing out of reference to structures
was correct, or alternatively overlooks the original indictment of the
structures and thinks these later paragraphs are the general conclusion,
in John Habgood, *Church and Nation in a Secular Age* (DLT 1983),
pp. 98–9.

tion of disestablishment is not on the agenda.' And the doors closed again.

All this is not unlike my original Northern Ireland comparison; I can now offer another. Outside criticisms of the establishment of the Church of England are like meteorites entering the earth's atmosphere. The atmosphere burns them up, and nothing solid survives to hit the earth's surface – and *terra firma* is protected from the catastrophes that would otherwise ensue. So it is with the criticisms. Only the truly enormous travelling with gigantic force survive their journey through the atmosphere and make any impact at all. Perhaps that mention at the end of the report above of 'State relations' is the minute surviving marble-sized meteorite which was all that was left to impact on the earth from the vast bulk with which it first hurled itself into our atmosphere.

Curiously enough, there is another small crater left by a meteorite which successfully brought some surviving small mass into contact with *terra firma* at the Lambeth Conference in 1988. The 'Dogmatic and Pastoral Concerns' section (around 140 bishops) included in their long statement the following:

15. The Christian way of being human is simply not compatible with any and every way of being human: it will at certain points be in conflict with aspects of the Indian or Melanesian or Irish or American way of being human. Being with Jesus by being with each other means that Christians are not going to be *uncritically* with, or on the side of, any one 'natural' culture for good and all. The Church is, by its nature, an uncomfortable presence anywhere. Because it has its own standards of human relations, it will not let itself be just the religious department of a nation-state – however often, as with the English Establishment, it has been lured into something dangerously like that role.[7]

One wonders what was the size and what the velocity of this meteorite at the point where it originally hit the atmosphere. The size of the crater left by the small fraction of the missile when it hit the earth, again suggests something enormous prior to its entering our atmosphere. Whilst it does look as though the protecting atmosphere will burn up most things thrown against it from outside, it is also clear that some very large meteorites are threatening us. So we *might* have to prepare for being shaken.

It is doubly paradoxical that we in England stand still at the hub of a world-wide Anglican Communion yet nursing this slightly guilty secret. We defend the position by telling others they will not understand the establishment because they have not had the benefit of it from birth. We can organize missionary societies, send the State-appointed archbishop on tours round the world, arrange prayer and support for church leaders in countries such as Sudan, South Africa and Kenya, where those leaders have had to confront their own State rulers. We gladly offer support in such cases, and applaud the courage of Anglican bishops, Synods, and ordinary lay-people. But no one from overseas can ever understand the joys and privileges which are ours in the established Church of England.

It is actually not difficult to set up hypothetical situations in which we in England would have to evaluate Christian Churches which were under direct State control in countries elsewhere. What would we have made of the South African government appointing bishops for the Anglican Church in that republic? How would we have defended a situation where Amin appointed bishops in Uganda? And Stalin and Hitler would have been automatically suspect. We have seen above that Anglican critics of Hitler's subversion of the 'German Christians' were inhibited in their criticisms by the State appointment of bishops in England.* Is there any hope that reversing the viewpoint would enable us to see ourselves as others see us? Or are we irretrievably and blindly stuck in our self-delusion?

However, it is not simply delusion that should worry us – a corporate *folie de l'église*. The difficulty is what it *does* to us. The first Christians were 'neither Jew nor Greek', not because they had lost all ethnic identity, or merged all individual characteristics in a single shapeless lump. They had become true internationalists, strangers and pilgrims on earth, worshippers in a temple made without hands, living on this earth but not captive to its institutions or its ways of thought. My fear is that established Anglicanism has just the opposite effect – we have a nationalistic account of our church life; we engage

---

*See the quotation on page 103 above.

in a justification of our State relationship which not only sets us up above other Churches in England for the wrong reason, but also gives a message to the rest of the world of effortless superiority. There *is* something about our attitude – all partners were right about that. But it may well be that the attitude is bound up with the structures, and the suppressed rationale for the structures. But in truth we are 'poor and wretched and blind and naked' – and cannot see it.

Of course, if we could see it, we would know we are not special as English, know that we, like others, are only sinners saved by grace – that all kinds of citizens of all kinds of nations have all alike come short of the glory of God, and are all alike justified freely through his grace through the redemption that is in Christ Jesus. That, I submit, is the key to being the worldwide Church, the basis of our true internationalism, our determination that all 'middle walls of partition' should come down, and we should find ourselves, with men and women of every race and language and law and culture, as the people of God subsisting throughout the world.

11. How Should We Get There?

Methods of de-colonization

There are three possible routes by which the Church of England may be free of State control. They compare to three de-colonization processes in the political world, and may be best understood by setting out those precedents:

1. A people may simply declare themselves free, and defy their previous oppressors to do what they will about it. The classic instance in British history is the revolt of the American colonies in the eighteenth century. The War of Independence followed, and the occupying power lost, and finally came to terms with the independence.

2. The occupying power may, for its part, simply declare that it will cease to occupy from a certain date, but may add that it will in time recognize any credible nation and leadership that may emerge. In broad terms this was the process at the termination of the Palestine Mandate in 1948 – Britain simply left, and, because there were two sides in the land, both wanting possession of the land and thus arming themselves to the teeth, a bitter war ensued. The nation of Israel emerged, and was duly recognized. But the end of the Mandate was a unilateral action, because there was no single 'interim' or other self-government of the peoples in the territory – there was indeed no credible institution which could speak for all the people, and, although in this case there were strong partisan forces, no negotiated deal could be done with them together, nor could one be preferred over against another. Yet the British government had become clear, for its own sake, that it could not continue – so it got out.

3. The occupying power may negotiate a constitutional settlement, in which the pattern of independence, on a constitutional basis, becomes an Act of the imperial Parliament, granting and conferring all powers previously held. The usual method in the British de-colonization process was to develop a constitution, run internal self-government as an

interim phase, and thus have all the organs of government
in place before final independence was granted.

If we work through these models, we can see how, in theory,
each would work in the process of 'de-colonizing' a Church
from State control.

First model: Ecclesiastical unilateral declaration of independence

In line with the first model the people of a Church could simply
walk out, and then, if the property was not alienable, they
would meet next door, declaring themselves to be still the
same Christian people. That was the pattern of the Scottish
Disruption in 1843 – it was also the process followed by Gray
in South Africa at the foundation of the Church of the Province
of South Africa in 1870. In the Scottish case, less than half
the Church left, but the process would have been the same
if the entire Church of Scotland had followed the lead.* In
Gray's case, the property was mostly locally owned and, in
effect, came with the people as they declared for independence.† The mustering was not total; and not only Bishop
Colenso, but also congregations up and down the country,
insisted that they still stood where they had stood before, not

---

*The 'Disruption' was a 'Disruption' *from* the State, and not a division
within the Church, and must be understood that way. The actual resultant
schism was a contingent regrettable outcome, not a phenomenon integral
to the Disruption itself.

†Curiously enough Bishopscourt, where all Archbishops of Cape Town
since Gray have lived, was *not* really locally owned. From funds provided
by a donor in England, it was held in Cape Town in trust for the use of
'a Bishop of the Church of England'. Gray, by his unilateral formation
of the new voluntary association, was deemed to have detached the Province of South Africa from the Church of England 'root and branch'. However, it was legal opinion that he was simultaneously Archbishop of Cape
Town *and* 'a bishop of the Church of England', on the grounds that he
had been consecrated in England. When the first Archbishop to have been
consecrated not in England but within the Church of the Province, Francis
Phelps, took up residence in 1931, then a series of court cases followed.
In these the final judgement was that the Archbishop of Cape Town did
not wholly conform to the terms of the trust, but that he was the nearest
approximation to a legally watertight occupant, and such Archbishops
could continue to use the property unless or until a better claimant to
the legal title appeared. And I believe that is still the position to-day.

subject to Gray's new Synod or Canons, but (by a sophisticated theory) still part of the Church of England.

Second model: Unilateral turning loose
In respect of the second political model above, Irish and Welsh disestablishment had many echoes of this method, though it was done with the Churches in a more principled way. (Obviously the earthly stakes were lower than in Palestine, though the issue of Irish Home Rule which lay behind the Irish was nearly as fraught.) But in 1871 and 1920 in these Church cases, history dictated this second method, as there were not present in the two Churches those organs of internal self-government to which we are accustomed today – in Ireland because it was too early in history in 1868–70, and in Wales because there had not been till then an ecclesiastical entity identifiable as 'Church in Wales'. The Westminster Parliament in effect said (and did so virtually without negotiation), 'on such and such a date, you cease to be directly governed by us. If you of your own voluntary decision then form the appropriate patterns of responsible self-government, we will convey the following assets to it . . .'

Third model: Negotiated freedom
In line with the third model, the Church of Scotland was in 1921 freed from the State, by agreed State action, under the Church of Scotland Act. This Act asserted the spiritual independence of the Church, and so empowered the General Assembly and lower courts as to ensure that the initial constitution could itself thereafter be amended by purely ecclesiastical action. This was the natural last step in the laying down of State control, as the General Assembly of the Church of Scotland was a highly developed governing body, very conscious of its own dignity and standing, and it was natural that the Church of Scotland Act should locate all governing powers in that Assembly with its subordinate bodies.

First model: A UDI by the Church of England?
How do these models bear upon us in the Church of England? The first is always possible, but it would have to be a secession of overwhelming weight to be worth doing. There have been nibbles in that direction, not least in the episcopate

defying Parliament after the 1927-8 defeats in the Commons. Perhaps if Parliament had last year been minded to block the ordination of women, we would have had a *cause célèbre*. Perhaps if a Prime Minister ignored the advice of the Crown Appointments Commission and nominated someone else, we *might* reach that theoretical point where an archbishop declined to consecrate, and the Church of England went into rebellion. But, whilst such cases can be imagined, they do not appear likely. There would, of course, be an amazing problem for the State, if the General Synod and the dioceses declared themselves voluntary bodies, held onto whatever property they actually owned, and walked out of the rest . . .

The point must be made that, in any Church which considered acting in this way today, there must always be the dissuasive that such a demonstration of people-power needs to be virtually total. Otherwise even small numbers holding on to the existing structures, buildings and synods, will have a valid claim to continue the life of the Church as it has been known, and will thus emerge as the true inheritors. As nothing constitutional is involved in a walk-out, the State Church (the existence of which is unrelated to numbers!) would still be there – and the claims to continuity by the secessionists would be vested solely in their own individual persons and in nothing else of substance.

Second model: Would Parliament turn the Church of England loose?

The second way to freedom has this attraction – that the patterns under which the freed Church then lives owe nothing to the colonists of pre-freedom days. The freed Church takes full responsibility for creating its own instruments of government and structures of ministry and decision-taking. The government merely contracts the frontiers of its own direct control to allow the emerging institution to create its own institutional life. But the circumstances which gave birth to both our precedents, i.e., both the political exit from Palestine and the disestablishment in Ireland and Wales, do not really obtain for the Church of England today. In particular, the existing process of devolution of powers from Parliament to Synod is already half-way to creating freedom on the third model. Furthermore, by definition, this second way to freedom would rarely if ever arise by a petitioning from the colony concerned – it is, in principle, a disdainful and patronizing act of unilateral naked power. The Church of England is in position to do rather more than merely petition, so it certainly should not find itself in a position of not even being allowed to do as much as petition.

The issue of unilateral action by the controlling power – i.e. the Westminster Parliament – is of more than passing interest here because three different members of the Commons in the years since the 1987 election did actually make attempts to cast us off. The three were Tony Benn (Labour), Simon Hughes (Liberal Democrat), and Michael Latham (Tory). These were in varying ways simplistic or coercive or both at once, simply as a result of the situation. In other words, it is not easy for an individual Parliamentarian, even with the best will in the world, to imagine *how* the State can unilaterally lift its control and fairly allow the Church to re-muster as a voluntary body. The complexity of the Church of England's corporate life is such that the very terms of lifting the controls themselves start to mark out the ways in which the people can or cannot then re-muster to remain in continuity with the previous body. The MPs would no doubt retort that they tabled their Bills as debating points, rather than with any serious expectation or hope that they might become law, and that if, by an amazing chance in a blue moon, the Commons had been able to debate these Bills, then the Committee process, and the parallel debates in the Lords, would have sorted out idiosyncratic features of the legislation. To this we can only reply: well, maybe. But the initial drafts which were tabled in the Commons do give us *some* idea of how at least one proponent of disestablishment sees the issues from a Parliamentary standpoint.

The first effort came from Tony Benn in 1988. His draft was headed *'English Church'*, and read in total as follows:

A BILL TO
Disestablish the Church of England

Be it enacted by the Queen's most Excellent Majesty, by and with the advice and consent of the Lords Spiritual and Temporal, and Commons in this present Parliament assembled, and by authority of the same, as follows:

1. On the day after expiration of six months, or such extended period as Her Majesty may fix by Order in Council,

not being more than twelve months, after the passing of this Act, the Church of England shall cease to be established by law, and no person shall, after the passing of this Act, be appointed or nominated by Her Majesty or any person, by virtue of any existing right of patronage, to any ecclesiastical office in the Church of England.

2. This Act may be cited as the English Church Act 1988.

Again, it may be that a draft Bill simply does duty to put a foot in the legislative door. However, it is immediately clear that in the issue with which the Act does deal – patronage – its provisions are hopelessly simplistic; and in the great cluster of issues with which the draft does *not* deal, we are greatly in need of guidance and rulings if anything like disestablishment (the Bill's intended end) is to result.

Tony Benn returned to the attack on 17 May 1991, and indicated that on the following Monday (20 May) he would be presenting his own Commonwealth of Britain Bill. The relevant part of this (stillborn) Bill read as follows:

PART XI
RELIGIOUS FREEDOM

45. The Church of England is hereby disestablished, and all the powers over faith, doctrine, liturgy, property, discipline and appointments shall forthwith be transferred, in their entirety, to the General Synod of the Church of England, to be exercised in accordance with any rules determined by that body.

46. [Abolition of blasphemy]

47. [Equality before the law of all persons of all faiths]

Well, again it might be simplistic. It would, of course, only come into force in the context of an enormous constitutional revolution abolishing the monarchy, the House of Lords, jurisdiction in Northern Ireland, and a host of other inherited features of the constitution. But it remains doubtful whether even the expanded range of the Benn disestablishment sufficiently meets the needs of the case. This Bill too has made no progress.

The second man in the breach was Michael Latham. His draft, headed '*Established Church*' and published in December 1991, was entitled:

A BILL TO:

Abolish the General Synod of the Church of England, on a
date to be appointed; to provide for the creation of a Church
of England assembly, consisting of a house of all diocesan,
suffragan and assistant bishops, and a joint house of clergy
and laity, to be directly elected by all Church of England
clergy and lay persons on parochial electoral rolls; to make
provision for the diocese of Sodor and Man; to empower the
Assembly to decide on all appropriate matters, except those
within the legal responsibilities of the Church Commissioners, without further reference to Parliament; to provide for the election of new bishops by members of the house
of bishops, saving the right of final approval of the chosen
candidate by the Crown; to abolish the Ecclesiastical
Committee; to abolish the automatic places of the bishops
in the House of Lords; to permit ordained clergy of the
Church of England, with the consent of a diocesan bishop,
to seek election to the House of Commons; and for connected purposes. [Then a host of clauses gives effect to the
above.]

Of this proposal, it has to be said that it retains much of the
existing establishment (notably the Crown's veto on appointment of bishops – which have to come back to Downing Street
– and the presumed continued answerability of the Church
Commissioners to Parliament). In addition it prescribes all
too much of church life thereafter (particularly in its absurd
'Assembly' and its provocative co-option of new bishops by the
existing House); and therefore it cannot well be viewed as
'disestablishing' – no, it is almost the opposite, an attempt to
reform the Church of England by naked Parliamentary power,
without any approach coming from the Church. It may have a
benefit for Parliament in view – for Measures would no longer
come to Parliament – but, as far as the Church of England is
concerned, in the Bill's interfering high-handedness, it is in
fact only comparable to the original Irish Bishoprics Act of
1833 or the Public Worship Regulation Act of 1874!

The third disestablisher was Simon Hughes in this present
Parliament. His Bill got its first reading on 10 March 1993.
The stated purpose came in his opening speech:

I beg to move
> That leave be given to bring in a Bill to terminate the establishment of the Church of England, to make provision in respect of the Temporalities thereof; and for connected purposes.
> The main purpose of the Bill is to allow the House to start to consider whether the time is ripe to disestablish the Church of England in England . . .

He stated that he was in no sense aiming to demote the role of Christianity in society. He then touched upon Parliamentary legislation, bishops in the Lords, the Prime Minister's appointment of bishops, and the place of the Throne 'one, two or more generations from now'. The Bill got no further at the time.

Now it has to be conceded not only that these Bills had no chance of success, not only that none of them accurately addressed the disestablishing issue, but also that they were attempts made on the basis of the wrong model. Of course the government of the day was not assisting them (the Tories at heart rather like having the Church of England established – it makes Britannia feel more secure). And of course they were clumsy as to *how* the imperial power can grant independence unilaterally without deeply affecting the independent institution thereafter. But their real problem was that they were starting from the Parliamentary end, instead of the Church end. For that we shall need to come to the third model.

Third model: Negotiated separation on the Church's initiative

As a matter of fact the Church of England *is* like a colony in the process of being de-colonized. It is fair to look for parallels in a large devolution of powers to a largely autonomous governing body prior to the full independence of the colony. The difference is this: that in the de-colonization process all devolution of powers came within a structured timetable of progress, a timetable which was to lead clearly and on a stated date to full independence; but in the Church of England's life that is not the case. We have been granted some powers; it is natural to conclude that we are some way along a process of full disestablishment; but this is far from agreed. Not only do some Parliamentarians and churchpeople alike talk as though any hint of disestablishment is treason, heresy and blasphemy, but even those who can view it with more equanimity have no idea when – because they have no idea how – it can happen. Furthermore, there are not a few Parliamentarians who talk as though the powers already devolved ought to be taken back, or at least viewed as the State's *ne plus ultra*. We are still at intervals reminded that we are under direct State control, and that not only is disestablishment not on the agenda, but it must never be. So we are left with enough separate corporate life to be able to formulate and take action where the powers have been granted to us, but with total corporate uncertainty as to whether or not we are actually in a principled move to the freedom that the gospel dictates.

Obviously, I believe that the only way out of this quagmire is to take purposeful action from the Church of England's own side. I return to that below. But there is another false trail that is sometimes unrolled for us. It is articulated thus: 'We should never seek disestablishment, but we should of course be ready to accept it if the State thrusts it upon us.' People who speak this way can make it sound as though disestablishment were a form of martyrdom – as though we should bravely face it, turn the other cheek to it when it happens, and emerge as wrongfully battered saints when it is over.

Let us be entirely clear about this. Parliament has power to act unilaterally. In power terms Parliament is sovereign. If Parliament decrees it, it matters little whether we want to turn the other cheek or not – it will still happen. A Liberal Democratic party in power (no, I do not stop to speculate on the chances of that or evaluate the politics involved) could disestablish us unilaterally. But *any* party or coalition in power could do the same, simply by allowing governmental time to a Private Member's Motion and a free vote on the matter at issue. For, quite apart from the reluctant tone of so many speakers in the debate on the ordination of women as presbyters, there is reason to doubt whether amongst the silent and absent Members there is at the moment strong support for the present establishment.*
On 4 September 1992 (i.e. during the lifetime of the present Commons, elected in April 1992) the *Church of England Newspaper* published a headline 'MPs say it is time to disestablish

---

*For an analysis of those speakers, see pp. 129–30 above.

the Church'. Apparently the company which does a regular survey of MPs' opinions, Access Opinions, polled a chosen cross-section sample of 100 MPs, and found a majority in favour of disestablishment – led by the Scottish and Northern Ireland members. That may be less than conclusive. What is clear is that support for the establishment is most likely to be found among Tories sitting for English constituencies (which is practically all of them); and it is unlikely that this figure will see an increase in any election of the next three years. So there could yet be a Bill making genuine progress through Lords and Commons. And there appear to be churchpeople waiting for it to happen – with this possibility of the half-thrill of martyrdom thrown in. There is a splendid summary of the 'we must wait for them to do it' stance in some remarks of Stanley Booth-Clibborn, last Bishop of Manchester, in a broadcast documentary:

> I think we have to recognize that we're hanging on to the establishment by our fingernails, so to speak. It's very tenuous now, and it is of questionable value. I myself believe that we should maintain the establishment until the time comes when the State itself, on its side, says to the Church, 'Look, we've had enough of this, it's a fiction' – and breaks the links.[1]

A fiction? Yes, we are all playing at 'Let's pretend'. But in that case why wait for the secular Parliament to make the first move? The odds are that from that quarter it will come at the wrong time, or alternatively not come for a long time, and very probably come in the wrong way and on the wrong terms. Furthermore, and this is the point of this whole section, it follows in principle the wrong model. And all the time there is a better method awaiting our employment of it.

Third model: How it could work

The third model is the constitutional devolution of total freedom and autonomy from the colonizing power to the former colony. This has usually been effected as the last stage in a process of getting the constitution right by negotiation, and of providing by constitutional means an interim government, sometimes an 'internal self-government', with which the final conversations are held and to which the full autonomy is given. This is roughly what happened in the almost total 'disestablishment' of the Church of Scotland in 1921. And the Church

of England has the organs ready for it – it only seems to lack
the will. But as long as it does not challenge or picket the
colonial power it acquiesces in its own captivity.

So how should the Church of England go about it? It has
the immense advantage, for the purposes of going to Parliament, that it can draft the enabling legislation itself, and
Parliament cannot then amend it. It is interesting to conceive
of one final Measure to end all Measures – the Church of
England super-inclusive exhaustive Miscellaneous Provisions
Measure. But it is more practicable to conceive of a plan by
which a rolling series of Measures were passed – planned as
a single campaign, worked through Synod by a rolling plan, and
laid before Parliament at regular and not too long intervals.

However it is done, the Church should be doing it. Of course
there would need to be negotiations. Perhaps the process by
which the Ecclesiastical Committee summons members of
Synod to give evidence to it could be reversed, and the Revision
Committees of Synod digesting and re-drafting the proposals
could ask the Ecclesiastical Committee for the time being to
give evidence to them. Perhaps an informal, once-off, conference between the Synod and the leaders of the political parties
in Lords and Commons could be set up – at our invitation. But
whatever method is used, what Synod needs to know is what
can be recommended to Parliament as a natural and obvious
concluding step down a path where up to now Parliament may
have been more keen than Synod to go.

One complicating point is that there might prove to be features of the establishment which could only be changed by a
Parliamentary Act, and not by Measure. Interpretation of the
limiting effects of the 1919 'Enabling Act', which created
the principle of legislating by Measure, would be needed. It
might well be that enabling clergy to sit in the Commons
(especially as the current prohibition is not restricted to
Church of England clergy) requires an Act to amend the 1801
and other legislation. I suppose there might be an argument
that winding up for good and all the provisions of the very
Enabling Act itself would require an Act.* But the precedents

---

*It was on the doubtful premise that the ordination of women as presby-
ters required an Act that the Church Society asked for a judicial review
of the laying of the Measure before Parliament – but lost. (See fn. on
p. 40 above.)

suggest that every part of devolution of powers, when it is done step-by-step, can be done by Measure – so one assumes that in general, if many such steps of devolution are taken at the same time, they can be done either by a comprehensive single Measure or by a cluster of specialized Measures. If at any point Synod were warned by the Ecclesiastical Committee that it was attempting to act *ultra vires* as the law now stood, then it would have to approach the government of the day with a request for a particular change to be put into an Act.

Immediate possibilities

At the time of writing I have awaiting debate in the Synod the following Private Member's Motion:

> That this Synod request the Standing Committee to bring forward proposals for the lifting of direct state control:
> (a) upon the appointment of diocesan bishops; and
> (b) upon the authorization of legislation coming from this Synod.

I tabled this in Spring 1992, and by November 1993 it had accumulated enough signatures to be running second in the list. However, it was not reached in the November 1993 session, and so has been held over till July 1994. At the time of writing, another Private Member's Motion had overtaken it, so it is at least possible it will not be reached this July.

The picture has been complicated by Southwark Diocesan Synod passing a motion calling for a Church and State Commission. I believe this came from a deanery that was worried about the Coronation Oath. The way in which, in November 1993, Southwark diocese was being advised to present its motion, was to table it as an amendment to mine. It would remove all the content of my Motion, and thus would be a substitute *alternative* to mine; but that in effect means that it becomes a wrecking amendment. The two centrepieces of the current colonial relationship between secular State and Christian Church of England are the two I have identified in my Motion. A Church and State Commission is bound to put out a load of ideology, but, when it has done so, it must either recommend the two changes I have requested – or it must evade doing so. Either way, Synod will be faced by exactly the same questions – but it is likely to be five, six, or seven years

further on that they are so. The rather wooden advice to Southwark diocese threatens at these two points simply to waste
the Synod's time.

On the other hand, if the setting up of a Commission does
not swamp my two thrusts, and is made *additional* to a reasonably swift handling of them in their own right, then there is
a real case for it. In my Motion I had hesitated to call for
total disestablishment, largely because it is not transparently
obvious what that means, and in particular it would clearly
have different meanings for different people, and thus cause
confusion. I might not have got the support I achieved for my
fairly sharp-edged, and certainly far-reaching, Motion – and,
even if I had had that support, I still ran the risk of the debate
drifting off into romanticized concern about the Royal Family
or barely relevant worries about baptismal policies, and thus
failing to grapple with the prime issues.

Longer-term goals

So, granted that I restricted my Motion to these two prime
issues, it would now be actual gain if a call for a Church and
State Commission were *added* to it. If the two clear issues in
the Motion can be promoted in an immediate and direct way,
but a Commission can pick up all other issues over a longer
period of time, then the Synod will be well served. If the call
for a Commission comes within such a Motion, it will, we may
hope, have terms of reference which would keep the goal of
disestablishment in view, and would indicate in detail the ways
of achieving it. This would in turn mean that the Standing
Committee could produce a five-year legislative programme.

It is difficult going to press shortly before such a vital debate.
But whether the Motion is amended or not, and passed or not,
the issue will not go away. As it sharpens, it becomes more
and more a question of straight obedience to God. Through it
we need a vision of a missionary Church of England, uniting
with her fellow-Christians, and witnessing to Jesus Christ in
secular, pluralist and superstitious times.

For that, the Church must be the Church, and the world the
world. And for *that*, cut the connection and 'let the Church of
England be free'. Soon.

Appendix A: Anglo-Catholics, Broad Church People, and Evangelicals

Whilst it is clear that opinion in all groupings in the Church is split, it does appear that each has within its theological armoury exactly the weapon to strike off the shackles that bind the Church of England to the State – yet each grouping, when it becomes defensive about its own position, starts to view the State as a last-ditch defence for that position against threatening tendencies within the Church itself. I attempt to illustrate the point from the standpoint of three main streams of Anglicanism.

Anglo-catholics

Anglo-catholicism was born in – and even out of – suspicion of State control. The Tracts bewailed the growing Erastianism of the times. The key category here was 'the Church'. The leaders of the movement denounced Parliament, denied the jurisdiction of the Judicial Committee of the Privy Council, and worked for the restoration of the Convocations as sacred synods of the Church. Their central thrust in the nineteenth century was to produce a Church with a profile which actually exhibited 'catholic' belief, and was visibly distinguishable from the State. The more the movement looked towards Rome, the less it could take the establishment seriously.

In the twentieth century this thrust was continued, as Gore's approach to the Enabling Act illustrates.* One recent advocate from this school is Valerie Pitt, who dissented from the Chadwick report. The most powerful exponent of recent years has been Eric Kemp, still in office today as Bishop of Chichester, but notable for his pleas for freedom twenty, thirty and more years ago, both in his *Counsel and Consent* and in his advocacy to the Church Assembly and the General Synod. Sadly, as with so many other Anglican Catholics, the actual decisions of General Synod in recent years appear to have turned him from his determination. Other prominent Anglican Catholics of recent years, as, for example, Roy Porter, Oswald Clark, John Gummer and George Austin, also seem to have drifted from their origins and to be ready to make a virtue of the establishment.†

But the issue remains. Is not a 'Catholic' ecclesiology, with its high concept of spiritual society, bonded by creeds and sacraments and led

---

*See p. 35 above.

†George Austin appears jaundiced about the Prince of Wales, rather than opposed to the establishment (see p. 144 above).

by episcopally ordained bishops and presbyters, such as to demand
that the Church's life should not be controlled or trammelled or loaded
by the organs or servants of a secular State?

Broad (or 'Central') Church people

The first instinct of the 'broad' Church, from Thomas Arnold onwards,
has always been to make the Church as inclusive as possible, and
therefore to work for it to be co-terminous with the nation. However,
there has also been within the strand of churchmanship a social
concern which has to be ready to confront the State, and, at its best,
an ideal of prophecy, as part of the Church's basic *raison d'être* within
a secularized society. Perhaps the best category of thought here is
'the Kingdom', a theme well explored, for instance, by F. D. Maurice.
A notable contributor was Hensley Henson (post–1928!), and in these
latter times David Edwards suggests that the strand of thought has
run on, even when the constituency has sometimes shown little outward sign of it. If the 'central' people are not Kingdom people, what
are they? And if they are Kingdom people, what is their relationship
to the kingdoms of this world?

Evangelicals

Evangelicals were always aware of the sluggishness of State decision-
taking, and it was that which led from the 1790s to the 1830s to the
formation of a greater welter of voluntary societies. Societies are not
our theme here, but their existence and their ecclesiology are a witness against Erastianism in an otherwise Erastian-looking Church.

However, the rise of anglo-catholicism had an Erastianizing effect
upon the evangelicals themselves. During the nineteenth century
they came to believe that God's truth had been delivered to the
saints in virtually final and finished condition in the Elizabethan
Settlement. They had constant appeal to law (and thus to formularies)
to check the advancing tide of Catholicism. And as they gradually
slid from power from around 1880 onwards, so they found they could
less and less trust the existent Church of England, its leaders and
even its lawyers. They came to rely more and more upon a Church of
their own construction, a pure sixteenth-century Church, but actually
an unreal figment of the imagination. And so in the present century
they have always been liable to lapse into Ulster-like parrot cries
'Hold fast! Hold fast!' (cries, I should quickly add, not wholly unjust-
ified as the tide moved against them so strongly). In the process
they have always abandoned that bright-eyed looking forward which
marks the true sons and daughters of the Reformation – and the
principle of *Ecclesia Reformata semper Reformanda*.

In the last fifty years evangelicals have been half-consciously domi-
nated by the half-conscious memory of those two stirring defeats of
the new Prayer Book in the Commons in 1927–8. The 'arm of flesh'
saved them then, and Parliament as the guardian of the laws of the
Reformation earned a kind of apotheosis in their eyes. As evangelical

bishops and others faded from the scene in the years after 1928 so the lines became clearer – Church decisions doubtful, State decisions God-given. It has taken a long time to pass away.* To be fair, some of the evangelical establishmentarians of recent years, including Timothy Hoare, Timothy Dudley-Smith, and Michael Alison, have held to a haunting dream, of a Christianly tinged nation, which is in no sense reducible to being trapped by the memory of 1928.

But evangelicals have also abandoned their account of society. Perhaps the evangelical resurgence of post-War years has been too Public School led (with a calm assurance that English society had plenty of godliness in its *mores*). Who knows? But evangelicals also have a differentiating principle – a concern for conversion and new birth – which must be their key theological category for confronting the State. They are also not without a social concern, though traditionally with little theory to back it. But above all they know you have to be twice-born to inherit the Kingdom. They know the whole world lies in wickedness and open sin. And so it is as they have become more confident of their place in the Church, so they have started to be suspicious of the establishment of the Church of England. Indeed, they are the people most keen to question indiscriminate baptism, to proclaim repentance and faith, and to bring to light a Church with a radical transformed Christian lifestyle and a mission to the nation. If their key category of thought is *either* the conversion of men and women, *or* (more Calvinistically) 'the Crown rights of the Redeemer', what does that imply for our captivity to an unconverted State?

---

*But see the fn. on p. 40 above, about Church Society's willingness to go to absurd lengths to bring the action of the Church into the test of Parliamentary law, and to hamper the living Church by the rusty shackles of appeals to law.

Appendix B: A Small Personal Fracas

In December 1988, the editor of the *Church of England Newspaper* asked me to write an 'alternative *Crockford's* Preface' for 1989 – the point being that, after the Gary Bennett business in late 1987, *Crockford's* had ceased to publish an anonymous Preface, and the *CEN* editor thought this gap could well be filled by some purposeful journalism. True to my last, I wrote a page, advertised as replacing *Crockford's* Preface, and it was published on 6 January 1989. It was a plea for cutting the connection with the State. In the course of it, I wrote:

> When it comes to genetic and sexual ethics, Parliament votes according to what it thinks the country will 'take', and when it comes to ideals for the life of society, the government of the day – and especially the government of *this* day – will follow its own doctrinaire economic theory... the state for its part clearly does not now acknowledge the God of the Old and New Testaments.

Normally this would have caused no raised eyebrows. But the publicity-conscious editor sent the article round Fleet Street in advance under an embargo, and with a label proclaiming it as an 'alternative *Crockford's* Preface' or something similar. Fleet Street responded to this label, as '*Crockford's* Preface' did catch the eye.

An amazing chain of events followed. On the next day, Saturday 7 January 1989, *The Daily Telegraph* had a column headed 'Bishop questions Thatcher's role in the Church', and it was relatively accurate. However, Nigel Reynolds, their political commentator, had interviewed Ivor Stanbrook MP, chairman of the backbench Tory Constitutional Committee, and he, on the basis of hearsay remarks, had exploded to Nigel Reynolds as follows:

> Dr Buchanan should resign from the Church immediately if he wants a different one from the one to which he is lucky enough to have been called. [He is] absolutely and fundamentally wrong, and totally misconceived in his views. The Church of England belongs to the people of England. It does not belong to any bureaucracy, and it certainly does not belong to the professional clerics who operate it. I wonder how he could have reached that position in the Church of England when he is in such ignorance of its nature.

I also found myself debating (so called) with Ivor Stanbrook on the *Today* programme at 8 a.m. on that Saturday morning on BBC Radio 4. I actually hardly opened my mouth as my critic shot himself in every limb he possessed. His best lines were that Parliament created the Church of England in Henry VIII's reign, and that only Parliament held it together, and that without Parliament we should all fly apart into little segments.

The biggest cumulation of nonsense happened in Birmingham itself. *The Birmingham Post* that same morning had banner headlines 'Thatcher Regime Godless – bishop'. All sorts of Birmingham notables came into play to attack me for this (none of them having read the original article, of course). The *Mail* that evening had another headline 'Caesar-like Thatcher – Fury at bishop's outburst'. The news item began 'Midland politicians and councillors today joined in the chorus of criticism ... The bishop's comments were condemned by angry Conservative MPs. Mr Patrick Cormack ... said "The man is plainly an ass ..."' Meanwhile the *Mail* had rung up Downing Street and had asked 'a spokesman' (perhaps Bernard Ingham?) what he (or the Prime Minister) thought, and the report of this went:

> A Downing Street spokesman immediately rejected the claim by the bishop that the Government 'clearly does not now acknowledge the God of the Old and New Testaments'. The Prime Minister has made her Christian beliefs known in the past, for instance at the General Assembly of the Church of Scotland ...

When I read this, I wrote to Bernard Ingham, the Prime Minister's Press Secretary, explaining that I had made no personal attack on the Prime Minister, and was ready indeed to honour her personal faith, which had nowhere been in question. But I was led to reflect that it was interesting that remarks about *Parliamentary* processes being godless had been understood as remarks about the *government* (I think some of the Tories concerned thought all Parliamentary processes *were* theirs); and I was further impressed with the profound ignorance of the Church of England displayed by virtually everybody who rose to the bait. In the case of Patrick Cormack, I sent him the original '*Crockford's* Preface', and he responded generously acknowledging that he had attacked me on the basis of considerable misunderstanding of what I had actually said. And after seventy-two hours the whole thing went away. He now thought I was wrong, but not an ass.

But, did the Tories rise in wrath because they think the Church of England is peculiarly their poodle? Why did they not ask to see what I had written before launching into battle? Is there something in the Tory subconscious which actually believes this Christian Church is run by them for the country's benefit, and that bishops and clergy should live in deferential gratitude to the political leaders? Or, alternatively, what do they fear?

And, finally, was I right or wrong to say that 'the State' (not one particular party) does not acknowledge the God of the Old and New Testaments? If I was right, why get so fussed? And if I was wrong, where is the *evidence*?

Appendix C: Clergy Sitting in Parliament

It is not clear that the clergy of the Church of England were debarred from sitting in the Commons after the Reformation, though the possibility that they might take seats there would have undermined the claims from Richard Hooker to Hugh Craig that it is a lay assembly. What is clear is that in 1801 Parliament was faced with an actually elected cleric, the Revd J. H. Tooke. He had made many attempts to win a seat in the Westminster constituency, but was at last that year elected for Old Sarum (a well-known 'rotten borough' in which he needed and obtained three votes to be elected). Parliament then passed the House of Commons (Clergy Disqualifications) Act. This banned membership of the Commons to clergy of the United Church of England and Ireland and of the Episcopal Church of Scotland, and also to ministers of the Church of Scotland. When Roman Catholics were allowed to sit in the Comons, the Act excepted those who are in Holy Orders. It appears that the ban on those ordained in the Church of Ireland still stands (because of the accident of history that in 1800, one year before Tooke got to the Commons, the union of Parliaments led to a union of Churches, and this item was not put into the disestablishment of the Church of Ireland). It is, however, at least possible that the Church in Wales does not come under the ban, not being in existence as an identifiable entity when the legislation was enacted. The whole stupid business appears to be an arbitrary move, not really connected with the theory of establishment at all. It does not prevent Anglican clergy sitting on Borough and County Councils, nor taking their seats as MEPs. Nor does it prevent ministers of non-Anglican Churches (except as mentioned above) being elected to the Commons. It would not even prevent an Anglican clergyman or clergywoman holding a living in the Church of England from being elected, provided that she or he had been ordained overseas (anywhere except Ireland or Scotland)!

It appears that until 1983, a disqualified person (i.e. a peer, lunatic, incarcerated criminal or cleric) could run for election, but could not take his seat. It was in this way that Tony Benn ran for the Commons in a by-election in his own previous constituency, when he was disqualified from the Commons through inheriting a peerage in 1963. However, this process was excluded by the provisions of the Representation of the People Act 1983, which required candidates for election to the Commons to state, along with their consent to be nominated, that they are aware of the categories of disqualification from sitting in the Commons, and they know themselves able to take the particular seat if elected.

This presents a very serious problem to a clergyman who wishes to run – as one I know does – for the Green party. The chances of election look slim; but the man must renounce his orders and be laicized if he would be a candidate. There was, it appears, a Mr Clemitson who represented Luton in the 1970s (not in the Green interest) who had taken exactly that step. But, of course, the prohibition is simply daft in the latter part of the twentieth century. For the sake of completeness we should note that an MP who was ordained as an NSM whilst serving in Parliament would not be unseated (it is *not* a new alternative religious Chiltern Hundreds!), because it is only *taking* one's seat that is excluded by the Act, and Tooke himself retained his seat until the next General Election.

The Chadwick Commission noted the point and recommended the abolition of all restrictions on ministers of any Church standing for Parliament and taking their seats if elected.* No action seems to have followed. One can only assume that the Standing Committee of General Synod was either unsympathetic or viewed the matter as beyond their purview. Clearly, even if it were just Church of England ministers involved, it is doubtful whether it could be done by Measure. As in fact it involves ministers of other Churches, and above all involves the character of the Commons, it would need an Act of Parliament, which General Synod has no power to initiate. That would not have prevented the Standing Committee from bringing forward a motion to call upon the government of the day to give justice at this point to all its enfranchised citizens. But no Standing Committee did so.

The matter was accordingly left to the initiative of private members. The General Synod at last debated it in November 1982, when Robert Dell, then Archdeacon of Derby, moved a Private Member's Motion:

> That this Synod believes that clergymen of the Church of England should be free like other citizens to offer themselves for election as Members of Parliament and, in accordance with the recommendation of the Church and State Report 1970, asks the Standing Committee to request Her Majesty's Government to seek a suitable opportunity to amend the relevant Act which forbids them to do so.

During the debate, the text was amended in two places. The first half then read '. . . other citizens to take their seats as elected Members of Parliament' (a point necessary to make prior to the 1983 legislation mentioned above); and the second half changed 'to seek . . . forbids them to do so' into 'introduce appropriate legislation to enable them to do so' (a point covering the fact that there are more Acts than one behind the prohibition, and that positive enabling legislation is preferable to going back to the doubts that existed before 1801).

Church and State 1970, pp. 57–8.

The debate was a sad one in that quite ridiculous points made by three opponents in a quite short debate appear to have made the Synod hesitate. These can be reduced to the following:

(a) clergy should not belong to political parties and get themselves compromised in that way;

(b) clergy are ordained to look after parishes full-time and should not abandon their cures;

(c) in a national Church, we ought to accept a small restriction in return for other privileges.

All three of these are self-evident exercises in idiocy. The first is bogus, not only because even independents can run for Parliament, but also because clergy can run under party colours in council and European elections anyway. The second is bogus, because it is totally outdated by the coming of non-stipendiary ordained ministry. The third is bogus, because simply to want to be handicapped as a Church for the sake of certain supposed privileges which are quite unconnected to the handicap is illogic at its zenith.

However, the motion was passed by 181 votes to 147. It does not appear that the Standing Committee ever acted upon it. Even less does it appear that any government of the day has ever taken any notice of it.

Redress is urgently needed.

Notes

Introduction
1 *Church and State 1970*, p. 2.
2 For a more detailed treatment of the various organizations, see Kenneth Thompson, *Bureaucracy and Church Reform* (Oxford 1970).

1 Phases of the Establishment: From the Reformation to the Enabling Act
1 From an unpublished paper by the Mennonite Alan Kreider, cited from Thomas Fuller (ed.), *The Church History of Britain from the Birth of Jesus Christ until the year MDCXLVIII* (William Tegg, London, 1868), Vol. II, pp. 576–7.
2 P. F. H. Bell, *Disestablishment in Ireland and Wales* (London 1969), p. 43.
3 *The disestablishment and disendowment of the Established Church in Ireland shown to be desirable under existing circumstances* (London and Dublin 1968), p. 8. (In Bell, *op. cit.*, p. 44.)

2 Phases of the Establishment: From the Enabling Act to the Present Day
1 They had this much justification: 'The nation at the centre of its life is more Protestant than the Church of England at the centre of *its* life' (Church of England Liturgical Commission, *Prayer Book Revision in the Church of England* (SPCK 1957), p. 12, summarizing the findings of G. K. A. Bell in his biography, *Randall Davidson: Archbishop of Canterbury*, p. 1354).
2 G. K. A. Bell, *Randall Davidson: Archbishop of Canterbury* (Oxford (3) 1952), p. 1359.
3 Archbishops' Commission on Canon Law, *The Canon Law of the Church of England* (SPCK 1947), pp. 215–23. With regard to Vaisey's comments on evidence by Davidson to the Royal Commission on Ecclesiastical Discipline at the foot of page 219, see my *Recent Liturgical Revision in the Church of England* (Grove Booklet on Ministry and Worship no. 14, Grove Books, Bramcote, 1973) p. 5, fn. 2.
4 Archbishops' Commission, *Church and State 1970* (CIO 1970), pp. 17–28.
5 I discuss this much more fully in my *Infant Baptism and the Gospel: The Church of England's Dilemma* (DLT 1993), pp. 76–80.

3 An Established Church in a Secular State
1 Peter Cornwell, *Church & Nation* (Blackwells, Oxford, 1983), p. 9.
2 Enoch Powell, 'The Church of England and Parliament' in Peter Moore (ed.), *The Synod of Westminster: Do we need it?* (SPCK 1986), extracts from pp. 117–26.
3 Hugh Craig, *Selecting Good Shepherds* (Church Society 1990), pp. 6–7.
4 Peter Brierley, *'Christian' England: What the English Church Census Reveals* (Marc Europe 1991).
5 *Church and Nation in a Secular Age* (DLT 1983), p. 1.
6 *Op. cit.*, p. 98.
7 *Op. cit.*, p. 103.
8 *Op. cit.*, p. 109.
9 (SPCK 1988), p. 20.
10 (SPCK 1993), p. 144.
11 From a transcript of a Radio 4 interview and discussion with COB, 26 October 1993.
12 From a transcript of the BBC Radio 4 debate on 'This House believes the Church of England should be disestablished', held in the debating chamber of Church House on 18 February 1992, and broadcast on 23 February 1992.
13 Adrian Hastings, *Church and State* (Univ. of Exeter 1991), p. 55.

4 The Appointment of Diocesan Bishops: The State's System
1 *Tracts for the Times* no. 59 (1835), pp. 4 and 6.
2 *Church and State 1970*, p. 42.
3 See the quotation from *Church and State 1970* on p. 86 above.
4 *The Times*, 8 April 1991.
5 *Church and State 1970*, pp. 35–6 (italics mine).
6 H. H. Henson, *Bishoprick Papers* (1946), p. 50.
7 Paul Oestreicher in General Synod, 13 November 1984.

5 The Appointment of Bishops: The Church's Own Task
1 Mark Santer, 'The Freedom of the Gospel' in Donald Reeves (ed.) *The Church and the State* (Hodder and Stoughton 1984), pp. 113–14.

6 Parliament
1 Hooker, *Laws of Ecclesiastical Polity*, Book VIII, Chapter vi *passim*.

7 The Monarchy
1 *Senior Church Appointments: A Review of the Methods of Appointment of Area and Suffragan Bishops, Deans, Provosts, Archdeacons and Residentiary Canons* (CHP 1993), pp. 20–34.
2 General Synod, *Report of Proceedings* (February 1993), p. 9.

3 General Synod, *Report of Proceedings* (February 1993), pp. 15–16.
4 *Church and State 1970*, pp. 70–1.
5 In *Church and State 1970*, see the major dissentient note by Valerie Pitt (pp. 68–79) and the additional notes by Peter Cornwell (pp. 79–82) and Denis Coe (pp. 82–4) which they contribute over and above their 'broad agreement' with the fully argued case of Valerie Pitt.
6 On BBC *Heart of the Matter*, 24 January 1993.

8 Parish Concerns

1 There is a vast stream of literature covering more than two decades within England itself to recommend this pattern. See, for instance: the 'Ely' Report, *Christian Initiation: Birth and Growth in the Christian Society* (CIO 1971), pp. 42–3; C. H. B. Byworth, *Communion, Confirmation and Commitment* (Grove Booklet on Ministry and Worship no. 8, Grove Books, 1972), pp. 16–17 *et passim*; the 'Knaresborough' Report, *Communion before Confirmation?* (CIO 1985), pp. 46–7. But there is also great pressure upon the Church of England from other parts of the Communion; and the above pattern is recommended in the statements of the International Anglican Liturgical Consultations, for which see (re IALC–1 at Boston) *Children and Communion* section III (found, among other places, in Colin Buchanan (ed.) *Nurturing Children in Communion* (Grove Liturgical Study no. 44, Grove Books 1985), p. 48), and (re IALC–4 at Toronto) the statement 'Walk in newness of life' published in David Holeton (ed.) *Christian Initiation in the Anglican Communion* (Grove Worship Series no. 118, Grove Books, 1991), and in David Holeton (ed.) *Growing in Newness of Life* (Anglican Book Centre, Toronto, 1993), pp. 245–7 *et passim*.
2 This is spelled out in the same literature cited in note 1 above. In particular see: the Ely Report, pp. 43 and 49; the Toronto statement, as e.g. in *Growing in Newness of Life*, p. 233 (and at the top of p. 118, where it is misquoted . . .). There exists a liturgical model for this in the Canadian *Book of Alternative Services* (1985), p. 120 (where the laying on of hands is not mandatory for those baptized as adults – yet they are fully initiated).
3 In the 'Powers and Duties' of churchwardens the whole list of powers is ecclesiastical, and there apparently remain no duties whatsoever in relation to the civil parish or community (see Kenneth M. MacMorran, E. Garth Moore and Timothy Briden, *A Handbook for Churchwardens and Parochial Church Councillors (1989 edition)* (Mowbray 1989), pp. 70–4).
4 COB, *Infant Baptism and The Gospel: The Church of England's Dilemma* (DLT 1993), pp. 63–72 and 80–90.
5 ASB Emergency Baptism service, section 106, p. 280.

9 Other National Considerations
1 *Church and State 1970*, p. 51.
2 *Church and State 1970*, p. 77.
3 Bernard Lord Manning, *Essays in Orthodox Dissent* (Independent Press 1939), pp. 137–8.
4 Edward Carpenter (ed.), *The Archbishop Speaks* (Evans Bros, London, 1958), pp. 66–7.
5 *Conversations between the Church of England and the Methodist Church: A Report* (CIO and Epworth 1963), p. 52.
6 The Anglican–Methodist Unity Commission, *Anglican–Methodist Unity: 2 The Scheme* (SPCK/Epworth 1962), pp. 95–7.
7 *Ibid.*, p. 98.
8 *Church and State 1970*, p. ix (italics mine).

10 Some International Perspectives
1 The Radio 4 debate was recorded in the Assembly Hall of Church House, Westminster, on 18 February 1992, and was broadcast on the Sunday evening following, 23 February 1992.
2 (Darton, Longman and Todd 1966.)
3 (Bodley Head 1989.)
4 *To a Rebellious House? Report of the Church of England's Partners in Mission Consultation 1981* (CIO 1981), pp. 27–8.
5 *To a Rebellious House?, op. cit.*, p. 36.
6 *To a Rebellious House?, op. cit.*, p. 47.
7 *The Truth Shall Make You Free: The Lambeth Conference 1988: The Reports, Resolutions, and Pastoral Letters from the Bishops* (ACC, London, 1989), p. 47.

11 How Should We Get There?
1 From a transcript of a BBC Radio 4 documentary, *A Holy Row*, broadcast on 30 November and 1 December 1989.

Bibliography (of Twentieth-Century Books)

The books and reports mentioned are set out in chronological order. There is no suggestion that the list is exhaustive! Note that official reports usually have a sub-title (or second sub-title) such as 'Report of the Archbishops' Commission on . . .', and such wording is sometimes omitted here. Occasions when it is useful to refer to the *Report of Proceedings* of General Synod, or to *Hansard*, the official record of Parliamentary debates, have to be divined from the text of the book. The official biographies of Archbishops of Canterbury – Davidson, Temple, Lang, Fisher and Ramsey in particular – will also assist.

'Selborne' Commission, *Report of the Archbishops' Committee on Church and State* (SPCK 1916).
 The Committee was appointed in the wake of difficulties in getting Parliamentary time for church affairs in the pre-War years ('The wheels of the ecclesiastical machine creak and groan and sometimes refuse to move', p. 2). A motion asking for it was passed in the Representative Church Council in 1913. Most of what came to pass in the 'Enabling Act' in 1919 is recommended here, including the word 'enabling'. Temple was a member of the Committee.
William Temple, *Christianity and the State* (Macmillan 1928)
 This book is a set of lectures delivered in Liverpool in January and February 1928, when Temple was still Bishop of Manchester. The specific question of the establishment of the Church of England is in an appendix, written in the heated aftermath of the December 1927 debate in the Commons – '. . . it is most emphatically not the business of the State to determine what is, and what is not, compatible with theological truth . . . the proper course for Parliament to pursue if it disapproves the Prayer Book Measure is not to reject the Measure, but to pass the Measure and then disestablish the Church' (pp. 194–5).
H. Hensley Henson, *Disestablishment* (Macmillan 1929).
 Henson reviews his previous pro-establishment stand, and indicates how and why he has done a 180-degree turn. (There are several other Henson writings from 1928 onwards which reflect his stance – for a fuller survey, see his biography by Owen Chadwick in 1983, cited below.)
'Cecil' Commission, *Report of the Archbishops' Commission on the Relations between Church and State* (Press and Publications Board 1935).
 Set up in wake of 1928 debacle. Perhaps opened the possibility of devolution of powers over liturgy to Convocations; also recommended that cathedral chapters be allowed to refuse Crown's nomi-

nee as bishop. There is a second volume of the written evidence
submitted.

Canon Law Commission, *The Canons of the Church of England* (SPCK
1947).

   The very thorough and detailed report (with a learned appendix on
   'Lawful Authority') which lay behind all Canon Law revision in the
   1950s and 1960s.

Cyril Garbett, *Church and State in England* (Hodder and Stoughton
1950).

   The then Archbishop of York wrote in his old age 'an argument for
   some readjustment in the existing relationship between Church
   and State'. The book is a 300-page hardback and includes historical
   information from Constantine onwards, and down through the
   Reformation. It has central chapters describing the details of
   the then contemporary establishment, and one asking 'Disestablishment or reform?' He envies the Scottish pattern, and wants for
   England at least reform in appointing bishops, and in various other
   areas in which progress has been made since his time. A delightful
   bit of work, but perhaps not chiming in closely with Fisher's views
   at Canterbury.

'Moberley' Commission, *Church and State: Being the Report of a
Commission Appointed by the Church Assembly in June 1949* (Church
Information Board of the Church Assembly 1952).

   The text of this report was typically cautious, and its main
   effects lay in the checks it recommended upon the proposed Canons
   to allow services alternative to those in the Book of Common
   Prayer to be authorized within the Church itself – the main
   gains, as compared with the 1947 draft Code, being the necessary
   concurrence of the House of Laity of the Assembly in such
   authorization. There were also effects in the area of ecclesiastical
   courts and the final appeal to the Judicial Committee of the Privy
   Council. But generally the shock-waves from the Commission were
   minimal.

Eric, W. Kemp, *Counsel and Consent: Aspects of the Government of
the Church as exemplified in the history of English Provincial Synods*
(SPCK 1961).

   A wonderfully clear and learned survey of church government in
   England from medieval times to 1960, demonstrating finally the
   Erastianism into which the Church of England had lapsed (and
   fearful of Parliament's likely role in the then imminent revision of
   the Canons). Sadly, the author appears in subsequent years to have
   backed off his enthusiasm for Synods, and to have reposed more
   trust in Parliament.

Charles Smyth, *The Church and the Nation: Six Studies in the Anglican Tradition* (Hodder and Stoughton 1962).

   The 'Six Studies' start with the Anglo-Saxons and finish with the
   Tractarians (plus, for some slight reason, Geoffrey Fisher's
   enthronement sermon of 1945!). To that extent, the book does not
   bear closely on present-day Church and State relationships.

Paul A. Welsby, *The Bond of Church and State* (SPCK 1962).

A slender paperback which, like his other writings, sets out the constitutional ground carefully, and leaves readers to judge what reforms, proposed or otherwise, are needed.

Leslie Paul, *The Deployment and Payment of the Clergy* (CIO 1964).

This is the famous 'Paul Report'. Whilst not directly touching establishment issues, it gives a very full picture of the statistical and organizational aspects of the Church of England as an institution thirty years ago.

'Howick' Commission, *Crown Appointments and the Church* (CIO 1964).

Proposed no change to appointments method, save advance consultation (which was granted by the setting up of Vacancy in See committees).

Peter Hinchliff, *The One-Sided Reciprocity: A Study in the Modification of the Establishment* (DLT 1966).

Written when the author was still in South Africa – a historical survey which subtly becomes a very judicious, but nevertheless devastating, disclosure of the idiocy of establishment – and demonstrates the way establishment appears from elsewhere in the Anglican Communion.

'Hodson' Commission, *Government by Synod: Synodical Government in the Church of England* (CIO 1966).

The foundation document for synodical government, which was finally instituted through the Synodical Government Measure 1969, and came to pass in 1970.

David Nicholls, *Church and State in Britain since 1820* (Routledge and Kegan Paul 1967).

This volume is a 'reader' in the subject, i.e. an anthology of notable writings or sayings on the theme. Its era covers Irish and Welsh disestablishment as well as the Scottish Disruption, and its authors include Anglican proponents and opponents of the establishment, as well as astringent Free Church and secularist appraisals.

'Chadwick' Commission, *Church and State 1970* (CIO 1970).

The report that recommended full devolution of powers over liturgy to General Synod, and offered two alternative ways of appointing bishops (the more radical discarding Downing Street, but both retaining the Crown's role). Three dissentients proposed the complete end of establishment.

Kenneth A. Thompson, *Bureaucracy and Church Reform: The Organizational Response of the Church of England to Social Change 1800–1965* (Oxford 1970).

A closely researched and scholarly investigation of three periods within the overall one. The last period – the Church Assembly years after 1920 is done most sketchily, whilst the middle period, of events leading up to the Enabling Act, is wonderfully satisfying; the nineteenth century first part is thorough, but not so relevant to this book.

Dewi Morgan, *The Church in Transition: Reform in the Church of England* (Chatto and Windus 1970).

About a sixth of this paperback is given to a chapter on 'Establishment'. What should be the attitude of the Church to the State? Why, says Morgan, the Church's duty is to *love* the State. But the chapter turns diffuse and descriptive where it promised to be tight and prescriptive. It ends with half a cheer for the imminent arrival of General Synod.

William Mackintosh, *Disestablishment and Liberation* (Epworth, 1972).

A closely researched book about nineteenth century conflicts on the issue, with a special charting of the Liberation Society and other associated movements and pressures.

Christopher Wansey, *The Clockwork Church* (Becket 1978).

A cartoon-style, arms-flailing, largely and deliciously autobiographical, broadside on the establishment and every connected feature of it. Not notable for either its finesse or its impact.

John Habgood, *Church and Nation in a Secular Age* (DLT 1983).

John Habgood is the ultra-anti-disestablishmentarian, but, of course, writes with the mature confidence of the one in possession. Actually only one chapter of the book is about the establishment, whilst the rest elaborates a series of tangible and intangible areas of connection and mutual responsibilities between Church and nation. His later collections of papers, *The Confessions of a Conservative Liberal* (SPCK 1988) and *Making Sense* (SPCK 1993), also include essays on the establishment.

Owen Chadwick, *Hensley Henson: A Study in the Friction between Church and State* (Oxford 1983).

Despite the sub-title, the book does not dwell disproportionately on establishment issues. There is, however, a long chapter on 'Church and State' which records and documents Henson's change of position on the issue, and is invaluable as history.

Peter Cornwell, *Faith and the Future: Church and Nation* (Blackwell 1983).

A slight paperback from one of the Chadwick dissentients. Theologically argued, no holds barred, and crying out ever since for an answer.

Donald Reeves (ed.), *The Church and the State* (Hodder and Stoughton 1984).

Nine lectures given at St James' Piccadilly, with establishment particularly blistered by Tony Benn from a secularist Parliamentarian's standpoint, and by Mark Santer from an ecclesial (and episcopal) standpoint.

George Moyser (ed.), *Church and Politics Today: The Role of the Church of England in Contemporary Politics* (T. & T. Clark 1985).

This is a rich repast of contrasting dishes – John Habgood does a Foreword, and Frank Field defends Parliament's role; but Peter Cornwell is a known opponent, and Anthony Dyson's professorial dissection of 'four Church and State Reports' leaves little to admire in the cautions and compromises of all four. Other essays touch on social and economic issues.

Colin Buchanan, 'Mission and Establishment' in Philip Turner and Frank Sugeno (eds.), *Crossroads are for Meeting: Essays on the Mission and Common Life of the Church in a Global Society* (SPCK, USA, 1986).

> This is the 'Seabury bi-centenary' volume arising from the pan-Anglican symposium on mission in Hartford, Connecticut, in 1984; my participation helped me to work out the hindrance that establishment is to mission, and to gather the evaluation of our Church–State relationship from Anglicans elsewhere.

Enoch Powell, 'The Church of England and Parliament' in Peter Moore (ed.), *The Synod of Westminster: Do we need it?* (SPCK 1986).

> Enoch Powell brings his massive intellect to bear in an essay devoted to a quite incredible fantasy – that somehow all England is 'C. of E.', and all should be governed in both their religious and their civil aspects by the Queen in Parliament. It is made more amazing still by the fact that Enoch Powell was in the Commons as Ulster Unionist MP for South Down, thus representing a constituency with plentiful churchgoing and no established Church.

Paul Avis, *Anglicanism and the Christian Church* (T. & T. Clark 1989).

> In this, as in his other books, the author digs deep into both history and Anglican self-understanding and ecclesiology, from the sixteenth century to the late nineteenth. Establishment issues are well highlighted in the coverage of Hooker and, particularly, of the Tractarians.

William Powell and Maurice Chandler, *Appointing our Bishops – Pastors and Focus of Church Unity? or Architects of Change and Schism* (Church in Danger 1989).

> A duplicated 16-page pamphlet from a somewhat paranoid anglo-catholic constituency, in which they recommend the removal of the Archbishops from the Crown Appointments Commission and their replacement with more representatives of the vacant diocese.

Stewart Lamont, *Church and State: Uneasy Alliances* (Bodley Head, London, 1989).

> A Scottish journalist visits seven areas to review relationships between Church and State. In many (e.g. Russia and South Africa) events have moved on since he went – but the Church of England ('The naked Empress') had not. He is a journalist (with small errors of fact), but he brings a sharply critical mind onto the pretensions and faded gentility of our Aunty-Empress. He also has a chapter on the Church of Scotland.

Edward Norman, 'Is there a Case for a National Church?' in *Churchman* (1989–4).

> A demanding Survey of Church–State relationships, demonstrating that Anglicans are without a satisfying ecclesiology, and thus more likely to fall for a pragmatic (but ultimately indefensible) State connection.

Hugh Craig, *Selecting Good Shepherds* (Church Society 1990).

This is a 16-page pamphlet from an entrenched establishment-arian, who treasures a rare persuasion that England is a 'still professing Christian State'. He wants a stronger lay voice in the consultative machinery, and a better theological balance in the outcome.

Adrian Hastings, *Church and State: The English Experience* (Univ. of Exeter Press 1991).

Four lectures given at Exeter make up this profoundly satisfying book, with a full theological examination of the roots by which Church and State have been bound together – leading to a demonstration of the great need for separation of them today, yet with a pragmatic refusal to advocate this in a 'blanket' way.

Allen Warren (ed.), *A Church for the Nation* (Gracewing, Fowler Wright, 1992).

A Symposium by largely conservative scholars, including one Roman Catholic and one Scottish Presbyterian, with a particular (if off-beam) point of reference in Gary Bennett's *Crockford's* Preface of 1987–8 and his subsequent suicide. There is a strong thread of 'a national church' running through the essays, and a chapter (by the Roman Catholic contributor, Derek Jennings) on 'The established Church'.

Bernard Palmer, *High and Mitred: Prime Ministers as Bishop-Makers 1837–1977* (SPCK 1992).

A fascinating look at 'bishop-making' from the Downing Street end, with a look at any consistent characteristics that marked particular incumbents' appointments. Despite the stated period of the subtitle there is a postscript on the Thatcher years.

'Van Straubenzee' Working Party, *Senior Church Appointments: A Review of the Methods of Appointment of Area and Suffragan Bishops, Deans, Provosts, Archdeacons and Residentiary Canons* (CHP 1992).

Proposals for separating these appointments from a Downing Street process, whilst still retaining a role for the Crown.

Tim Bradshaw, *The Olive Branch: An Evangelical Anglican Ecclesiology* (Paternoster, Latimer Monograph, 1993).

This pioneering work touches at intervals upon Church and State relationships, and appears to be ready to make a virtue of the present position – in fact betraying a rather more uncritical approach to this issue than he adopts in most others.

Parliamentary Weekly (5 and 14 April 1993) *The House Magazine: Church and State* – articles by the Archbishop of Canterbury, John Gummer, Peter Pike and Simon Hughes.

George Carey thinks disestablishment 'would ... take spirituality off the national agenda'; John Gummer is, naturally, too vexed about a certain recent decision of Synod to get his focus credible; Peter Pike would be ready for step-by-step separation; and Simon Hughes wants it much quicker than that. All write as Christians. There is also a description of the work of the Ecclesiastical Committee of Parliament by its secretary, Clive Mitchell.

Adrian Pepper, *On the Parish: The Report on the Church of England* (Adam Smith Institute, London, 1993).

The publishers are committed to the market benefits of privatization, and Adrian Pepper cheerfully applies their criteria to church attendance. You know before you start that the Pepper view will be that the Church of England needs to be disestablished (for 'monetarist' reasons); what you perhaps do not realize is that you will pay £17 sterling for 38 pages, which almost means you bid for it one page at a time at Christie's. It is superficial and adds little to any argument.

1993 Church Statistics: Some facts and figures about the Church of England (Central Board of Finance of C. of E. 1993).

The most recently available statistics indicate the size of the worshipping 'core' of the Church of England, and the likely size of the supposed 'fringe'.

Michael De-la Noy, *The Church of England: A Portrait* (Simon & Schuster 1993).

This is a journalist's self-indulgence, painting a 'portrait' simply in terms of what interests him. It includes lengthy chapters on 'By Law Established' (though he interprets the atmosphere as much as the structures) and on 'The Making of a Bishop' (though he is as interested in the work of a bishop as in the tortuous State process of appointment). A 'portrait' is not of itself an advocacy, though one as colourfully unflattering as this might suggest a least a facelift. There is some journalistic inaccuracy.

Ted Harrison, *Members Only? Is the Church becoming too exclusive?* (Triangle/SPCK 1994).

A journalist urges that our boundaries should be fudged, our worship non-sacramental, and our clergy out visiting. Baptism should be for all – no questions asked. So far, predictable journalism. But there is an extraordinary twist – he favours disestablishment. Whether it is compatible with his otherwise reactionary programme is very doubtful.

Name Index

Index of Commissions, Reports and Official Documents

Index of Subjects